CABINET STUDIES: A READER

Also by Valentine Herman

PARLIAMENTS IN THE WORLD: A REFERENCE COM-
PENDIUM
WORKBOOK FOR COMPARATIVE GOVERNMENT
  (*co-author with Jean Blondel*)
THE BACKBENCHER AND PARLIAMENT
  (*co-editor with Dick Leonard*)

CABINET STUDIES:
A READER

Edited by
VALENTINE HERMAN

Lecturer in the Department of Government
University of Essex

and

JAMES E. ALT

Senior Research Officer to the British Election Study
University of Essex

First published 1975 by
THE MACMILLAN PRESS LTD
London and Basingstoke
Associated Companies in New York Toronto
Dublin Melbourne Johannesburg and Madras

SBN 333 14433 3

Typeset in Great Britain by
PREFACE LIMITED
Salisbury, Wilts
and printed in Great Britain by
LEWIS REPRINTS
London and Tonbridge

To Betty and Reg

and

To Elaine and Rachel

Contents

The Contributors   *page*   ix

Introduction   xi

PART ONE: THE LIFE OF THE CABINET

1 The Making of Cabinet Ministers   1
   Richard Rose

2 Continuity, Turnover, and Experience in the
   British Cabinet, 1868–1970   33
   James E. Alt

3 Comparative Perspectives on Ministerial Stability
   in Britain   55
   Valentine Herman

4 Resignations   77
   P. J. Madgwick

5 Personal Views of Ministerial Resignation   103
   Lord George-Brown
   Lord Thorneycroft

PART TWO: THE ENVIRONMENT OF THE
CABINET

6 Cabinet Ministers and Senior Civil Servants: Mutual
   Requirements and Expectations   121
   Bruce Headey

7 Her Majesty's Shadow Government: Its Evolution
   and Modern Role   140
   R. M. Punnett

8 The Cabinet and the Lobby   157
   Colin Seymour-Ure

9 Two Styles of Government—Press Relations   184
   Jeremy Tunstall

PART THREE: THE CABINET AT WORK

10 Reflections on Cabinet Government   193
    Lord Butler interviewed by Norman Hunt

11 On Being a Minister   210
    Roy Jenkins

12 Two Imaginary Cabinet Meetings   221
    Lord Gordon-Walker

13 Cabinet Reform since 1914: Major Trends   242
    Hans Daalder

14 The Brains behind the Throne   277
    James Fox

    Bibliography   293

    Index   297

The Contributors

Richard Rose is Professor of Politics at the University of Strathclyde.

P. J. Madgwick is Senior Lecturer in Political Science at University College of Wales, Aberystwyth.

Lord George-Brown was Deputy Leader of the Labour Party, 1960—70; First Secretary of State and Secretary of State for Economic Affairs, 1964—6; and Secretary of State for Foreign Affairs, 1966—8.

Lord Thorneycroft was President of the Board of Trade, 1951—7; Chancellor of the Exchequer, 1957—8; Minister of Aviation, 1960—2; Minister of Defence, 1962—4; and Secretary of State for Defence, 1964.

Bruce Headey is Lecturer in Politics at the University of Strathclyde.

R. M. Punnett is Senior Lecturer in Politics at the University of Strathclyde.

Colin Seymour-Ure is Senior Lecturer in Politics and Government at the University of Kent at Canterbury.

Jeremy Tunstall is Professor of Sociology at the City University.

Lord Crowther-Hunt has been Fellow and Lecturer in Politics at Exeter College, Oxford, and since October 1974, Minister of State at the Department of Education and Science.

Lord Butler of Saffron Walden is Master of Trinity College, Cambridge. He was previously Under-Secretary of State for Foreign Affairs, 1938—41; Minister of Education, 1941—5; Minister of Labour, 1945; Chancellor of the Exchequer, 1951—5; Lord Privy Seal, 1955-9: Leader of the House of Commons, 1955—61; Home Secretary, 1957—62; First Secretary of State, 1962—3; Deputy Prime Minister, 1962—3; and Secretary of State for Foreign Affairs, 1963—4.

Roy Jenkins was Minister of Aviation, 1964—5; Home Secretary, 1965—7; Chancellor of the Exchequer, 1967—70; Deputy Leader of the Labour Party, 1970—2; and has been Home Secretary since 1974.

Lord Gordon-Walker was Secretary of State for Commonwealth Relations, 1950—1; Secretary of State for Foreign

Affairs, 1964—5; Minister without Portfolio, 1967; and
Secretary of State for Education and Science, 1967—8.
Hans Daalder is Professor of Political Science at the University of Leiden, the Netherlands.
James Fox is a writer for the *Sunday Times Magazine*.

The editors are grateful to their contributors, and to the
many people who advised them in the compilation of this
reader. A special debt of gratitude is owed to Jacqueline
Bayes for her invaluable assistance in the preparation of the
manuscript.

Introduction

Political scientists at the moment probably ought to be concerned less with assessing the Prime Minister's power than with simply describing his job.[1]

Our purpose in presenting this collection of readings on the Cabinet and Cabinet ministers is a reflection on and application of Anthony King's prescription for the study of the Prime Minister. His call for a redirection of research, away from unverified (and, we suspect, ultimately unverifiable) assertions of the sources of the Prime Minister's power toward detailed descriptions of how this power is, and has been, used in specific instances, applies equally well to the study of the Cabinet, particularly as it is primarily with members of this body that the Prime Minister is compared. We are by no means the first to point out the need for more imagination, care, and rigour in the study of the Cabinet and the ministers who comprise it. Nor are we the first to note that it is both possible and desirable to separate the role of the Cabinet from the role of the Prime Minister. We agree with Colin Seymour-Ure's[2] argument that, in recent times, the Cabinet has not received the detailed scrutiny given to other institutions of the British political system, and that this neglect is largely attributable to the disproportionate emphasis placed on disputing the question of the Prime Minister's power.

This volume is not explicitly concerned with contributing to the debate on the power of the Prime Minister vis-à-vis the Cabinet or, for that matter, any other institution. It is our contention that not only is the power of the Prime Minister difficult, if not impossible, to describe accurately — for it changes over time, over different policies, and with individual Prime Ministers' varying conceptions of their office — but also that we lack at the present time sufficient descriptive information of the office and the job to advance anything but highly tentative statements. Furthermore, some may feel that, despite its title, this volume is not really concerned with the Cabinet. Such a view, we feel, would be part of an unfortunate tendency in past studies of the Cabinet: a failure to look beyond the formal boundaries of the institution. We insist that the study of the Cabinet must take account of the fact that the Cabinet is one of a complex system of institutions, and furthermore that the ministers comprising the Cabinet have responsibilities going beyond whatever transpires in Cabinet meetings at No. 10 Downing Street and inter-departmental meetings elsewhere. To refuse to study the individuals comprising such a collectivity as the Cabinet, and to restrict attention only to the activities of the collectivity as a whole, is to invite sterility in research. Hence, the chapters of this volume cover both the Cabinet as a whole and the ministers comprising it.

It is also necessary to make another disclaimer. This volume is not advanced as a definitive work on the Cabinet: the changing nature of the institution leads us to doubt whether it is possible, or even worthwhile, to make such a claim. Our aim in editing a series of readings entitled *Cabinet Studies* is far more modest. In combining some recently published work with a number of original contributions which deal with various aspects of the Cabinet, our purpose is to encourage people to think, more systematically and more rigorously than has been the case in the past about the Cabinet as an institution. As students and teachers of politics we believe that, on the one hand, it is continually necessary to update our understanding of the Cabinet and, on the other hand, that it is useful to bring a series of readings about the institution and its members together under one cover. The scope of this volume suggests the sort of areas where significant work has been undertaken in recent years, and where more is needed in the future. If the publication of this collection of readings in any way results in political scientists undertaking more systematic and more rigourous research on the Cabinet than has recently been the case, we shall be well satisfied.

The study of the Cabinet

In the last decade a small number of studies have appeared which have been exclusively devoted to various aspects of Cabinet government in Britain, and new insights into the

institution have been offered by John Mackintosh, Hans
Daalder and Lord Gordon-Walker (a former Cabinet minister).[3] Other material on the Cabinet has appeared in the
popular press, scholarly journals, and general books on
British government and politics. Compared to a much larger
volume of works on Parliament, the Prime Minister, elections
and political parties, the relative neglect of the Cabinet is
somewhat surprising and not a little disqueting. It might be
the case that this neglect reflects the unimportance of the
Cabinet in the governmental process, but this can only be
advanced as an assumption which, because of the absence of
detailed studies on the institution, we are not in a position
seriously to accept or reject. Until more research has been
undertaken on several aspects of the Cabinet we are unable to
say whether, for example, the Cabinet is more or less
important in the decision-making process than Parliament or
the Prime Minister, or whether the Cabinet has or has not
been decisive in such areas as international relations or trade
union reform. The panoply of secrecy (to which we return
later) surrounding many of the Cabinet's activities con-
tributes most directly to the existing state of affairs:
compared to other aspects of the political system such as
Parliament or elections, the Cabinet is far less visible and
much more difficult to approach. The fact that the Cabinet is
less visible and more difficult to study than other parts of the
political system should not mean that, on the one hand, all
attempts to study it should be postponed indefinitely, or, on
the other hand, that if they are to be conducted, they must
proceed in a cautious and piecemeal fashion.

An examination of the major existing works on the
Cabinet reveals that attention is usually focused on five
major topics. The first of these is the *functions* of the
Cabinet. Graham Moodie, to quote one author who has
commented on this aspect of Cabinet government, notes the
following three functions which the Cabinet performs:

(1) final determination of policy to be submitted to
    Parliament;
(2) supreme control of the national executive in accordance
    with policy endorsed by Parliament;
(3) co-ordination of the activities of Departments of
    State.[4]

These are very general and all-embracing functions which the Cabinet performs. A moment's reflection on them reveals that the Cabinet is intrinsically involved in the decision-making process and, given this, we must draw attention once again to the surprising neglect of the Cabinet by students of politics. The central position of the Cabinet in the drafting, controlling, and implementing of policy is such that it cannot be ignored in any consideration of policy-making or politics.

A second aspect of the Cabinet which is frequently referred to (and one to which we have already drawn attention) is its *power* relative to that of other persons or institutions. In *The Government of Great Britain*[5], Graham Moodie divides his chapter on 'Cabinet Government' into five approximately equal parts, two of which deal with conventions of responsibility, and the other three with the Cabinet's relationship to, respectively, the Monarch, the Prime Minister, and the Commons. Moodie is not the only author to look at these relationships in terms of power; Sir Ivor Jennings' classic study, *Cabinet Government*, is an historical examination of the Cabinet and the Monarchy,[6] John Mackintosh and G. W. Jones have debated at length power relationships of the Cabinet and the Prime Minister,[7] and the late H. V. Wiseman's *Parliament and the Executive* reviewed relationships between the Cabinet and the Commons.[8] What is common to all these works is their consideration of the question, 'who has power over whom, at what time, and with regard to what matters?' The answers have generally been framed in terms of historical conventions or precedents which govern the relationships between these institutions. In his *Government and Politics of Great Britain*, John Mackintosh considers yet another power relationship, that between the government and the public.[9] Mackintosh's concern is with describing various channels of communication between the government and the people: these include interest groups, opinion polls, and the mass media. What is markedly absent from what is otherwise a very sound discussion is an analysis of the effects that these channels have had on the making or implementing of important national policies (on, for example, Northern Ireland, the European Economic Community, Concorde, etc.) at the Cabinet level.

shortcoming of these works is that they tend to be descriptive rather than analytic or theoretical. The analytic failure stems from production of insufficient systematic historical evidence to permit discovery of significant trends and changes and an almost total lack of comparative analysis. However, without such evidence and analysis, it is impossible to proceed to theorising about the consequences of the background, experience, and tenure of British Cabinet ministers for the policy-making process.

In this connection all of the following questions could well and legitimately be asked. What difference does it make to the business of government if Cabinet ministers are recruited from Oxbridge rather than other universities, or no universities at all? In what ways are decisions taken by ministers with a public school education different from decisions taken by ministers with a grammar school education? Is it important in any way if the average age of Cabinet ministers is fifty-five rather than forty-five? Questions such as these are rarely raised, let alone answered, in the literature, and yet there remains at least a nagging suspicion that background, experience, and tenure variations are related to what the Cabinet does and how it does it. A more thorough investigation of such variations than currently exists is at least a necessary precondition for more successful investigation of such suspicions.

Alternative strategies for the study of the Cabinet

The review of the existing literature suggests that certain aspects of the Cabinet have been emphasised at the expense of others. These emphases have, in our opinion, had unfortunate consequences for the study of the Cabinet. In general, the following reorientations would produce more interesting and more useful research.

(1) A reduction of concentration of the *formal* powers of the Cabinet and their evolution, and a consequent increase in attention to actual *behaviour*. For instance, this could take the form of establishing how often, under what circumstances, and with what consequences the Prime Minister *does* replace or reshuffle a large part of his Cabinet, rather than

pointing out that, *in principle*, he could sack or reshuffle all of his ministers without resigning himself. Similarly, instead of citing the Cabinet's function of ultimate determination of policy, what ought to be studied is the extent and manner in which this function is performed. This requires knowledge of what Cabinet meetings are like, what sort of matters come before the Cabinet, and how often in the creation of a policy the issues involved are considered. While the secrecy surrounding Cabinet minutes prevents the obtaining of the actual discussion until many years after the event, a great deal of information could be gained, or pieced together, through interviews with the participants involved.

(2) As a consequence of reducing the amount of energy spent studying formal powers, more attention can be paid to the actual *relationships* between the Cabinet and other institutions of government. This question is by no means answerable solely in terms of whether or not one body controls another. Instead, the Cabinet should be seen as the centre of a *system* of interrelated parts, all concerned to a greater or lesser extent with the formulation and implementation of public policy; a system which includes, at least, Parliament, the shadow Cabinet, the civil service, interested groups, other governments, international organisations, and the mass public. What is of importance in the study of the Cabinet is the extent to which the component parts of this system have changed, how changes in one part of the system modify the behaviour of another part, and how each of the parts interacts with others in the formulation of government policies. It is plausible to argue, for instance, that Britain's entry into the EEC has greatly enlarged the number of relevant actors in policy formulation, may considerably reduce the speed with which a policy is put through (because of the need for international negotiations), may considerably alter the knowledge and skills required of civil servants, may affect the strategies which the government communicates with the public, and so on. Assessment of these arguments requires a great deal of information not currently available, and a fuller understanding of the role of the Cabinet in the policy-making process.

(3) More attention ought similarly to be given to the internal *structure* of the Cabinet. This is not only a question

of institutional developments such as committees, but also a question of power. Discussions of the power of the Cabinet must cover two lines of inquiry: one is concerned with the power of the Cabinet vis-à-vis other institutions, the other with the power of individual Cabinet ministers relative to each other. Despite problems of secrecy and lack of detailed information, most attention has been paid to the former; however, research into power relationships within the Cabinet is likely to be far more profitable, but it is discomforting to observe from the existing literature that little attention has been paid to this subject. D. J. Heasman, in a perceptive analysis,[15] has pointed out that the Cabinet is not an amorphous collection of individual positions, but rather is a hierarchy of jobs underpinning ministers' careers with the premiership at the top of the hierarchy. The hierarchy defines patterns of recruitment of senior ministers, who are provided with the experience necessary for efficient policy-making; at the same time, it provides possibilities of promotion for junior ministers who aspire to more senior positions. Heasman ably documents the major lines of conflict that the hierarchy generates, but leaves unresolved several related problems of considerable importance. These include such concerns as the actual nature of the hierarchy; which, if any, are commonly-taken paths to certain senior positions; whether or not any positions appear to be critical in the attainment of other positions; or which posts are immune to frequent changes.

Common sense and observations suggest that a minister's power is related to characteristics of both the individual concerned and the office he or she holds; both of these will require investigation in the future. This could take the form of attempts to assess the relative *importance* over time of the many positions which have been included in the Cabinet. To do this requires producing great amounts of evidence on different subjects; moreover, the answer is likely to be complicated by the fact that different Cabinet positions are likely to appear more and less important when different measures are used. The following are probably the most useful of these measures. Firstly, the amount of expenditure controlled and size of permanent civil service staff which are reliable indicators of the volume of business done by a department and thus a part of its importance. Secondly, the volume of legislation introduced into Parliament may indicate another side of a department's business, while, thirdly, the volume of parliamentary questions directed at a department indicate its importance at any time as perceived by other MPs. Indicators of the importance of a ministry over time include the proportion of time that the post is included in Cabinets as well as the relative seniority of the minister in charge of it. Patterns of promotion of individual ministers from one post to another could be used to elucidate relationships among posts in determining the structure of relationships within the Cabinet.

(4) More attention must also be paid to the *personal characteristics* of individual ministers, in discussing either power within the Cabinet or the Cabinet's performance as an institution. This is related to the point made previously that the Cabinet should not be studied only as a collective body but also as a collection of individuals; similarly, their other activities (for instance, service on Cabinet committees) should be studied as part of the working of the Cabinet and not merely as detractions from the power of the Cabinet as a whole.

The study of Cabinet ministers is markedly undeveloped. It is by no means clear that much (outside of biographies, autobiographies, and diaries) is known about why individuals seek Cabinet appointments, how they perceive the nature of their responsibilities as Cabinet ministers, what they perceive to be the function of the Cabinet as a whole, or whether or not these perceptions have altered over time. Nevertheless, any and all of these could have significant bearing on the power and performance of the Cabinet. Similarly, while speculations abound on the increasing need for specialists and people competent to deal with technical information, it is rare to find anywhere suggestions of exactly what background, skills, or experience are necessary or useful in the performance of a minister's job. Finally, to make such suggestions requires knowledge of exactly what a minister's job is likely to involve, and how this varies among different Cabinet-level positions and departments.

(5) Underlying all the above is a major recommendation — that probably the most important reason for

studying the Cabinet is that *it is essential in any investigation of the making of public policy*. Policy-making is an exceptionally complicated matter; as Stephen Bailey suggests in the American context

> Legislative policy-making is ... almost unbelievably complex ... [and] appears to be the result of a confluence of factors streaming from an almost endless number of tributaries: national experience, the contribution of social theorists, the clash of powerful economic interests, the quality of Presidential leadership, other institutional and personal ambitions and administrative arrangements in the Executive Branch, the initiative, effort and ambitions of individual legislators and their governmental and non-governmental staffs, the policy commitments of political parties, and predominant culture symbols in the minds of both leaders and followers in the Congress.[16]

Notwithstanding institutional differences between the American and British systems of government, this list is suggestive of the contents of an examination of policy-making. The researcher is generally interested in ascertaining a number of things about the policy-making process: what the outcomes of the process were, how these decisions were reached, what alternative policies were rejected and why, under what circumstances the policies were initiated, formulated, and implemented, and, finally, what contributions various institutions made to all these features of a policy decision.

Policies are, in principle, not made in a haphazard or chaotic fashion, but are the products of conscious activities of political actors. Despite this, policy studies in Britain are markedly undeveloped, and there is little detailed information available about exactly what contributions the Cabinet — or, for that matter, any other institution — makes to the policy process. Furthermore, much of what has been written on the Cabinet to date — matters of responsibility, composition, institutional developments, and so on — is (while it remains only tangentially related to questions of policy performance) largely uninteresting unless the connection with policy matters is explicitly investigated.

In the context of the study of the Cabinet, the most important questions that need answering are the following:

(1) At what stages in the formulation of a policy and in what ways was the Cabinet involved?

(2) What interchanges took place between ministers and civil servants?

(3) Who were the ministers involved? What were their backgrounds and skills? What sort of contributions were made by the ministers responsible for the policy?

(4) What inter-departmental discussion, compromise, and agreement took place?

(5) To what extent were Cabinet-level discussions held in committee rather than in plenary session?

(6) To what extent and with what effect were members of other institutions in the wider circle of policy-making involved?

Even this partial list, if fully answered, would be inadequate, for this sort of research requires both historical and comparative counterparts to be truly profitable. Only when the development of decision-making processes in Britain is understood, and has been compared with the experience of other countries, can one adequately begin to assess the role and effectiveness of the Cabinet in the British system of government. Moreover, only when that assessment can be made would a political scientist be in a position to tackle seriously what Colin Seymour-Ure has called the 'neglected' question of Cabinet reform.

The organisation of this reader

In selecting passages for inclusion in this reader we have deliberately and consciously ignored the distinction which is often drawn between, on the one hand, the Cabinet as an institution and, on the other hand, Cabinet ministers who derive their titles from membership of that institution. Our reason for doing this is simply our insistence that the study of the Cabinet requires attention to both. To focus on one at the expense of the other seems to avoid discussion of many of the central aspects of the Cabinet. For reasons of easy availability elsewhere — and the desire not to contribute further to what is already a large literature — we have not included sections which specifically focus on either the power of the Cabinet (especially vis-à-vis the Prime Minister) or the historical development of the institution. We realise that the contents of this reader are at the same time both limited and novel: they are limited because much of what is traditionally associated with the Cabinet is not included here; and they are novel because our focus is markedly different from existing studies, and because many of our selections appear in print here for the first time. The reader will soon become aware that the material we have included is mainly of a descriptive and analytic, rather than a prescriptive, kind. Although we have taken advantage of our editorial position to adopt a prescriptive tone in this introduction we share the belief that description and analysis must precede prescription, and our choice of material reflects this belief.

The suggestions made in this introduction underlie the organisation of the remainder of this volume. There are three principal sections. The first of these, 'The Life of the Cabinet', focuses on the characteristics of Cabinet ministers. Background, perceptions of office, skills and experience brought to office, length of tenure in office, and reasons for leaving the Cabinet are all considered; as far as possible, attempts are made to provide sound historical and comparative perspectives on these topics. The second section, 'The Environment of the Cabinet', deals with the relationships between Cabinet ministers, individually and collectively, and members of other institutions. Civil servants and the shadow Cabinet are the parts of the government which are considered, and selections are also included on the Cabinet's relationships with the public. In the latter case, the emphasis is on strategies adopted by the government in dealing with the public through the mass media. The final section is entitled 'The Cabinet at Work'; unlike the first two, it contains no previously unpublished material. Three former ministers discuss, respectively, the nature of Cabinet government, the nature of certain ministers' jobs, and, through imaginary examples, what takes place in Cabinet meetings. In the final chapters Hans Daalder reviews the major institutional de-

Part One

THE LIFE
OF THE CABINET

1 The Making of Cabinet Ministers*

PICHARD ROSE

> Ministers are very busy and harassed people. Some of them
> encourage their staff when presenting their work to make
> what is complex appear to be simple, to draft papers
> composed of short sentences and cut up into short
> paragraphs, so that they can be taken in almost at a glance.
> This process (which has its dangers) is as far removed as it is
> possible to be from the deliberate and exhaustive methods
> of formal scholarship. That is why the proceedings of
> bureaucrats appear to the academic mind to be so
> superficial.
>
> Lord Strang, formerly Permanent Under-Secretary,
> The Foreign Office

The executive branch of British central government consists
of three groups unequal in size and in the attention given
them: the Prime Minister, the senior civil service and Cabinet
ministers. In the past decade, the work of the Prime Minister
has been the subject of considerable journalistic and
academic scrutiny. The chief book about the Cabinet, John
P. Mackintosh's study, concentrates attention upon the
collegial role of Cabinet ministers and not upon their position
as departmental executives. Mackintosh concludes by
emphasizing the power of the Prime Minister vis-à-vis others
in Cabinet.[1] The Fulton Committee voluminously chronicles
many things about the recruitment and work of senior civil
servants, but it avoids consideration of the relationship
between administrators and the ministers they are meant to
serve.[2] The very substantial literature about the social origins
and career patterns of men in ministerial office[3] tells the

*Reprinted from the *British Journal of Political Science*, Vol. 1 (1971)
pp. 393–41, with the permission of the Cambridge University Press and the
author. An earlier version of this paper was presented at the VIIIth World
Congress of the International Political Science Association, Munich, 4 September
1970. In preparing it, the author has benefited from comments made by Bruce
Headey, Anthony King and R. M. Punnett. The research on which this paper is
based did not require any research grant.

1

reader much more about where ministers come from than it does about what they do once they get into office. All three types of studies have one characteristic in common: the isolation of one aspect of executive government from its other parts. Yet in theory and practice, central government is a collective process; its activities are the result of the inter-action of civil servants, departmental ministers and the Prime Minister.

The purpose of this article is to concentrate attention upon the least studied part of the executive: departmental ministers. The choice can be justified because, while ministers lack the unique status of the Prime Minister, they have about twenty times the energy and time to devote to the working of a particular department of state. These departments are the chief building blocks of central government. Because the Prime Minister is a non-departmental minister, there is little that he can do of an executive character without the active collaboration of one or more departmental ministers. To note this is not to denigrate the importance of his central co-ordinating role or, for that matter, of non-departmental ministers in co-ordinating and advisory roles. Moreover, both departmental ministers and the Prime Minister are overshadowed numerically by the hundreds of senior civil service advisors with whom they must work. Whether they are overshadowed in terms of influence is a matter of long-standing debate.

The making of a minister involves two important and distinctive elements: the experiences that an individual has while qualifying for selection and the tasks that confront him once he has been appointed to office. The minister's potential capability for meeting the demands of office is thus conceived as a ratio between the skills gained in recruitment, and the demands made upon him once he has been recruited. The approach differs from many socialization studies in that the emphasis is upon role socialization in a political environment rather than upon pre-political socialization. It differs from many recruitment studies in that the emphasis is not upon the politician's career as dependent variable but as intervening variable. The dependent variable is the executive process of government. Its structure and conventions influence the recruitment of individuals, which in turn, affects the process. The first section reviews the way in which individuals are recruited for ministerial work, and the second reviews the structural demands and constraints upon a minister once he gains office. The concluding section considers the consequences of existing procedures for British central government.

Within the space available and material at hand, one cannot provide a definitive description of what ministers do in office. But one can reasonably infer the limits of their activities and influence. Analysis involves inference, but the chain of inference is far shorter than that involved, say, in studies of the relationship of social origins to ministerial behaviour. If a relationship is to be established by that means, then one must show: (i) people of the same (or similar) social origins will, upon gaining office, be able to influence the executive activities of government; (ii) they will influence it in a similar manner; (iii) such actions will lead to predictable outcomes; (iv) these outcomes will be advantageous to their group of origin. Analysis of legalistic conventions concerning ministerial work involves a much shorter chain of inference, but studies have increasingly emphasized the gap between the 'dignified' convention of ministerial responsibility and the 'efficient' activities of ministers.[4] Inferences about what an individual does immediately prior to gaining office and what he does immediately afterwards cover a much shorter timespan than that employed in studies of social origins; moreover, drawing inferences about later behaviour from earlier behaviour is logically very different from inferring behaviour from constitutional norms. The logic of analysis is the same as it might be in a study of the making of university professors. For example, one might find a university in which professors were recruited from careers in party politics and cleared by party headquarters, rather than from schools giving specialist professional training and appointed by committees of professional peers. In such circumstances, one would infer that the skills of the individuals concerned are not what conventional labels imply. In redefining the job of a professor, one would also be re-formulating the idea of a university.

I

In analyzing the making of Cabinet ministers one might choose either of two contrasting approaches. A deductive approach emphasizes the substance of the job, as in management theory. The job of the minister is first defined and characteristics necessary or relevant to success are specified. Given this, one can then ask to what extent individuals recruited into ministerial posts have these characteristics, and/or what kinds of individuals in a society are likely to have them, whether or not they are made ministers. The great advantage of the deductive approach is that it avoids tautological reasoning of the form: What characteristics are necessary for ministerial success? The characteristics that successful ministers have. Its limitation is that analytic abjectivity is achieved by standing outside the system as it has evolved and operates at present. An inductive approach emphasizes the selection of ministers as the product of a series of conventions and rules that have evolved in the course of time, without a coherent plan or rationale. Instead of asking what kind of person ought to become a minister, one asks: What kind of people does the process throw up?

In a society in which a Constitution was being newly written or substantially revised, then reasoning from first principles would be entirely appropriate; it would also be necessary, if no appropriate foreign models were availabe for imitation. But England, pre-eminently among Western regimes, is a land in which the chief rules of government were not worked out deductively but have evolved through the centuries. Hence, there is substantial justification for analyzing the process as it is, before considering the criteria that might be invoked in making ministers.

The formal identification of ministers is a straightforward task, for appointments are always officially gazetted. Differentiating non-departmental from departmental ministers is more difficult, because nearly every minister of

Cabinet rank has one or more assigned responsibilities. The Leaders of the House of Commons and the Lords do differ from most of their colleagues in that they are managing Parliament, instead of large administrative agencies. The Chancellor of the Duchy of Lancaster, with the task of negotiating British entry into the Common Market, is also free of many conventional administrative responsibilities. The Lord Chancellor and the Lord Privy Seal in his role as head of the Civil Service Department have responsibilities relating to large bureaucratic activities. Even an individual described as a Minister without portfolio, such as Lord Drumalbyn in the Heath administration, may have specific responsibilities assigned to him and, in the noble Lord's case, a desk at the Department of Trade and Industry. Reciprocally, the head of a large government complex, such as the Department of Environment, may have less routine work than expected, because of the extent to which his responsibilities are delegated to subordinate ministers and his principal concern that of co-ordinating a federal ministry. Lord Mills, a personal confidante of Mr Harold Macmillan, appears to be one of the last of the 'duty-free' non-departmental ministers. Nearly all Cabinet ministers — except the Prime Minister — have assigned departmental duties.

The number of persons styled ministers has been growing primarily because of the increase in the numbers of ministers outside the Cabinet. In recent years, the number of ministers of Cabinet rank outside the Cabinet has been about as numerous as those in the Cabinet. Some of these officeholders are in charge of autonomous but minor departments, e.g., the Solicitor General; others hold subordinate posts in large departments, e.g., Ministers of State in the Foreign and Commonwealth Office. Another tier of official appointees — parliamentary secretaries and under-secretaries — are unambiguously junior ministers. Their status, as measured by salary or departmental authority, is usually well below that of the highest ranking civil servants in a department, and their effective influence is usually very limited too. Collectively, these individuals form the government, i.e., the ministry of the day. The lowest stratum of political appointees — parliamentary private secretaries of individual ministers — is unpaid and not formally recognized by legislation. Informally it is well established, and increasingly, the PPS is expected to be bound by conventions regulating the behaviour of ministers.[5] In this paper, the term ministers is used to refer to the parliamentary appointees of the Prime Minister, except parliamentary private secretaries. The term Cabinet minister refers restrictively to the twenty or so men in the Cabinet. All ministers will be assumed to have departmental responsibilities, currently or at some point in their Cabinet career.

Although the Prime Minister is formally but one among a number of members of Cabinet, in this study he must be treated separately, because he makes the Cabinet, in the formal and practical sense of naming other ministers. While he may be assisted in some appointments by advice from the Chief Whip or occasionally from other senior ministers, a Prime Minister cannot allow others to determine the composition of the Cabinet, for if it is not his, then he risks deposition from office. Because the power of appointment is concentrated in the hands of one individual, then the criteria for appointment are inevitably subject to fluctuation, as one Prime Minister succeeds another or even as an individual Premier's outlook changes during his tenure of office. As Britain has had only seven Prime Ministers since 1940, the source of data for generalization is both small and heterogeneous. At least three major criteria can be identified. The first is *representativeness* in relation to political factions and tendencies as well as social origins. The convention of collective responsibility gives the Prime Minister an immediate incentive to include political opponents in his Cabinet, to silence criticism and to implicate them in what is done by the government. This tactic will fail if an individual refuses an appointment, as Iain Macleod did from Sir Alec Douglas-Home in 1963, or resigns, e.g., Aneurin Bevan in 1951. There are occasionally individuals who, by actions or words, rule themselves outside the bounds of co-option, e.g., Enoch Powell in 1970. Representativeness of social groups is most clearly evident in the Labour Party, where traditionally a Co-operator, a woman and a prominent trade unionist, as well as a Scot and a Welshman, have been included in each Cabinet. A representative Cabinet ensures a Prime Minister maximum support by opinion leaders in the parliamentary party; it also brings a wide variety of views to bear in Cabinet. Reciprocally, it might be suggested that part of Harold Wilson's troubles with the Industrial Relations bill in 1969 arose from the paucity of working-class trade union representatives in Cabinet. A second criterion is *loyalty to the Prime Minister*. If potentially disloyal colleagues are appointed to gain silence, they must be counterbalanced by the appointment of individuals whose loyalty can be relied upon by the Prime Minister. There is always a tendency to err on the side of caution to ensure a maximum of personally loyal colleagues. Loyalty may be founded in personal friendships, well established status relationships, e.g. of senior patron to junior, or in alliances of convenience or of principle. A third criterion of selection is ministerial *competence*. At the start of an administration, a Prime Minister will have fewer clues about the competence of ministers than at the end, when promotion and dismissal can be used to sort those with demonstrated competence and incompetence. (The situation is thus the reverse of an American administration, for a President can hope to recruit the most talent for a new government, whereas, at the end of his term in office, he will have only short-term and relatively unattractive commissions to offer.) Competence is, however, a highly abstract term. It begs the question: What kind of competence — oratorical? administrative? technocratic? The only posts with formal qualifications are relatively minor: the English and Scottish law officers must be qualified lawyers. By contrast, there is no expectation that the Chancellor of the Exchequer must have formal training in economics or finance. Of thirteen post-war Chancellors of the Exchequer, nine have had no formal economic training, one did some economics at University, and three had worked as economists.

The attributes that gain an individual a ministerial appointment may be singular or several. In theory, an individual can be representative, loyal and competent; alternatively, he may be so outstandingly loyal or velopments of the Cabinet over the last sixty years, and James Fox considers the role of the Central Policy Review Staff. If any or all of these selections serve to inspire further thought or research on the Cabinet, our aim in presenting this Reader will have been achieved.

Notes

1. A. King, 'Introduction', A. King (ed.), *The British Prime Minister* (London: Macmillan, 1969) p. ix.
2. C. Seymour-Ure, 'The "Disintegration" of the Cabinet and the Neglected Question of Cabinet Reform', *Parliamentary Affairs*, vol. 24 (1971) p. 196.
3. J. Mackintosh, *The British Cabinet*, 2nd ed. (London: Stevens, 1962); H. Daalder, *Cabinet Reform in Britain 1914–1963* (Stanford: Stanford University Press, 1964); Lord Gordon-Walker, *The Cabinet* (London: Fontana, 1972).
4. G. C. Moodie, *The Government of Great Britain* (London: Methuen, 1964) p. 75.
5. Ibid.
6. Sir Ivor Jennings, *Cabinet Government*, 3rd ed. (Cambridge University Press, 1959).
7. The debate can be found in King (ed.), *The British Prime Minister*, pp. 168–210.
8. H. V. Wiseman, *Parliament and the Executive* (London: Routledge and Kegan Paul, 1966).
9. J. Mackintosh, *The Government and Politics of Great Britain*, 3rd ed. (London: Hutchinson, 1967) pp. 69 *et seq.*
10. G. Marshall and G. C. Moodie, *Some Problems of the Constitution* (London: Hutchinson, 1967) pp. 60–74.
11. S. E. Finer, 'The Individual Responsibility of Ministers', *Public Administration*, vol. 34 (1956) pp. 377–96.
12. Lord Gordon-Walker, *The Cabinet*, esp. Chapters 2 and 3.
13. For instance, D. N. Chester and F. M. G. Willson, *The Organisation of British Central Government* (London: George Allen and Unwin, 1968).
14. See sources cited in Chapters 1–4, below.
15. D. J. Heasman, 'The Prime Minister and the Cabinet', *Parliamentary Affairs*, vol. 15 (1962) p. 479.
16. S. Bailey, *Congress Makes a Law* (New York: Columbia University Press, 1950) p. 236.

representative or competent that this one attribute alone
assures him a place in government. The less qualified a man is
on one or two counts, then the more important it is that he
show qualities on another. In the extreme case, there may be
an inverse relationship between two attributes: an individual
may be very loyal but incompetent, or very competent but
disloyal. Just as an individual may combine within himself
several attributes, so too a Prime Minister will combine
within a Cabinet people with a mixture of attributes. If he
cannot find individuals who are simultaneously
representative, loyal and competent, then he must appoint
some individuals primarily for their competence, some for
their representativeness and some for their personal loyalty.

Two of the three criteria elucidated above are concerned
with solidary aspects of government; ministers who are loyal
and/or representative will help to hold a government together
by virtue of their following among some backbenchers or
their concern with supporting the Prime Minister. Only one
of the three attributes, competence, is immediately relevant
to instrumental goals extrinsic to Westminster, such as
'restructuring the economy'. In other words, what is in the
self-interest of the Prime Minister need not be in the interest
of the ministry collectively.[6] Because a Prime Minister has no
fixed term of office, he has good institutional incentive to
concern himself with party solidarity. Unlike an American
President, a Prime Minister cannot reckon he is secure in
office for four years. Instead, his standing in the party can be
eroded substantially in a few months by private, public and
leaked mutterings against him by his nominal colleagues and
subordinates. This may not lead to an open defeat in the
House of Commons. The mode of 'retirement' of Harold
Macmillan, Sir Anthony Eden and Sir Winston Churchill
suggests that Prime Ministers may resign when Cabinet
colleagues indicate that there is not much point in going on;
domestic politics can occasion 'diplomatic' illnesses as well as
foreign affairs. It could be suggested that the best security a
Prime Minister has for retaining office is that his Cabinet
consist of competent ministers. The limitation upon this
argument is that the more successful senior ministers become,
then the more readily comparisons may be drawn between

them and the Prime Minister, to the disadvantage of the latter. In other words, a Prime Minister does not want around him as senior ministers a large number of men who are 'too' competent, for fear that he is promoting his successor sooner. Among post-war Prime Ministers, only Churchill has been secure enough (and old enough) to allow a single heir-apparent to remain prominent for years. One explanation for the calibre of a number of appointments to the most senior posts of Chancellor or Foreign Secretary is that it would hardly be conceivable that the party would oust the Prime Minister to make such men Premiers.

There is an institutionalized incentive for senior ministers to consider their prospect of becoming Prime Minister tomorrow, should their leader be forced to retire by health or other considerations. The survival of most Prime Ministers for years is a reminder that ambitious princes also face difficulties. It need not diminish the effect of *feeling* insecure upon Prime Ministers. Such feelings can explain such things as the Macmillan purge of July 1962, not to mention some of the more puzzling of Harold Wilson's reshuffles. The subjective way in which the Prime Minister can decide the fate of his colleagues can breed insecurity among ministers threatened with instant dismissal by loss of favour. The omission of a single name in a reshuffle brings little cause for complaint in a party, and principally stigmatizes the man left out. The aggregate and diffuse sense of insecurity would seem likely to stimulate suspicion and conflict in circumstances that are not intrinsically harmonious, as departments inevitably compete against each other for scarce supplies of money, parliamentary time, publicity and party favour.

Because the Prime Minister is the sole initiator and authorizer of ministerial appointments, then his patronage powers are of intense importance to all MPs who hope for preferment in government. Because of the convention of collective responsibility, all who accept this patronage are bound to show the outward signs of loyalty, private thoughts and remarks notwithstanding. There is, of course, nothing new in the use of patronage to maintain support within Parliament. What is particularly noteworthy in twentieth-century Britain is the extent to which the Prime

Minister's patronage power has increased (Table 1.1). In 1900, sixty persons held paid appointments; the number increased by one-third in the First World War, and then declined to pre-1914 levels. The Second World War raised the number of appointees. In the two decades following, the number of ministers remained at the level previously reached only in the First World War. The return of a Labour government under Harold Wilson increased by two-fifths the number of ministers in paid posts. Mr Heath commenced his administration with fewer men on his payroll than Mr Attlee had found necessary in 1950 or Mr Macmillan in 1960. If parliamentary private secretaries are counted as part of the government, then the growth in patronage in this century is greater, for their numbers have more than trebled in the period.

The impact of patronage in the House of Commons has risen disproportionately in the past seventy years. The number of paid posts given individuals in the House of

TABLE 1.1

The growth of ministerial appointments — 1900–70

	1900	1910	1917	1920	1930	1940*	1950	1960	1967	1970†
Cabinet ministers	19	19	5	19	19	9	18	19	24	18
Non-cabinet ministers	10	7	33	15	9	25	20	20	27	25
Junior ministers‡	31	36	47	47	30	40	43	43	58	36
MPs in paid posts	33	43	60	58	50	58	68	65	92§	68§
Peers in paid posts	27	19	25	22	12	19	13	18	23	11
Total paid posts	60	62	85	81	58	74	81	82	115	79
PPSs	9	16	12	13	26	25	27	36	30	32
Total MPs appointed	42	59	72	71	76	83	95	101	122	98

*Chamberlain.
†Heath.
‡Includes political appointments in the Royal Household.
§Includes paid assistant whips.
Sources: D. E. Butler and J. Freeman, *British Political Facts, 1900–1968* (London: Macmillan, 1968) p. 57 and author's calculations.

Commons has doubled from the time of the third Marquess of Salisbury to that of Mr Heath; it almost trebled from the time of the third Marquess to that of Mr Wilson. If those who serve as PPS are also included as recipients of patronage, then the importance of patronage in the House of Commons has grown even more. The most immediate reason for the increase in the number of MPs in government is the decline of the number of peers. In the Conservative ministry of 1900, 45 per cent of paid posts were held by persons in the House of Lords; in the Conservative government of 1970, the proportion had dropped to 14 per cent, 6 per cent lower than under Labour in 1967. Because the average size of the majority party in the Commons has declined from 387 in 1900–14 and 414 in 1918–39 to 344 since 1945, the proportion of formally eligible MPs receiving posts has further increased. The third Marquess of Salisbury gave jobs to 8.4 per cent of his MPs in 1900, whereas Mr Heath gave paid posts to 20.6 per cent of those in receipt of the Conservative whip in the Commons. As the circulation of ministers rises, that is, the speed with which they move from post to post, the total number of appointments that a Prime Minister will make during a fixed period of time increases. The apparent tendency of more Members of Parliament to regard this job as a full-time career will also increase the desire for patronage within the Commons, as appointment to a ministerial job contitutes promotion in career terms. Moreover, self-conscious and ambitious backbenchers looking for their first appointment can show the outlook of a ministerialist by virtue of anticipatory socialization, hoping that their adoption of this outlook while not yet in receipt of patronage will help gain them a government appointment.

From the Prime Minister's point of view, the substantial increase in the patronage that he dispenses to MPs is valuable to increase his support within the parliamentary party. Insofar as he can claim the formal loyalty of those who accept his patronage, he will have a substantial block vote for use when questions of confidence are raised in party meetings. A Prime Minister such as Harold Wilson needed to add to his 'payroll' vote the endorsement of only one-quarter of Labour MPs not in receipt of patronage in order to be sure of a majority within the Parliamentary Labour Party. Mr Heath similarly knows that if he is challenged, ministerial appointees constitute almost two-thirds of the numbers needed to form a majority among Conservatives in the Commons. The use of such support to defeat critics does not assure a Prime Minister of freedom from criticism by backbenchers or, for that matter, by colleagues speaking off the record. It does leave him in possession of formidable institutional powers to maintain the endorsement, if not the assent, of his fellow partisans in Parliament.

From a detached point of view, the increase in the number of ministers drawn from the Commons has as a corollary a decline in selectivity in making appointments. Everything else being equal, the more men who must be appointed from a fixed number of applicants, then the lower down the scale of qualifications the selector must go, by whatever standards individuals are ranked. In the time-honoured phrase of constitutional lawyers, the Queen's Government must be carried on; someone must be given each office to avoid declaring political bankruptcy because of an insufficiency of talents. It may be that there has been a gradual rise in the level of ministerial ability among MPs. In the absence of clearly defined and operational criteria and evidence, one cannot confirm such an assertion.[7] Moreover, executive leadership depends upon the ratio of individual talents to job requirements. The demands of ministerial posts have risen greatly in this century; they may have risen faster than the pool of ability in the Commons. The most realistic working assumption is that the capabilities of MPs have expanded neither more nor less than the demands of the job since 1900.

The pool of potential ministers is confined to Parliament and, increasingly, to the House of Commons, by the traditional convention that each Cabinet Minister, excluding the minor posts of Scottish law officers, must be a Member of Parliament. In a House of 630 members, a minimum of 315 MPs are thus formally available for a ministerial job. In practice, various conventions and practical considerations substantially reduce the number of MPs eligible for appointment.[8] Except in wartime, ministers are rarely appointed without having already established membership in Parliament.[9] There is an equally strong convention against appointing newly elected MPs to ministerial posts. In 1951 and 1970, none of the junior or senior ministers in the new Conservative government was a freshman MP, and, excluding Frank Cousins, no one had this status in the 1964 Labour government, notwithstanding the considerable turnover in government on both occasions. The number of 'veteran' MPs elected when a new government is returned is, by definition, less than a majority, further discounted by the consequences of retirement by some previously sitting MPs. For example, Mr Heath had 269 veteran MPs in his Commons majority in June 1970 and Mr Wilson 235 in his majority in 1964.

Age is a second restriction upon ministerial eligibility, operating by custom, if not by force of law or convention. If one assumes that MPs above the age of seventy or below the age of thirty are outside the appropriate age brackets for office, eighteen veteran MPs in the 1964 Labour government were disqualified from consideration, and two MPs in Conservative ranks in 1970.

A third category of MPs are effectively disqualified from appointment on personal grounds. In a handful of cases, this involves extreme political views. Extremists seem to have declined greatly on the Labour side since the heyday of fellow travelling MPs in the 1940s. On the Conservative side, the numbers may be rising, with racists and 'hardline' Ulster Unionists potentially outside the pale. A larger number of MPs are ruled out on grounds of unsuitable personal characteristics, such as poor physical or mental health, drinking problems, questionable business association, sexual delinquencies, etc. One might estimate that perhaps five per cent of all MPs are ineligible on personal grounds. The same proportion might be ruled out because of the inability to handle administrative tasks, even with the maximum of assistance from civil servants. (It would assume unvarying and overriding elitism among constituency associations to assert that every one chooses a candidate of ministerial standard or the egalitarian Jacksonian belief that the minimum required of a minister is so low that every MP will meet the standards.) There are some MPs who do not wish office, perhaps a tenth of the House. They may prefer the freedom to criticize on the backbenches to the constraints of a parliamentary secretaryship at Public Building and Works. Business or professional considerations, e.g., as a lawyer or journalist, may make participation in government less attractive, psychologically or financially, than dual roles inside and outside Westminster.

The total number of MPs in the majority party who are *de facto* ineligible for a ministerial appointment ranges from one-third to two-fifths, depending upon circumstances fluctuating from Parliament to Parliament. This means that a Prime Minister is left with a pool of potential ministers so small that he must give ministerial appointments or the status of PPS to half or more of all MPs who are not unsuited to receive an appointment. There is, of course, competition and choice for higher offices, especially in Cabinet. But competition here, as in a closed classics scholarship, is among a very restricted pool of competitors. Difficulties are more likely to arise in determining *what* job many MPs will have, rather than deciding whether they will be offered posts.

The compulsion to draft about half the eligible MPs into government means that the calibre of a ministry is to a large extent determined by the character of membership in the House of Commons. In the period from 1868 to 1958, F. M. G. Willson calculated that the median minister spent about fourteen years in Parliament before entering Cabinet.[10] Things have changed little since. In the Cabinet that Harold Wilson named after the 1964 general election, the median number had been in the Commons for 19 years. In Heath's 1970 Cabinet, the median appointee entered the Commons in 1953; only one Cabinet minister had entered the House after 1959. After reviewing the period 1958–68, Wilson concludes:

> Whatever developments there may have been within the British political system within the last ten years, whatever subtle shifts of power and/or influence may have taken place between institutions, there is clear evidence that in one enormously significant area — the recruitment and career backgrounds of its most senior political

members — the pattern not only remains overwhelmingly similar to that established over the last hundred years but if anything moved slightly towards more orthodoxy in terms of parliamentary and administrative experience.[11]

The characteristic of Commons seniority is even stronger among Prime Ministers, for post-war Premiers average twenty-five years from first election to Parliament until entry into Downing Street.

The duration of role socialization in the Commons is important, if one hypothesizes that those most successful in gaining ministerial posts are likely to be most strongly committed to the institutions within which they achieve success. This commitment reduces the effect of differences in social origin between Etonians and sons of coal miners or builders, just as it enhances the impact of political institutions upon ministerial outlooks. The House of Commons is thus not only a chamber for electing a Prime Minister, but also a school for ministers. What training does the Commons give an MP? The chief skills that are emphasized in the Commons concern personal relations and the effective oral presentation of ideas. The art of working with people at Westminster is different from the 'glad handling' associated with electioneering. It involves the ability to work with other full-time politicians both co-operatively and competitively. Verbal skill goes beyond mere verbal fluency or rhetorical tricks. It also includes the ability to show conviction and in some cases, knowledge of complex matters.

The expansion of the committee system in the House of Commons gives the backbench MP some opportunity to acquire familiarity with the subject-matter of government, though not infrequently in pathological situations. But he is not so well placed as a civil servant to learn about departmental work. Yet even senior civil servants are subject to official criticism for not having enough specialist knowledge about the problems that they and their ministerial overlords are supposed to solve. It is noteworthy, moreover, that frontbench MPs in both parties have strongly opposed efforts to give backbench MPs and potential ministers greater knowledge of the workings of the executive side of British government. The work of a British MP is certainly no more (and probably less) a preparation for involvement in the executive side of government than is membership in the United States Congress. The difference between Westminster and Washington is that the President rarely chooses his executive aides and Cabinet from the legislature, whereas the Prime Minister nearly always does.[1][2]

Activities in the House of Commons do not lead naturally to the work of a departmental minister as prep-school leads to public school. A minister's job differs in important respects from that of an MP. In addition to dealing with people, he must also deal with mountains of paperwork. Instead of dealing with intimates on a face-to-face basis, he must delegate many tasks to civil servants whom he hardly knows, without losing influence upon their actions. On *a priori* grounds, it would seem that the skills needed for managing a large government department might as well or better be learned in the management of a large organization, whether profitmaking or non-profitmaking, or even in another part of government.

The existence of an established hierarchy of titles among the ranks of ministers provides a clear progression of jobs within the executive. It makes it possible and probable for Cabinet ministers to undergo intensive role socialization for a substantial number of years prior to reaching Cabinet, first as an MP, then progressing from the status of PPS to junior minister and then to a ministerial office outside the Cabinet before becoming a Cabinet minister at the top of a government department. It is historically indisputable that the job of a junior minister was *not* designed as a training ground for Cabinet ministers.[1][3] The fact that service in such a post is today virtually *sine qua non* for Cabinet office does not assure that the time spent in these qualifying posts necessarily imparts skills useful in higher offices. There is no conscious apprenticeship training in a junior ministerial whether profitmaking or non-profitmaking, or even in another part of government.

II

To note that the job of an MP does not offer specialized preparation for excutive work in government does not answer the question: What task or tasks are ministers expected to perform? If ministers are expected to do nothing but manage people and present oral justifications of policies, then the skills acquired in qualifying for appointment will be necessary and sufficient for success once selected. If this is not the case, then the question arises: What happens to the work that ministers are poorly prepared to undertake?

The roles that ministers, especially Cabinet ministers, may perform are multiple and demanding. Formally, each minister is responsible in several senses of the term for all that is done in his department, including matters of detail that may be politically explosive. He is also expected to speak on behalf of his department in the House of Commons, both to advance departmental causes and to defend the department against criticism. A third role is representative of the department in inter-departmental negotiations and at Cabinet. Such negotiations not only affect administrative details, but also competition for two scarce resources: public funds and parliamentary time for the passage of departmental bills. Another role of the minister is spokesman and chief negotiator with interest groups affected by departmental measures. The minister can also present and publicize the department in the press and on television. In theory, at least, there is the expectation that from time to time a minister may contribute to Cabinet discussion on matters not directly connected with his own department, e.g., sale of arms to South Africa, or a Profumo-type crisis. In addition, a minister also has two personal political roles not immediately connected with departmental business: as a constituency MP, and a politician concerned with his future career.

The multitude of time-consuming and difficult tasks that confront a Cabinet minister gives him some freedom of choice in what he does. Because there are not enough hours in a week to do everything that could be done, a minister must, consciously or unthinkingly, give priority to some roles rather than others. It could be argued that the most important decision a Cabinet minister makes is how to allocate his time as between competing roles.[14] On this hinges much that follows during his ministerial career.

A series of interviews with present and past Cabinet ministers undertaken by a Strathclyde colleague, Bruce Headey, has identified three departmental roles as of special importance.[15] One basic role is that of *departmental representative* to the outside world, both in inter-departmental negotiations and in dealings with special publics, whether interest group spokesmen, MPs or journalists. This role fits well with previous training in the House of Commons, for it requires both skill in presenting ideas orally and the ability to relate meaningfully to other individuals. Success in this role means that the minister has a good image outside his department. A second basic role is that of departmental *chief executive*. As an executive, he will become involved intimately in the details that constitute the core of the administrative process. As chief executive, he will be able to make discretionary decisions when the administrative process presents him with problems involving alternative choices. In this capacity, a minister will concentrate attention upon expending and improving the flow of work through the department. In a place such as the Home Office, simply keeping up with all that is going on within the department can be difficult or even impossible. Such an individual may climax his ministerial career by a major departmental reorganization or a legislative measure which makes for the more efficient despatch of business.[16] A third basic role is that of the *key issues* minister. He concentrates what discretionary time exists upon a few key issues for which his department has primary responsibility. The key issue may be forced upon a minister by its crisis character (e.g., Northern Ireland in 1969) or it may be chosen by a minister on other grounds (as Northern Ireland might have been prior to 1969). A corollary of the key issues role is that the individual minister ignores as much as possible many other issues for which his department is responsible. In some instances, he may have capable junior ministers to whom some tasks can be delegated. Alternatively, civil servants can sort the files, recommend courses of action and present him with documents designed to facilitate choice or formal approval. Headey's interviews found that the largest group of ministers see themselves as devoting substantial time to key issues. It does not follow that this subjective perception is matched by an objective account of what they will or can do with their time in office.

The role that best fits the conventional picture of a Cabinet minister is that of the key issues man, for this is the role in which an individual politician makes his influence felt most, by initiating programmes consistent with his own and his party's values. By contrast, the chief executive does little to alter positively the on-going activities of his department; the distinction between the minister and his Permanent Under-Secretary is blurred, for the latter as well as the former could choose between options identified as equally practicable by the departmental machine. The politician primarily active as a departmental representative may influence individuals outside his department on its behalf. But it does not follow that the policies he promotes are his, or even his party's policies. Given existing constraints, the more time and energy a politician devotes to his representative role, the less resources he has to invest in influencing the content and administration of the policies he promotes.

Typically, a minister takes charge of a department with limited subject matter expertise in the field, and occasionally, little experience of running a government department. The development of a formal Shadow Cabinet, with departmental posts assigned, recognizes that something more than twenty-four hours notice is required before an individual can realistically be said to be in charge of a major government department. But in Mr Heath's 1970 Cabinet, nine of the eighteen members were assigned to work that did not match their most recent shadow post.[17] Moreover, the median shadow minister spends limited time upon his departmental brief, and the opposition party provides much less support than would be necessary for the preconditions of party government to be met.[18] Once in office, the multiple and time-consuming character of the job greatly limits time available for thinking about policies in anything other than a reactive manner. There is no time and some danger in trying to anticipate the problems of one's next department, if one is a serving minister with a chance of being promoted or moved in the next Cabinet reshuffle. By concentrating closely upon departmental work at hand, there is a danger that the minister may become, in Oakeshott's terms, a 'mere empiricist',[19] reacting to whatever is set in front of him, with little or no time or ability to anticipate or initiate events within his department.

In so far as government is something more than movement from crisis to crisis — a few departments, such as the Foreign Office, may primarily involve just that — then one can consider what is the minimum time required for a minister to carry a major new policy within his department. At least three years would be needed to achieve this. It would take one year for the minister to understand the technical intricacies of his department sufficiently well to settle the administrative and not unimportant details of a bill, a year to push it through Parliament and/or secure Treasury authorization for expenditure, and a year to establish guidelines for administering the resulting policy so that administration can subsequently be routinized and thus delegated to others. Such an estimate assumes that consultation with affected interest groups, including local authorities, and publicity designed to mobilize or simulate popular support can be undertaken simultaneously with these steps, or has already been done. If not, the period of time required to see a policy through will be even longer. If a minister enters office without a clearly defined objective but simply wants to do something, then he may need a year to find out what it is he wishes to do. He may also need to learn what is unworkable about what the party says he ought to do. In short, the three-year estimate of official responsibility is a minimum estimate, rather than a generous one. It may be reduced in a limited number of policy areas, or if a minister takes over and sponsors as his own a measure that departmental officials or ministerial predecessors have slowly been nurturing in committees, both appointive and civil service.

Time is further constrained by particular institutional features of British elections, with their attendant consequences for new governments and new Cabinets. Uncertainty about the timing of an election means that a government may be formed on very short notice, unable to present many perfected bills of its own in the first year's session of its Parliament. The absence of a period of two months for transition between Opposition and office, such as exists in the United States,[20] means that individuals must simultaneously become familiar with new jobs and also find time to identify key issues and formulate policies for such issues. The bulk of the first year may therefore be spent in 'learning the ropes' and not in making effective choices. Uncertainty about the timing of the next general election means that pre-election preparations have no fixed time limit. In 1963—4 and 1965—6 the amount of time spent in pre-election manoeuvres meant that few key issues were resolved then. The sight of the Prime Minister 'clearing the legislative decks' in December, 1969, for an election that need not have occurred for fifteen months indicates that the first two instances are not unusual. Something like two years in four or five are likely to dedicated to dealing with electoral preparations and their consequences; this quantum of time is not different in magnitude from that expended in the United States. In short, a Cabinet minister must move fast in the life of a new Parliament to have a three-year uninterrupted time span in which to advance a measure of his own.

The custom of British government anticipates that Cabinet ministers will be moved from department to department with some frequency. The term 'Cabinet reshuffle' aptly connotes the idea of movement as an end in itself, rather than as a means to an ulterior policy objective. The prime purpose is often to maintain the solidary equilibrium of the Cabinet. Taking departments persisting across the years, in the period between the 1955 and 1970 general elections — a time spanning four Prime Ministers, three elections and one party change in office — the average duration of a holder of eleven departmental posts normally in the Cabinet was twenty-six months, well under the three-year minimum stipulated as desirable. An individual who initiates and presents a major bill is thus unlikely to remain in the department long emough to see to its implementation. The duration of a Cabinet Minister's stay in a single office is shortening while government becomes more complex. In the period 1900—14, which also involved four Prime Ministers, three elections and one change of government, the average tenure of the same posts was thirty-four months (Table 1.2). The rate of turnover in Britain is unusually high by the standards of Western nations. It ranks thirteenth out of seventeen in the amount of time ministers remain in a major office, according to data compiled for the period since 1945 by Richard Lowe.[21] Only France, Finland, Italy and Belgium, all ruled

TABLE 1.2

Duration in ministerial offices 1900—14 and 1955—70

Office	Ministers 1900—14	Average months per minister	Ministers 1955—70	Average months per minister	Difference in months
Foreign Secretary	2	82.5	8*	22.5	−60.0
Chancellor of the Exchequer	5	33.0	7	25.7	−7.3
Home Secretary	5	33.0	6	30.0	−3.0
Defence	5†	33.0	7	25.7	−7.3
Local Government and Housing	4	41.2	6	30.0	−11.2
Education	6	27.5	10*	18.0	−9.5
Board of Trade	6	27.5	8	22.5	−5.0
Scottish Secretary	5	33.0	4	45.0	+12.0
Agriculture	5	33.0	5	36.0	+3.0
Postmaster General	6	27.5	6	30.0	+2.5
Public Building and Works	4	41.2	9	20.0	−21.2
Averages	4.8	34.4	6.9	26.1	−9.7

*A minister who held the same post with other appointments intervening is counted twice.

†This figure averages turnover rates for the Admiralty and the War Office, each of which had five men in charge in the period, 1900—14.

(Time spans calculated from November 1900—July 1914 inclusive, 165 months; and from June 1955—May 1970 inclusive, 180 months.)

Sources: Calculated from Butler and Freeman, *British Political Facts, 1900—68*, pp. 50—7 and public statements subsequently.

by unstable coalitions, have lower scores than Britain. The median turnover rate for all nations is nine months higher than in Britain. The disruptive effect of high rates of turnover is accentuated in Britain by the practice of moving a man from one department to another in the course of giving him promotion. By contrast, the American pattern of promoting appointive officers emphasizes movement from assistant secretary to under-secretary and upwards within the same department.[22] One argument often used to justify frequent moves is that politicians need the reward of rapid promotion, or the goad of rapid demotion. This argument emphasizes the use of Cabinet appointments for solidary political purposes rather than managerial ends.

Constitutionally, the problem of high ministerial turnover is resolved by assuming that all Cabinet ministers are interchangeable in their values and capabilities. Whatever the utility of this assumption as constitutional theory, it is hardly plausible descriptively. The very concept of a key issues minister implies a personalization of choice. It would be surprising if all members of a Cabinet had the same idea of what is a key issue in a given department. Partisanship can create a commonality of outlook between men in a single party, thus making individual politicians more easily interchanged. There appear to be few issues on which front benchers show monolithic unity in private as well as in public. The prospect of rapid mobility would seem to encourage Cabinet ministers to think in terms of short-term benefits when making decisions, whether benefits be perceived as accruing to themselves in terms of favourable publicity, or to clients of their department.

If one assumes that ministers will invest their efforts where they will find their skills most profitably employed, then it follows from the character of the recruitment process that most ministers are likely to find it most rewarding to take the role of departmental representative, for this will make use of prior paralimentary experience in managing people and presenting ideas orally. Skill in interdepartmental representations will gain an individual the respect of ministerial colleagues and civil servants, inasmuch as he will help make government run more easily, and/or show himself a worthy advocate of departmental claims in conflict with other departments. Skill in public representations will gain a minister a good press and the accolade of lobby correspondents, who write frequently about ministers from a House of Commons vantage point. There is no necessity that the verbal formulae advanced in these representations be unambiguous and administratively practicable. The growing proportion of journalists and publicists in the Commons (and the impact of television upon MPs generally) may be encouraging an increasing reliance upon representations that are no more than verbally plausible formulae.

The role of efficient chief executive within a department is not one for which MPs are specially trained, but a substantial proportion of Cabinet ministers appear to regard it as important. The job of an efficient administrator requires three very general skills. One is the ability to work with other people or to see their point of view; here, parliamentary training is useful. A second requirement is an analytic mind, capable of seizing the essentials of a problem. Constant public speaking may be helpful in this respect, especially for persons who also have a legal training. The third essential is the ability to read large masses of paper quickly and abstract essentials from the printed (or handwritten) page. Here, parliamentary life is not helpful; it is part of an oral tradition, and provides no experience in moving files of papers. With the dominance of graduates in Cabinet today and the removal of working-class early school leavers this skill need not be difficult for ministers to acquire.

The role for which prior parliamentary work offers least preparation is that of a key issues minister. This not only requires skill at verbal representations and moving paper, but also the ability to identify problems before they reach crisis stages, and initiate the exploration of programme alternatives that will not already be part of the routine or recognized world of the bureaucrat. Once a desirable solution is identified for a key issue, only one-third of the work is completed. There still remains the difficult task of relating general principles to administrative structures in a way consistent with the requirements of legislation and civil service administrative codes. Last and not least, the formal enactment of an act must be followed up by considerable pressures to ensure that the money, administrators and goodwill are forthcoming so that the desired consequences are likely to follow. The skills most suited to these ends are those of the expert administrative politician and are most easily learned by role socialization as an administrator, whether in Whitehall, local government, extra-Whitehall public agencies or the profit-making sector of the economy.

There is nothing in parliamentary work that provides this experience to MPs before they become ministers.

Because all three basic roles have some positive contribution to make to the operation of British government, it is misleading to think in terms of all-or-nothing evaluations of the best role or the best mix of roles. One must allow for at least two situational variables. One is the intrinsic capabilities of the individual who is (or must be) given a Cabinet appointment. One cannot easily make an expert administrator out of a lifetime debater, or a key issues minister out of a man who is by nature timid and respectful of tradition. A second variable is the political context: a single department cannot be continuously altering its major policies. Popular satisfaction or dissatisfaction will encourage inertia at one point in time, and require a show of action, whatever its form, at another. Differences between departments may also be considered a variable. In a non-departmental sinecure office such as the Lord President of the Council, skill in working with others is primary, inasmuch as committee concerns will be his first duty. In other posts, such as Education, the ability to move large masses of paper may be crucial, to keep in contact with all parts of a massive system requiring co-ordination. In the Home Office or the Scottish Office, with extremely heterogeneous responsibilities, an individual minister may need the capabilty of a key issues man, so that he can turn his attention away from many unrelated actions, in order to focus on one or two things where he wishes to leave his mark decisively. The secular growth in government responsibilities suggests that the number of departments where affairs can be left to run themselves is shrinking, or even disappearing. The growth of super-ministries, such as Environment or the Department of Health and Social Security, indicates that heterogeneity is increasing. If this is the case, there is thus a rise in the demand for if not in the supply of key issues ministers.

III

In so far as resources are scarce, and this is certainly true of ministerial time and effort, then the concentration of attention upon representational and administrative roles will result in a limited amount of attention being given to key issues by Cabinet ministers. A minister may significantly intervene in only two stages of a multi-stage process of policy-making. He may identify a problem as requiring a departmental response, saying 'prepare a plan to do x to problem y' or 'prepare a plan to do something about problem y'. And he may approve the recommendation or choose between alternatives set before him by civil servants concerning problem y. In canvassing alternatives and implementing policies in the field, ministers appear to have little chance to intervene. Given the difficulties of co-ordination in large organizations, not least where initial cues from ministers may be vague, it would be surprising if ministerial influence were not limited. One does not need to subscribe to a theory of synoptically reviewing all possible alternatives to think that the key stage in disjointed incremental decision-making may come *before* the reduction of alternatives to a paired comparison, especially one as simple as that between 'this thing' and 'no-thing'. In short, the structure of British Cabinet government tends to foreclose greatly the options of a minister to choose policy alternatives. Instead, he can become the salesman of policies of his department's devising (but not necessarily of his own, or of his party) and/or the efficient administrator and signator of a multitude of routinized papers produced by the bureaucratic process.

The pattern of recruitment identified above is the result of a great many influences, both historical and contemporary. The writings of those persons most involved in British government treat these influences as constants. Yet in terms of social science theory they are best conceived as variables, i.e., conditions that are potentially capable of change. The low probability of any of these influences changing, because of the inertia of the *status quo*, does not detract from the analytic value of examining the chief props of the present arrangements. Three conventions, none of them sanctioned by anything as rigid as statute law, are particularly important in determining the kind of men who are placed in charge of departments of state in Britain today.

(i) *The convention that ministers must also be Members of Parliament.* This not only stipulates that an individual must be given a seat upon appointment, but also that an individual must serve an apprenticeship in Parliament prior to appointment. The apprenticeship averages about 15 years prior to entry into Cabinet.[23] There is practical justification for this: only by experience in the House of Commons can a minister learn how to represent a department adequately in parliamentary debates. Failure to master parliamentary forms is harmful to a minister and to his department. Yet, important as this skill is, it concerns only one role: representation of a department. This skill has no necessary relationship with skill in other roles. Given the increasing demands upon the time of an MP, an individual who masters the technicalities and moods of the Commons is likely to have less time to devote to other extra-parliamentary roles, including those specific to decision-making in large organizations. The convention is most important for those it excludes: persons who hold leading positions in other major institutions of society, such as trade unions, financial institutions, and non-profit organizations. Some individuals have been co-opted into government as advisers on a full-time or part-time basis. But in so far as they have gained power, they have not been assigned responsibilty and accountability. This might be done in more than one way. The House of Lords already provides a place in Parliament for a minister brought in from outside the Palace of Westminster. One might even establish in politics as in the law a divided profession, with specialists in public pleading, analogous to trial barristers, speaking for departments in the Commons, and specialists in departmental decision-making, analogous to solicitors, managing other tasks. One might even suggest that this already happens, but that the decision-maker is not a minister, but rather, the Permanent Under-Secretary.

(ii) *The convention that ministers of the Crown should not disagree with each other publicly, because of collective responsibility.* One consequence of this dignified aspect of British government is that it 'privatizes' conflicts between decision-makers in the executive. (The alternative is to assert that no conflict exists, i.e., that the Cabinet is not a political institution!) Yet increasingly, ministers use leaks to the press and other covert devices to signify personal views to a wide audience, or to dissociate themselves from blame.[24] A more serious consequence is that the 'privatizing' convention extends to activities of civil servants, including their ministerial relationships. One can hardly have it known that civil servants disagree among each other and offer conflicting advice to ministers, if the latter are always to be treated as in agreement. This privatization tends to reduce public influence until *after* decisions are collectively promulgated in the name of the Cabinet. Yet it is precisely at the moment in which ministers and their advisers disagree that outside interventions may be most influential and, potentially, most desirable. (Interventions may also be useful even when no internal dispute exists.) In recent years the executive has been moving toward a less commital form of policy pronouncement, by such devices as 'Green Papers' for policy discussion. Private consultation continues with what the department regards as relevant people and groups. Unless one believes in departmental omniscience or a hidden hand mechanism guiding such consultations, one must doubt the maximum efficiency of such consultations. It is noteworthy that the Fulton Commission, while criticizing privatization, could do no more than call for yet another committee to consider reducing its effects.[25]

(iii) *The movement of ministers and Prime Ministers in and out of office without notice.* The uncertain tenure of a Prime Minister is likely to encourage a sense of insecurity and make him give greater attention to patronage as a device for ensuring personal loyalty and survival than would be the case if he had a fixed term of office. Logically, the choice of a Prime Minister for a fixed period of office is independent of the direct election of a Prime Minister. The Commons could be asked to make such a choice more easily than the electorate. Creating a fixed-term Parliament without simultaneously fixing the tenure of the Prime Minister would increase his insecurity, because there could be no sanction of dissolution to intimidate those trying to supplant a Prime Minister. The insecurity of individual ministers in their membership in Cabinet and charge of a particular department is a disincentive for an individual to become deeply involved in the work of his department. It would not require legislation or a major change in constitutional conventions if Prime Ministers began to give more attention to the 'career development' of Cabinet ministers, as their civil service counterparts are now expected to do.

Comparing procedures for making Cabinet ministers among Western nations having parliamentary forms of government emphasizes that the British process is not the only one consistent with parliamentary institutions, but one among a number of variants. In some Continental countries, ministers are not recruited exclusively or overwhelmingly from the lower chamber of Parliament. They may come from local government, civil service, universities or other major institutions within society, bringing with them little experience of parliamentary discourse, but offering other skills. In some countries, such as Norway, it is made a condition of appointment that an individual resign his seat in Parliament if he receives a ministerial appointment. The emphasis on privacy is also not inviolate. Sweden provides an extreme illustration of willingness to make information public about the deliberations of government. The change of leadership that can result from coalition instability in countries lacking a majority party is not conducive to instability in departmental leadership. On this count, Britain shows greater instability than most of its Continental neighbours.

To show that the present method of making Cabinet ministers in Britain is not inevitable is not to demonstrate that it could or should be easily altered. Such judgments must depend upon other criteria. One of the most important is assessment of the consequences of existing practices for the system of central government as a whole. Because of the inter-relationship of the work of MPs and ministers and civil servants, any alteration of one part of this triad would be expected to have consequences for the work of the other two. Unfortunately, questions of the reform of Parliament or of the civil service often proceed without considering indirect and systemic consequences. Whether reform is considered desirable depends less upon the consequences that the recruitment process has for ministers and more upon its consequences for central government. In particular, one must ask: If the Cabinet ministers do not settle key issues, who does? The most obvious candidates, in the sense of proximity to ministerial authority, are civil servants. They have the very real responsibility of seeing that the Queen's government is carried on. Yet civil servants lack the political legitimacy or the career incentives of a minister. If forced to handle key issues, they are likely to opt for a policy which minimizes conflict and criticism, for they are debarred from public controversy and it would hardly be loyal to involve their ministerial superior in a controversy without his knowledge and consent. Since many courses of action are likely to cause controversy, the tendency to maintain equilibrium and avoid change is likely to be strong. The result is a form of government that may be described in David Apter's terms as a 'reconciliation system' or alternatively, as 'directionless consensus'.[26]

Ironically, the long-term consequence of an equilibrium outlook is unintended change, unless the environment be as unaltering. as governmental conventions. The absence of adaption in one part of a complex system is just as much a source of change in function as in an intended initiative. Since the Reform era of more than a century ago, the demands made upon the individual Cabinet minister — both within and without his department — have grown enormously. No longer can a Foreign Secretary read and answer in his own hand 'every report, every letter, and every despatch received . . . down to the least important letter of the lowest vice-consul' as Palmerston did in 1830. By 1846, Palmerston found the business of the Foreign Office had grown too much for the prompt despatch of replies by his own hand.[27] The House of Commons was also making great demands upon his ministerial time. Latterly, the management of party, of publicity and of constituency relations have forced ministers to spread their efforts more widely than was necessary in the days when a man might literally own or inherit his seat. The change in the life of ministers has also been accompanied by two major changes in the status of their administrative assistants. The first was the decline of patronage appointees in administrative roles, these Benthamite administrative reformers, styled by Kitson Clark 'statesmen in disguise',[2][8] could, in effect, serve as key issues ministers. A second change in administrative personnel was the growth of a technically proficient and increasingly large civil service. This has become the residuary legatee of the minister's powers — in so far as these can be transferred. One can hardly be surprised by changes in the relationship of ministers, civil servants and Parliament in such a timespan. It would be extraordinary if the consequences of conventions affecting the selection of Cabinet ministers in the days of Queen Victoria would be unchanging in the days of her great-great-grandchildren.

Notes

1. Cf. John P. Mackintosh, *The British Cabinet* (London: Stevens, 1962); D. N. Chester, 'Who Governs Britain?', *Parliamentary Affairs*, Vol. 15 (1962) pp. 519—27; A. H. Brown, 'Prime Ministerial Power', *Public Law* (1968) pp. 28—51, 96—118; and P. Gordon Walker, *The Cabinet* (London: Cape, 1970).

2. For a comment see, e.g., G. K. Fry, 'Some Weaknesses in the Fulton Report on the British Home Civil Service', *Political Studies*, Vol. 17 (1969) pp. 484—91.

3. See items cited in the bibliography of Richard Rose (ed.), *Policy-Making in Britain* (London: Macmillan, 1969) pp. 369—71.

4. Cf. S. E. Finer, 'The Individual Responsibility of Ministers', *Public Administration*, Vol. 34 (1956) pp. 377—96; and G. Marshall and G. C. Moodie, *Some Problems of the Constitution* (London: Hutchinson, 1959).

5. See R. K. Alderman and J. A. Cross, 'The Parliamentary Private Secretary', *Political Studies*, Vol. 14 (1966) pp. 199—208.

6. Cf. Mancur Olson Jr., *The Logic of Collective Action* (Cambridge, Mass.: Harvard University Press, 1965).

7. See, for example, the data on university education among MPs and Cabinet ministers in Richard Rose, 'Class and Party Divisions: Britain as a Test Case', *Sociology*, Vol. 2 (1968) pp. 129—62, Tables 12—13.

8. See F. M. G. Willson, 'The Routes of Entry of New Members of the British Cabinet, 1868—1958', *Political Studies*, Vol. 7 (1959) pp. 222—32, and by the same author, 'Entry to the Cabinet, 1959—1968', *Political Studies*, Vol. 18 (1970) pp. 236—8.

9. In 1964 Harold Wilson appointed five individuals from outside the Commons to posts at the level of Minister outside the Cabinet or higher. The results did not inspire emulation by Mr Heath; in 1970 he named only Lord Aberdare to a ministerial post without substantial parliamentary experience.

10. Willson, 'The Routes of Entry', p. 227.
11. Willson, 'Entry to the Cabinet, 1959—1968', p. 238.
12 Cf. Willson, 'Entry to the Cabinet, 1959—1968', and David Stanley, Dean E. Mann and Jameson W. Doig, *Men Who Govern* (Washington: Brookings Institution, 1967) Table 3.1.
13 D. J. Heasman, 'Ministers' Apprentices', *New Society*, 16 July 1964.
14. See, for example, the personal accounts by Ernest Marples and Patrick Gordon Walker contained in Rose (ed.), *Policy-Making in Britain*, pp. 115—31.
15. Headey's research will be reported in a book-length study of the roles of Cabinet ministers. See also Bruce Headey 'Cabinet Ministers & Senior Civil Servants: Mutual Requirements & Expectations', Chapter 6 below
16. An analysis of a year of parliamentaty legislation found that the number of 'administrative' bills was as great as that of 'policy bills'; ministers need not be the initiators of the former—or of the latter—type of bill. Cf. I. F. Burton and G. Drewry, 'Public Legislation: a Survey of the Session 1968—1969', *Parliamentary Affairs*, Vol. 23 (1970) pp. 154—83.
17. A book-length study of the evolution of the Shadow Cabinet is currently being undertaken by R. M. Punnett of the Politics Department of the University of Strathclyde. See also R. M. Punnett, 'Her Majesty's Shadow Government: Its Evolution & Modern Role', Chapter 7 below.
18. Cf. Richard Rose, 'The Variability of Party Government: a Theoretical and Empirical Critique', *Political Studies*, Vol. 17 (1969) pp. 413—45.
19. Cf. M. J. Oakeshott, *Political Education* (Cambridge: Bowes & Bowes, 1951) p. 10.
20. Cf. Laurin Henry, *Presidential Transactions* (Washington: Brookings Institution, 1960).
21. See Richard Lowe, 'Political Instability in Western Nations' (Glasgow: University of Strathclyde Politics Department, unpublished manuscript, 1969).
22. Cf. Stanley *et al.*, *Men Who Govern*, Tables E.1—12.
23. See Willson, 'Entry to the Cabinet, 1959—1968', p. 238.
24. For a good discussion of the tactics of leak in the Wilson Cabinet, see Gordon Walker, *The Cabinet*, pp. 167 ff.
25. The Civil Service: Report of Lord Fulton's Committee (London: HMSO, 1968, Cmnd. 3638) Vol. 1, paragraphs 283—4.
26. See Rose, 'The Variability of Party Government', pp. 440 ff., for a more detailed statement of this argument. For Apter's term see *The Politics of Modernization* (Chicago: University Press, 1965).
27. The quotation is cited from Henry Parris, *Constitutional Bureaucracy* (London: Allen & Unwin, 1969) pp. 107 ff.
28. Cf. G. Kitson Clark, 'Statesmen in Disguise', *The Historical Journal*, Vol. 2 (1959) pp. 19—39

2 Continuity, Turnover, and Experience in the British Cabinet, 1868-1970

JAMES E. ALT

Introduction

It is perhaps more difficult to place this study in the context of the academic literature on the Cabinet than to show that it covers a topic of some importance. The topic is the experience of Cabinet ministers and the extent of continuity and turnover displayed in their appointments. By 'experience' is meant the amount of time that an individual has served in one or another Cabinet; by 'continuity', the amount of time that ministers retain their individual appointments; by 'turnover', the frequency of changes in appointments. The arguments about continuity in office are familiar: on the one hand, a minister must hold a departmental office for time sufficient to master it in order to be effective; at the same time there is much to be said for Cabinet ministers having experience in a number of areas, in order to have a better idea of the scope and nature of governmental activities. While experience has its uses, it might also be held desirable for the Cabinet to contain people with new ideas and, perhaps, greater energy. What is required is presumably some sort of balance, but it has been suggested[1] that in the modern British Cabinet there is too little continuity and too much turnover. This study makes no recommendations about how much continuity is enough, or good, but it is hoped that anyone wishing to argue one way or another will find its conclusions useful.

Moreover, these topics figure in a number of contemporary debates. For instance, the power of the Prime Minster is sometimes taken to be reflected by frequent changes in cabinet appointments,[2] and sometimes taken to be enhanced by the uncertainty created by frequent changes.[3] Similarly, the inexperience of Cabinet ministers and their vulnerability

to removal from the Cabinet might be offered to account for
the decline of Cabinet government or the failure of a
Government to fulfill its policy objectives.[4] In addition,
there has recently been considerable discussion of reforms in
Cabinet procedure, changes in the nature of ministerial
responsibilities and powers, and the size of Cabinets.[5] One
can find research into the background, experience, and
professional paths to office of Cabinet ministers,[6] and the
nature and frequency of ministerial resignations.[7]

Finally there exist a small number of findings about
continuity and turnover in Cabinet appointments. These take
one of two forms. One finds either contrasts between
Governments (well over a majority of the Cabinet held their
posts throughout Baldwin's 1924—9 Government; only four
ministers did so between 1964 and 1970),[8] or tables which
show that average tenure in Cabinet appointments has
declined between the beginning of the century and recent
years by perhaps 25 per cent or slightly more.[9]

These suggestive findings are assumed to be correct,
though insufficient. Moreover, they raise all the questions
usually raised by comparisons of selected short periods. Take,
for instance, the comparison of 1900—15 with 1955—70.
What are these periods taken to represent? It could be that
each is meant to be typical of a longer period about it. If so,
what is it? Equally possibly, each period might represent the
outcome of trends in preceding periods. Again, we do not
know what these trends were or how long they lasted. Are
there certain characteristics associated with each period? If
so, how long after 1915 did the characteristics associated
with 1955 appear? Furthermore, what are they? If they are
only a lower level of continuity and higher turnover, then did
these change smoothly over the intervening forty years, or
were there distinct turning points? And if there were, what
were they? To answer questions like these, what is required is
historical perspective — an analysis of continuity over a
longer period to ascertain what, if anything, is really new,
and to identify crucial turning points and trends.

However, this study also has wider implications. Some of
the works cited above suggest that low continuity and high
turnover are recent phenomena, and argue that they are

connected to other features of recent governments like failure to fulfill certain policy initiatives.[10] Such an argument merits attention for which sufficient space is unavailable in the present study. However, one point must be made: if low continuity is not of recent origin, then the argument must be revised; either policy failures are a consequence of low continuity but not recent, or policy failures are a recent phenomenon but not simply or obviously connected to low continuity. This point holds for a variety of features of British government said to be connected to low continuity, all of which will be discussed in the concluding section below.

The first purpose of this study, however, is to provide an accurate historical description of phenomena of considerable importance in the study of British politics. Attention is focussed on members of the Cabinet since 1868, a date sometimes taken to mark the beginning of the modern era of British politics.[11] Principal questions of interest are: Is the experience of Cabinet members and their continuity in office on the decline? If so, since when and by how much?

Data and indexes

Data for this study comes principally from three sources: Woodward[12] for Cabinet experience before 1868, Ensor[13] for the period 1868–1900, and Butler and Freeman[14] for 1900–68. Where ambiguities required resolution, and for the last five years, other sources[15] were used.

The first step taken to investigate these topics was the construction of two indices, presented in Figure 2.1. The first of these, the lower line, is the *continuity index*. Its construction is straightforward. In each month since the formation of Gladstone's Cabinet in December 1868, for each Cabinet post, the number of months that it has been held continuously by the same person is counted; these individual continuity scores are then added together and divided by the number of Cabinet posts, yielding an average continuity score. Thus, the *continuity* of a hypothetical Cabinet of three ministers, holding their respective present appointments for four, six, and fourteen months is $(4 + 6 + 14)/3 = 8$

months. On those occasions when sources indicate one person simultaneously held two Cabinet posts, one of these (if held for different lengths of time, the more recent appointment) is excluded from the computation. It must be noted that this index assumes that the Cabinet is a collection of jobs rather than individuals (though it seems reasonable to view an exchange of jobs between two ministers as a discontinuity rather than otherwise). Moreover, no attempt is made to differentiate between posts on grounds of importance, and only posts formally of Cabinet rank are considered. Finally, like all unweighted averages, this one does not distinguish between 'some large and some small' and 'all in the middle': equal continuity scores are obtained for each of two hypothetical cabinets, in one of which all members have served twelve months, and in the other of which half the members have served twenty-four months and half are newly-appointed. This may appear a weakness, but any effort to distinguish situations like these robs the index of any straightforward interpretability it might be claimed to have.

Most loosely, this index reflects the extent over time that the Cabinet has looked much as it does, in terms of job-specific appointments. High values of continuity, then, suggest that few changes have been made in appointments since the formation of the government. The index gives an accurate idea of how long the average Cabinet member has held his present post. If one were to argue, for instance, that it took a minister two years to master a department,[16] this index would show, for a Cabinet, on average, whether this condition were being met: it would be, if the index stood at two or more years. Periods of *continuity* are revealed by the index line moving upward without interruption; changes in Cabinet appointments are reflected by horizontal or downward movements. In general, the larger the drop, the greater the *discontinuity*; when a new government is formed, the continuity index almost always falls to zero. (Throughout this study, a *government* is defined by party support, irrespective of changes in Prime Minister.)

The second index, the upper line in Figure 2.1. is the *experience index*. It too is measured monthly, and over the same time period. In this case, not posts but individuals are

considered; for each member of the Cabinet, the number of
months that he has been a member of the Cabinet (any
Cabinet, any position, regardless of party, and not necessarily continuously) are counted; these are added together
and divided by the number of ministers in the Cabinet to give
an average. The same exclusion is made in cases of one
individual holding two simultaneous appointments. This
index reflects, simply, experience in Cabinet-level positions,
and thus, to some extent, whether a government is 'experienced' or not. Unfortunately, it does not take account of
potentially useful experience gained inside or outside
Parliament, while not in the Cabinet, and it would probably
be helpful, though extremely difficult, to incorporate such
information in the index. Moreover, it could well be argued
that a person stops gaining useful experience after a certain
time ('what you don't know after fifteen years isn't worth

FIGURE 2.1

Upper line = Average experience; Lower line = Average continuity

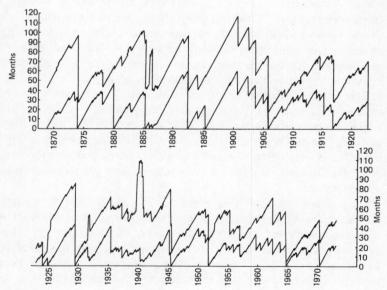

knowing'); employing such a criterion would of course be arbitrary, though no more so than not employing it.

This said, the interpretation of the experience index is quite staightforward. In any month, its value reflects the amount of Cabinet-level experience among all ministers in the Cabinet. A value, for instance, of five years shows that, on average, Cabinet ministers have five years experience in one or more Cabinet-level positions. Again, ths index is indeterminate between situations of a few very experienced ministers and many moderately experienced ministers; experience of two years is obtained in each of the following three hypothetical ten-member cabinets: all ten with two years experience; five members with four years experience, and five newly appointed to their positions; or one member with twenty years experience and nine new members. However, there is only one instance (Churchill's Cabinet, 1951—4) when the experience of one man might be said to render a misleadingly high level of collective Cabinet experience. (The continuity index is, of course, less affected by this situation.) Constant uninterrupted increases in the index of Cabinet experience are consistent with either continuity in office over the Cabinet, exchanges of position between ministers (where Cabinet personnel remain constant), or (very rarely) replacement of one minister by another with exactly the same amount of experience. Vertical upward movements reveal a shift to more experienced personnel, either by their replacing less experienced persons, or by the latter being dropped from the Cabinet. Vertical downward movements indicate the opposite, i.e., sudden shifts to less experienced personnel. Note that the experience index does not necessarily move in the same direction as the continuity index: indeed, when the latter falls to zero, the former may rise, if the new Cabinet's personnel have greater previous experience.

The advantage of this method is simply historical perspective. In the first place, one gets a visual idea of the extent and frequency of changes. Moreover, one can see whether certain periods have much in common, and which appear to be aberrations. Most importantly, one gets a sense of continuity and of patterns, unavailable through inspection of tables. The next two sections examine patterns of continuity and experience over the last century.

The continuity index

Consider first the continuity index. Its greatest values in the last century are sixty months, achieved by Lord Salisbury's second and third Governments, in mid-1892 and mid-1900. Since 1905, there have been five occasions on which governments have been both long-lasting and stable enough for their members to have been, on average, thirty-six months or more in their positions: 1914—15 (Asquith), 1928—9 (Baldwin), 1935 (MacDonald), 1945 (Churchill), and 1950 (Attlee). On the other hand, after May 1915 it is over twelve years before the Cabinet again reaches an average continuity of thirty months: after May 1935, this level is again not reached until July 1944. Furthermore, thirty months average continuity is only twice reached, and never maintained for over three months, after the resignation of the Labour Government in 1951. A first conclusion, then, is that a level of continuity in Cabinet appointments reflected by, on average, a Cabinet minister having been thirty months in his job has been comparatively rare for over half a century.

From an inspection of Figure 2.1, one sees that higher levels of continuity were achieved, and were maintained a greater proportion of the time, before 1900. While it is tempting to account for this by the possible longer tenure of governments then, this explanation cannot hold up, particularly in view of the long governments following 1905, 1931 and 1951. It is also unlikely that the requirement that a new Cabinet member (appointed in mid-term) stand for re-election could account for the difference; this rule was in force well into the twentieth century. If an explanation of this decline in continuity is to be given, it appears likely to lie in the changing nature of requirements of Cabinet activities, and in the dispositions of powers of Prime Ministers. In any case, the following fact remains (see Table 2.1): when governments had been in office long enough to permit an average continuity of thirty months (and they have been for over sixty years in the time period of our study), then this

TABLE 2.1
Achievement of thirty months continuity

Period	Proportion of time government in office over 30 months	Proportion of possible time that continuity was greater than 30 months
Dec 1868–Apr 1915	58.9%	78.1%
May 1915–Jun 1970	60.2%	19.3%

level of continuity was achieved 78 per cent of the time before May 1915 and only 19 per cent of the time since. That is to say, a government must be in office for thirty months before the continuity index can reach that level. Governments have been in office for at least that long about 60 per cent of the time before and after 1915. But of that time, a continuity average of thirty months has been achieved only one-fourth as often after 1915. Furthermore, inspection of Figure 2.1 reveals that average continuity has hardly changed since then; after 1915, it is simply lower, but not particularly decreasing.

Let us turn from *levels* of continuity achieved to *patterns* of continuity. As mentioned above, a government is taken to be determined exclusively by its party support. If one adopts this definition, Britain has had twenty[17] governments in the time period covered by this study, of which five[18] did not last long enough to allow continuity of Cabinet appointments to be sensibly discussed. Of the remaining fifteen governments, thirteen can be said to reveal three patterns of continuity. The remaining two governments (1895–1905, 1931–40) are mixed, in that the pattern of continuity revealed in the first half of their existence differs considerably from that of the second: in each case, a period of sustained continuity is followed by a prolonged period of frequent changes in Cabinet appointments.

The three patterns of continuity are as follows. The first is 'smooth', or a pattern of prolonged continuity: there may be changes at the beginning or end, but once established, the Cabinet carries on without change. The second pattern is of 'change in the middle': the Cabinet does not change for the first half of its existence; it is then subject to a major change,

TABLE 2.2
Patterns of continuity

Pattern	Government	Date
Smooth	Conservative	1886—92
	Conservative	(1895—1900)
	Conservative	1924—9
	National	(1931—5)
Change in the middle	Liberal	1868—74
	Conservative	1874—80
	Liberal	1880—5
	Liberal	1892—5
	Labour	1929—31
Continued or repeated change	Conservative	(1900—5)
	Liberal	1905—15
	Coalition	1915—22
	National	(1935—40)
	Coalition	1940—5
	Labour	1945—51
	Conservative	1951—64
	Labour	1964—70

or a number of minor changes, after which it continues again unchanged. The third pattern is 'continued or repeated change': throughout the existence of the government, changes are made in Cabinet appointments. These changes may be major ones, repeated at relatively short intervals, or a long series of more minor changes, perhaps punctuated by larger ones. Table 2.2 lists the governments under consideration by pattern of continuity they reveal; the two governments mentioned above as 'mixed' are each indicated in two places, with relevant dates enclosed in parentheses.

The 'smooth' pattern does not imply total absence of changes, though this is the case in the Salisbury Cabinet of 1895—1900. It is really intended to distinguish governments which may have been changed at the beginning or end of their terms (like the Conservative governments of 1886 and 1924) from those which changed abruptly in mid-term (like the Conservative government of 1874 and the Liberal government of 1880). There is a fairly sharp partisan division between these two patterns before 1935; speculatively, one might be tempted to attribute it to different dispositions on the part of Salisbury and Baldwin on the one hand and perhaps Disraeli and Gladstone on the other. Equally, it could be argued that what makes the difference is the presence or absence of sharp policy divisions in the Cabinet. In this case, whether or not an abrupt change occurs in mid-term appears to depend on whether or not issues reflecting such divisions emerge.

The pattern of continuous or repeated change, while dominant in postwar Britain, is not really very new: it is also the dominant pattern in the first quarter of the twentieth century. If one singles out the most discontinuous Cabinets (from Figure 2.1, those whose continuity over a long period of time is constant or declining), they are found to be spread over the last seventy years: 1900–5, 1935–40, and 1951–64. Not only is continuous or repeated change not new, but also the inference of a progression from smooth continuity to continuous change since 1868 must be resisted. The first two decades covered by this study contain only governments subject to mid-term discontinuities or too short-lived to be considered. Moreover, had the Attlee government lost the election of 1950 (or, just possibly, won it by a greater margin), its profile would resemble most of all that of the Liberal government of 1868.

Smooth continuity over the term of a Cabinet is simply uncommon. At the same time, there does appear to be a shift, occurring between 1900 and 1935, towards the pattern of more continuous change. This may be clarified by trying a different approach, which focuses on the nature and frequency of discontinuities. This is developed in a subsequent section, but first, the experience index is examined for similar patterns.

The experience index

As we have seen, the question of continuity in Cabinet appointments is complicated; on the other hand, it is the case that in the twentieth century it has become uncommon for the average Cabinet minister to have held his appointment for as long as thirty months. At the same time, quite clearly, continuity in office measures only a part of the 'experience' a

TABLE 2.3
Cabinet experience and size

Govt and date of formation	Average Cabinet experience (in months)	Proportion of members with previous Cabinet experience (%)	Proportion of members with 5 years Cabinet experience (%)	No. of ministers in Cabinet
1868 Liberal	42.5	53.3	26.6	15—16
1874 Conservative	25.7	83.3	0	11—13
1880 Liberal	63.3	64.2	35.7	12—15
1885 Conservative	41.5	60	33.3	16—17
1886 Liberal	75.7	71.4	57.1	13—14
1886 Conservative	39.8	85.7	28.5	14—18
1892 Liberal	39.3	70.5	29.4	16—17
1895 Conservative	54.9	57.8	57.8	17—20
1905 Liberal	16.8	36.8	5.2	19—20
1915 Coalition	70.5	77.2	50	19—24
1922 Conservative	18.2	50	12.5	16—20
1924 Labour	6.9	10	5	20
1924 Conservative	33.2	80.9	14.2	20—21
1929 Labour	7.5	63.1	0	19—21
1931 National	35.3	70	25	10—23
1940 Coalition	106.8	80	60	5— 9
1945 Conservative	41.6	56.2	37.5	16
1945 Labour	14.6	40	5	16—20
1951 Conservative	27.3	43.7	12.5	16—24
1964 Labour	3.8	17.3	0	21—24
1970 Conservative	29.8	55.5	27.8	17—19

government has at its disposal. Presumably, some parts of the job of being a minister are common to all Cabinet posts, and therefore it might be well to have some idea of the amount of experience in the Cabinet (in any position) possessed by its members at any time. Table 2.3 gives (for each government since 1868, at the time it came to office)[19] the average Cabinet experience (in months) of its members, the proportion of its members with any previous Cabinet experience, and the proportion of its members with at least five years previous Cabinet experience, as well as the number of ministers in the Cabinet.

The Governments whose members have the least previous experience are, not surprisingly, the four Labour governments of the twentieth century. Only two members of the 1924 Labour government had been in the Cabinet before, and only one of these (Viscount Haldane) had as much as five years experience. Most of the members of the second Labour government had served in the first, which lasted less than one year. More experienced was the Attlee government, the only Labour Government to take office with as much as (on average) one year's previous experience. The Wilson government was the least experienced of all; less than one-fifth of its members were ever in the Cabinet before, and none of them for as much as three, let alone five, years, a fact entirely attributable to their length of time out of office, during which most veterans of earlier Labour governments had either died, left Parliament, or been superseded by younger members of the Labour Party.

Apart from these, only two other governments have ever taken office with more than half their members in a Cabinet for the first time: the Liberal government of 1905 and the Conservative government of 1951. Both these governments were also relatively inexperienced, and had very few members indeed with long Cabinet experience. To see why this was so, one must look at Table 2.3 in terms of what can be called the 'aging' of party ministries. Cabinet personnel are drawn from the leadership of a party. If possible, they retain their positions of leadership, particularly when the party is governing. When out of office, desire to retain office presumably corresponds to the likelihood of regaining office. However, at some point, due to age and the rigours of office, the leadership group must retire and be replaced by less experienced personnel. Thus, the experience index in Figure 2.1, and Table 2.3, reflect successive 'generations' of leaders within parties. The concept is imprecise, as any government is a mixture of older and newer members, but the evidence for it is reasonably clear.

Take the example of the Liberal Party in the nineteenth century. In 1868, just over half its members had previous Cabinet experience, one-fourth had five years experience, and the overall average was about three-and-a-half years. All these figures increased in 1880, and again in 1886, when the average experience was over six years. In 1892, the average experience had fallen, due to absence of two very senior members of the previous government; however, over 70 per cent of the Cabinet had previous experience. In 1905 (with only three years in office in the previous two decades), there was virtually a new generation in the Cabinet; only one member of Campbell-Bannerman's Cabinet (the Marquis of Ripon) had a great deal (130 months) of previous Cabinet experience. A similar argument could be made to account for the 1951 Conservative government: it would point to the 'aging' of the Conservative (National) Government in the 1930s, some of which is still reflected in the May 1945 government, but which has (but for Churchill and Eden) disappeared by 1951. Finally, a similar pattern is revealed by the Conservative Party between 1874 and 1929. Disraeli's Cabinet was full of people with previous Cabinet experience, none of whom had much of it. Successive Conservative governments appear more and more experienced. This reached a peak (see Figure 2.1) in September 1900, when no member of the Cabinet had less than five years experience, and the average experience was almost ten years. This is almost halved during the upheavals of the next five years: when Balfour's government resigns its average Cabinet experience is over six years. When the next fully Conservative government is formed in 1922, it is again inexperienced.

Perhaps the most striking feature of the experience line in Figure 2.1 is the absence of most of the contrasts in the continuity index. It is true that in the twentieth century there were periods when the Cabinet was unprecedently inexperienced, but over the time period as a whole, the best description of average Cabinet experience appears to be one of a very gradual decline, from an average of perhaps five-and-a-half years in the late nineteenth century to perhaps four-and-a-half years in the 1950s and early 1960s. (Though its experience was comparatively low, by June 1970 even the Wilson Cabinet had an average of five years Cabinet experience.) It is very difficult to find any clear turning points, particularly as the Salisbury government is unusually experienced by the standards of either the nineteenth or twentieth centuries.

Willson[20] shows that the average minister was likely to have spent slightly more time in the House of Commons if he entered the Cabinet before 1916 than since. At the same time, since 1916 new Cabinet entrants have, on average, four-and-a-half years previous non-Cabinet ministerial experience; before 1916 the corresponding figure was three-and-a-half years. If one couples these figures with the above (a decline of one year in average Cabinet experience), it appears that, since 1868, overall ministerial experience has hardly changed at all. It appears likely that Cabinet ministers would have spent about ten years in some ministerial capacity. This last change, in all probability, can be attributed to increased competition: the number of ministerial appointments have, over time, increased faster than the size of the Cabinet (cf. Table 1.1.)

Two other features of Figure 2.1 deserve comment. First is that at two points in the 1930s — August 1931 and September 1939 — there are rapid upward shifts in the experience index. Both of these are 'crisis' governments, and, as has been pointed out elsewhere,[21] in crises there is a tendency to resort to small Cabinets. It appears from these two instances that crisis Cabinets are not just small, but also particularly experienced. On the other hand, if one looks at Lloyd George's inner or war Cabinet of 1916—19 (not shown in Figure 2.1), a rather different picture emerges. Initially, Lloyd George was its only member with over twenty months Cabinet experience; it is not until 1919 (with three members having been in continuously and Austen Chamberlain added) that the inner Cabinet becomes significantly more experienced than the Cabinet as a whole.

One further pattern does appear in Figure 2.1. Consider, in any month, the vertical distance between the continuity and experience indexes, and see, in the course of a government whether these two lines remain equidistant, or become further apart, or move closer together. The two lines, over an extended period of time, appear to move further apart at certain times: 1909—15, 1917—22, 1959—62, and 1964—70. In these periods, while continuity was low, collective experience was increasing. As it is highly unlikely that, over time, less experienced ministers were being replaced by more experienced personnel, it appears that these were periods in which individuals were most frequently shifted between different appointments. This subject, often termed reshuffling, is developed in more detail below.

Major discontinuities

Attention is now turned from patterns of continuity and experience to 'turnover'. In particular, is the British Cabinet becoming more subject to major discontinuities in appointments? Furthermore, has the nature of these discontinuities changed over time? At this point, a number of definitions are required.

We can define a *discontinuity* in the existence of the Cabinet as a collective body to be any point at which changes occur in the status or occupancy of the posts in the Cabinet. 'Changes' are taken broadly: they include a Cabinet minister giving up his job to another, who comes into or remains in the Cabinet; the demotion of a post to non-Cabinet status without a change in appointment, or the creation of a new post at or promotion of an existing post to Cabinet rank. A *major discontinuity* is then defined as an event in which such changes affect at least *one-fourth* of the posts in the Cabinet. In view of the time scale of this study, it does not appear sensible to insist that major discontinuities must occur all at a time: in fact, all cases are included where one-fourth of the Cabinet changes within two months, though in 80 per cent of the cases considered, the changes did in fact occur within a week or two.

If one accepts this definition of a major discontinuity, there have been no less than fifty-eight major discontinuities in the Cabinet since the formation of Gladstone's government in December 1868, suggesting that they occur, on average, once in slightly less than every two years. In fact, there have been only nine occasions in the last 104 years when the Cabinet existed for as long as three years without a major discontinuity; four of these nine occasions were in the nineteenth century when, as Table 2.4 suggests, major discontinuities occurred less frequently.

Different sorts of events precipitate major discontinuities. At this point, it will suffice to point out three possibilities: *changes of government, changes of Prime Minister*, and *reconstructions*. As before, a change of government is taken to occur whenever the partisan basis of the Cabinet changes, whether this involves the establishment or breakup of a coalition or simply an exchange between parties, for instance

TABLE 2.4
Major discontinuities

| Period | Change of govt | Change of Prime Minister | | Reconstruction | | Total | Average months between major discontinuities |
		Reshuffle	Replacement	Reshuffle	Replacement		
Pre-1900	7	1	0	2	1	11	34.3
1900—45	10	3	2	3	11	29	18.6
1946—70	3	0	2	6	7	18	16.6
Total	20	4	4	11	19	58	

after an election. As distinct from this, there is the possibility of a change of Prime Minister (and perhaps many other ministers) while party support remains unchanged. Finally, a reconstruction occurs when a Prime Minister makes changes in his Cabinet affecting at least one-fourth of its posts. (Later, a further distinction is introduced between *reshuffles* and *replacements*, depending on the extent of retention of *personnel* in a major discontinuity.) It is well to note that as a consequence of this classification, the establishment of Asquith's coalition in 1915 is a change of government, while Lloyd George's taking the Prime Ministership eighteen months later is a change of Prime Minister, even though the discontinuity was greater; the formation of Chamberlain's War Cabinet in September 1939 is a change of neither government nor Prime Minister.

Table 2.4 reveals the major discontinuities of the last century, classified by type and the time at which they occurred. Several comments are in order. In the first place, the last column reflects what was already clear from Figure 2.1: that major discontinuities are much more frequent after 1900, but that their frequency has not particularly increased in the course of the twentieth century. What has increased, on the other hand, is the extent to which major discontinuities are changes of neither government nor Prime Minister, but reconstructions: from 27 per cent (3 of 11) before 1900 to 48 per cent (14 of 29) in the middle of the period to 72 per cent (13 of 18) in the postwar years. In the nineteenth century a major change in the Cabinet was likely to be a change of government: this is clearly no longer the case.

TABLE 2.5
Type and extent of major discontinuities

Proportion of Cabinet posts affected (%)	Change of government	Change of Prime Minister	Reconstruction	Total
90–100	17	1	0	18
50–89	3	3	8	14
25–49	0	4	22	26
Total	20	8	30	58

On the other hand, as Table 2.5 reveals, there is a considerable difference in the likely scale of the major discontinuities. Changes of government, as one would expect, are always large: in three-fourths of the twenty instances, all Cabinet posts changed hands, and never less than 78 per cent of Cabinet posts changed. Changes of Prime Minister are much more variable in scale. In one case (Lloyd George in 1916) 92 per cent of Cabinet posts were affected. On the other hand, one change of Prime Minister (Eden in 1955) was not even a major discontinuity: only four posts in a Cabinet of eighteen were affected, though much greater changes were made shortly before and after he took office. Reconstructions are predominantly smaller, though it is not uncommon for over half the posts in the Cabinet to be affected.

Up to this point, discussion has centred on posts affected. However, major discontinuities also vary in the extent to which personnel are retained while appointments are altered. Depending on this extent, major discontinuities are either reshuffles or replacements. The concept of a Cabinet reshuffle, though the term is frequently used, is difficult to define with precision. To provide a notion worth discussing it seems that two criteria ought to be met: first, that a reshuffle ought to involve a major discontinuity in the occupancy of Cabinet posts and second, that continuity of Cabinet personnel ought to be considerably great, despite changes in specific ministerial appointments. As before, it seems intelligent not to insist that a reshuffle happen all on one day, but rather that it happen in a relatively short period of time.

Let us define a *reshuffle* as follows. A major discontinuity occurs, i.e., within a period of two months or so the status or occupancy of more than one-fourth of the posts in the Cabinet is changed. Of the occupants of the posts undergoing changes, however, at least two-thirds are still in the Cabinet after the changes take place. The choice of 'two-thirds' is, of course, arbitrary, but seems reasonably in accordance with usage of the term. If less than two-thirds of the former occupants of posts undergoing changes are still in the Cabinet, the major discontinuity was a *replacement*.

In practice, this is what is involved in a reshuffle, using the example of July 1960. The Minister of Aviation went to the Commonwealth Relations Office, whose previous incumbent went to the Foreign Office while abandoning the post of Lord President, which he held jointly with the CRO. The previous Foreign Secretary became Chancellor of the Exchequer; the previous Chancellor left the Cabinet. The Minister of Agriculture, Fisheries and Food became Minister of Labour; the previous Minister of Labour became Lord Privy Seal, while the previous Privy Seal (also Minister of Science) retained the latter post while also becoming Lord President of the Council. The ministries of Agriculture, Fisheries and Food and Aviation are taken by men not in the Cabinet immediately before the changes, though one has previous Cabinet experience. In short, eight Cabinet posts (out of 22) are affected; of the seven people holding these posts before the changes, five are still in the Cabinet after them. It seems reasonable to label this event a reshuffle.

From Tables 2.5 and 2.6, it is possible to detect changes in the relative frequencies of reshuffles and replacements.

TABLE 2.6
Principal reshuffles

Date	Government	Date	Government
Dec 1882	Liberal	Feb 1942	Coalition
Jan–Mar 1887	Conservative	Oct 1959	Conservative
*Mar 1894	Liberal	Jul 1960	Conservative
*Apr 1908	Liberal	Oct 1961	Conservative
Oct 1911	Liberal	Aug 1966	Labour
*Jun 1935	National	Mar–Apr 1968	Labour
Nov–Dec 1935	National	Oct–Nov 1968	Labour
*May 1937	National		

*Occurred at the time of a change in the Prime Ministership.

Virtually by definition, and certainly in practice, a change of government cannot be a reshuffle. Of the remaining thirty-eight major discontinuities, however, fifteen were, under the present definition, reshuffles: these are listed in Table 2.6. Of these, three occurred before the turn of the century, a further two during the Liberal Government of 1905—15, three between 1935 and 1937, one during the Second World War, and a group of three in each of the Macmillan and Wilson governments.

Four of the reshuffles (those marked * in Table 2.6) occurred at the time of a change in the Prime Ministership; in each case, the reshuffling is attributable either to the new Prime Minister's wishes for his Cabinet or to a chain of promotions starting from the need to fill the vacancy left by his elevation to the Prime Ministership. Table 2.4 suggests (though the small numbers involved reduce confidence in any interpretation) that over the period of this study the tendency has been for changes of Prime Minister to constitute replacements rather than reshuffles: it is tempting to ascribe this to the Prime Minister's increasing pre-eminence over his Cabinet colleagues and his greater freedom to replace them at will.

The 1882 reshuffle originated in Gladstone's resigning as Chancellor of the Exchequer, which post he had held jointly with First Lord of the Treasury. The second reshuffle of 1935 comes so quickly after Baldwin becoming Prime Minister that it is tempting to consider the events as one. The 1887 reshuffle is touched off by Lord Randolph Churchill's resignation (policy reasons) and continued by Hicks Beach's resignation (health). This leaves a set of eight reshuffles, of which six are very recent. From Figure 2.1 it can be seen that these reshuffles rarely occur within the first two or three years of a government. With the exception of October 1959, they do not follow long periods of continuity in Cabinet appointments. Moreover, with the exception of 1911, they take place in governments supported by large majorities. They affect both more and less important posts, and more and less experienced persons. On average, about one-third of the Cabinet is affected. Finally, as above, for them to occur with great frequency is a relatively new phenomenon, though

whether they will continue to be so common an occurrence is
an open question.

Conclusions

The first conclusion of this study is that, on the question of
continuity or stability of the British Cabinet in the last
century, the path of easy generalisations is strewn with
pitfalls. Continuity in office has declined since 1868; the
great decline is between 1900 and 1905, continuing through
to 1915, after which the present patterns can be seen to be
well-established. This must be seen in the context of the fact
that average Cabinet experience has declined slowly since the
late nineteenth century; if non-Cabinet ministerial experience
is added to this, there has been virtually no change. In the
last half century, governments have displayed a pattern of
more continuous or repeated changes in appointments.
Another way to put this is as follows: while the British
Cabinet has never in this period been free from relatively
frequent major discontinuities, these have become more
common and tended to occur more frequently outside a
change of government or Prime Minister. In particular,
reshuffles, though existent in the nineteenth century, are
very much a recent phenomenon.

Anthony King suggests these consequences of rapid turnover in ministerial appointments:

> ... at any given moment a large proportion of the
> government will be relatively ignorant and inexperienced
> particularly since changes almost always take place
> between departments ... Ministers new to their subjects
> are that much more likely to be managed in effect by their
> civil servants. The inflow of ministers into departments
> may bring a certain freshness to a government, but the
> temptation for some ministers to try to make instant
> reputations must be overwhelming. More important, stable
> relationships within government and between Britain and
> other countries become extremely difficult to establish if
> new faces are constantly appearing at the conference
> table — and if everyone knows that the existing faces are
> unlikely to be around for long.[22]

In the first place, as this study suggests, lack of continuity is not the same as lack of experience, and the two appear to have followed somewhat different patterns over the past century. On the other hand, lack of continuity in appointments probably has all the disturbing consequences King suggests. However, the 'era of rapid turnover' in which this situation exists is not something that began in the mid-1950s. All the analysis in this study points to the conclusion that, in the past century, lack of continuity has almost always been present, and has remained at its present level since around the turn of the century. Through both World Wars continuity in Cabinet appointments was at a level comparable to that of the 1960s.

In this case, only two possibilities remain for those who wish to argue that low continuity has dangerous consequences for British politics. On the one hand, it could be that for some reason — and it is not at all clear what that reason might be — lack of continuity has only recently come to have this sort of consequences. The sort of reasons that might be advanced include changes in the party system, the growth of mass electioneering, or the increase in government responsibilities, but each of these arguments would require a great deal of evidence in order to be convincing. If such cases cannot be established, then one must come to the conclusion that these consequences have been features of the British political system for a great deal longer than most people appear to suspect. In either case, it is clear that this is a subject deserving considerable examination.

Notes

1. For instance, by Anthony Crosland in M. Kogan (ed.), *The Politics of Education* (Harmondsworth: Penguin, 1971) pp. 158—9.
2. D. J. Heasman, 'The Prime Minister and the Cabinet', *Parliamentary Affairs* Vol. 15 (1962) p. 479.
3. H. Daalder, *Cabinet Reform in Britain 1914—63* (Stanford: Stanford University Press, 1965) p. 125.
4. This appears to be the point of Crosland's argument in Kogan (ed.), *The Politics of Education.*, pp. 155—9, and part of the argument of R. H. S. Crossman in his 'Introduction' to W. Bagehot, *The English Constitution* (London: Watts, 1964).
5. See, for example, Daalder, *Cabinet Reform in Britain.* or D. N. Chester and F. M. G. Willson, *The Organisation of British Central Government* (London: George Allen and Unwin, 1968).

6. For instance, Bruce Headey, 'Cabinet Ministers & Senior Civil Servants: Mutual Requirements & Expectations', Chapter 6 below, or F. M. G. Willson, 'The Routes of Entry of New Members of the British Cabinet 1868–1958', *Political Studies*, Vol. 7, (1959) pp. 222–32.

7. For instance, R. K. Alderman and J. A. Cross, *The Tactics of Resignation* (London: Routledge and Kegan Paul, 1967), or S. E. Finer, 'The Individual Responsibility of Ministers', *Public Administration*, vol. 34, (1956) pp. 377–96, or P. J. Madgwick, 'Resignations', Chapter 4 below.

8. Cited, for instance, by Crosland in Kogan (ed), *The Politics of Education.*, p. 159.

9. R. Rose, 'The Making of Cabinet Ministers', Chapter 1 above, or A. King, 'Britain's Ministerial Turnover', *New Society*, 18 Aug 1966, pp. 257–8.

10 See note 4 above.

11 For instance, by J. Mackintosh, *The British Cabinet*, 2nd ed. (London: Stevens, 1968).

12 E. L. Woodward, *The Age of Reform 1815–1870* (Oxford: Clarendon Press, 1946) pp. 633–93.

13. Sir Robert Ensor, *England 1870–1914* (Oxford: Clarendon Press. 1963) pp. 606–14.

14. D. Butler and J. Freeman, *British Political Facts 1900–1968* (London: Macmillan, 1969) pp. 1–98.

15. Principally various numbers of *The Times* or *Hansard*, and occasionally individual memoirs or biographies.

16. Crosland, in Kogan (ed), *The Politics of Education* p. 155.

17. The Formation of the Chamberlain War Cabinet is not counted as a new government, since party support was the same. The Lloyd George 'inner' Cabinet is not included in Figure 2.1

18. Conservative (June 1885), Liberal (February 1886), Conservative (October 1922), Labour (January 1924), Conservative (May 1945).

19. The figures for the National Government refer to its membership in November 1931.

20. F. M. G. Willson, 'Routes of Entry'.

21. Chester and Willson. *The Organisation of British Central Government*, pp. 310–11.

22. King, 'Britain's Ministerial Turnover', p. 258.

3 Comparative Perspectives on Ministerial Stability in Britain*

VALENTINE HERMAN

The establishment and maintenance of a stable political order is one of the most central and crucial problems which political systems face. Since the days of the Greek city states, philosophers, statesmen and citizens have experimented with various formulae of authority designed to promote stable, legitimate and effective government. The search for a stable political order is common to all contemporary and historical societies irrespective of their levels of political and socio-economic development, structures of government, and ideological persuasions. In the context of democratic political systems in advanced industrial societies the concept 'stability' can refer to three separate, but nonetheless related, phenomena. It can, to begin with, refer to the regime or form of authority: this usage encompasses notions of the persistence of a particular pattern of government or constitution over time. Secondly, stability can refer to the tenure of office of government and personnel, and the procedures whereby changes in these are made in an orderly fashion. Finally, stability can refer to societies as a whole, and the absence of violence in these societies to make illegal changes in the regime, the government and personnel, and the policies of these societies.[1]

A comparison of British and French political experiences reveals how the stability profiles of these nations differ at each of these three levels.[2] In France, regime changes have been relatively frequent, often bloody, and have involved the adoption of a series of constitutions each one different in several important respects from its predecessor. In Britain, by contrast, the unwritten constitution has peacefully evolved over the ages and major discontinuities in the pattern of

*The author is indebted to James Alt, Ian Budge, Jean Blondel, Mattei Dogan, Anthony King, Juan Linz and Lester Seligman for their helpful comments and suggestions.

government have been unknown. At the level of governmental stability, ministries and ministers came and went in the years of the Fourth French Republic at such a rate that they were the subject of many music hall-type jokes. Between the years 1945 and 1958 Britain had four governments and four Prime Ministers, while France had twenty-seven governments led by twenty different Prime Ministers.[3] At the level of societal stability, the experiences of the two countries has also differed considerably. France has undergone a series of revolutions since 1789, Britain has undergone none; in France peasants, students and workers have frequently protested violently in the streets against the government and its policies, while in Britain such manifestations of collective violent discontent have been relatively unknown; in France many assassination attempts (often successful ones) have been directed against leading political figures; in Britain, once again, such manifestations of individual violent discontent have been almost unknown. This much abbreviated survey of political events highlights how the experiences of the two countries differ at each of the three levels of stability we outlined earlier, and serves to illustrate popular perceptions of the political instability of France and the political stability of Britain.

In this chapter our concern is with the second type of stability outlined above, the stability of governments[4] and their personnel. Our task is to show, on the one hand, how stable British governments have been relative to those of a number of other Western parliamentary democracies, and, on the other hand, to undertake a comparative analysis of various aspects of the turnover of cabinet ministers in these countries.[5] Before approaching the first of these problems we need to define a 'government'. Our definition of a government follows Blondel's:[6]

> . . . any administration was considered as a government which fulfilled two conditions: that of being headed by the same prime minister, and that of relying on the support of the same party or parties in the chamber.

We measure *governmental stability* by calculating the average duration, in months, of all those governments which came to

TABLE 3.1
Governmental stability

	Stability (months)	Rank orders All countries	Rank orders Commonwealth countries	Rank orders European countries
Sweden	69.5	1		1
Canada	63.6	2	1	
New Zealand	60.0	3	2	
Australia	52.8	4	3	
Ireland	47.7	5	4	
BRITAIN	45.3	6	5	2
Norway	44.8	7		3
Austria	44.7	8		4
Germany	38.1	9		5
Luxembourg	37.7	10		6
Iceland	29.8	11		7
Holland	29.3	12		8
Denmark	26.2	13		9
*France 5	22.3	14		10
Belgium	22.1	15		11
Finland	11.0	16		12
Italy	10.8	17		13
*France 4	5.8	18		14

*France 4 and France 5 are the Fourth and Fifth French Republics in this and subsequent tables.

office between the formation of the first post-World War II government following free elections and the end of 1971.[7] At this stage, we deliberately equate stability with longevity as this seems to us to be the most satisfactory — though by no means the only — way of measuring the phenomenon. In later sections we examine alternative conceptions of stability.

The stability of governments which formed in the postwar years in eighteen Western parliamentary democracies is presented in Table 3.1. In the first column, the average duration of these governments in months is presented, in the second a rank ordering of governmental stability for the eighteen countries included in this study, in the third a rank ordering for five Commonwealth countries,[8] and in the fourth an ordering of governmental stability for fourteen European countries. Britain has been included in each of the three sets of rankings to facilitate our comparative analysis.

Table 3.1 allows us to consider the relative stability of

British governments. Britain ranks fifth out of the eighteen parliamentary democracies, fifth out of five Commonwealth countries, and second (after West Germany) out of fourteen European countries. It is noticeable that the Commonwealth countries occupy five out of the top six places on the governmental stability ranking. Their high rankings suggests that the Commonwealth pattern of governmental stability is quite different from the European pattern. In the ensuing analysis we will compare separately various aspects of the turnover of British Cabinet ministers with their counterparts in the Commonwealth and in Europe.

In the next sections of this chapter we turn our attention away from the stability of governments to an examination of ministerial stability. Our attention will be focused on the following aspects of ministerial stability:

(A) *Ministerial turnover.* Do British Cabinet ministers have a shorter or longer tenure of office than their Commonwealth and European counterparts? Has Britain had more or fewer ministers of Defence, Foreign Affairs and Finance than other countries in the postwar years?

(B) *Ministerial reorganisations.* Are Cabinet ministers in Britain subjected to more or less Government reorganisations than ministers in other countries? Are British ministers less likely to hold a particular portfolio for the duration of a Government than their counterparts elsewhere?

(C) *Structural and personnel continuity of ministries.* Are British ministers more or less likely to hold the same portfolio in successive administrations than ministers in other countries? Are they more or less likely to be promoted or demoted to different portfolios in successive administrations than their Commonwealth and European counterparts?

In the final part of the paper we offer some tentative thoughts on some of the consequences of various patterns of ministerial turnover, reorganisation and continuity.

(A) Ministerial turnover

Our conception of ministerial turnover is related to longevity in the same way as is our conception of governmental stability. We measure *ministerial turnover* by calculating the average duration (again in months) that individuals occupied eight 'key' ministries in the same postwar period: in addition to the Prime Minister, the holders of the portfolios of Foreign Affairs, Trade, Defence, Interior, Finance, Agriculture and Education. The average duration in office of these various ministries is presented in Table 3.2.[9] Before we comment on the pattern of turnover of British ministers a few comments about the construction of Table 3.2 are necessary. The principle of classification has been to group ministries into functionally comparable categories. For example, a country may not have a department of state titled the Ministry of the Interior, but where a department exists in that country with a different name (the Home Office in the United Kingdom) and performs approximately equivalent functions to differently named departments in other countries, it has been included as one of the eight ministries irrespective of its title. To qualify for inclusion in Table 3.2, a ministry had both to be in existence and to be of Cabinet status for at least 60 per cent of the time period under consideration. Thus these ministries are not only functionally comparable, but also among the most important portfolios that exist in each country.

We now turn our attention to the pattern of turnover of British ministers. How does this pattern compare to that of other Commonwealth countries? How does it compare to that of other European countries?[10]

(A.1) Commonwealth comparisons

We have already observed that British governments remain in office for fewer months than governments in Ireland, New Zealand, Canada and Australia. We now examine whether British ministerial appointments remain in office as long as their counterparts in the other Commonwealth countries. The average period that the eight selected ministers held

TABLE 3.2

Ministerial turnover (months in office)

Prime Minister			Foreign Affairs			Trade			Defence		
Commonwealth countries											
New Zealand	75.0	1	Ireland	71.5	1	Australia	79.2	1	New Zealand	66.0	1
Ireland	71.5	2	New Zealand	66.0	2	New Zealand	37.7	2	Ireland	35.8	2
Canada	63.6	3	Canada	45.5	3	Ireland	35.8	3	Canada	35.3	3
Australia	52.8	4	Australia	31.7	=4.5	Canada	35.3	4	Australia	31.7	4
BRITAIN	*45.3*	*5*	BRITAIN	31.7	=4.5	BRITAIN	*24.4*	*5*	BRITAIN	*22.6*	*5*
European Countries											
Sweden	139.0	1	Sweden	92.7	1	Sweden	92.7	1	Sweden	92.7	1
Luxembourg	75.5	2	Iceland	74.5	2	Germany	89.0	2	France 5	52.0	2
Germany	66.8	3	Holland	73.2	3	Iceland	50.0	3	Denmark	44.8	3
Norway	62.8	4	Luxembourg	60.4	4	Austria	44.7	4	Luxembourg	44.5	4
Austria	62.6	5	Norway	52.3	5	Luxembourg	33.5	5	Germany	39.6	5
BRITAIN	*45.3*	*6*	Austria	52.2	6	Holland	32.6	6	Austria	37.4	6
Denmark	44.8	7	France 5	52.0	7	Norway	31.4	7	Norway	34.9	7
France 5	39.0	8	Belgium	51.5	8	France 5	25.2	8	Belgium	34.3	8
Iceland	37.2	9	Germany	49.8	9	BRITAIN	*24.4*	*9*	Holland	29.3	9
Holland	36.6	10	Denmark	39.2	10	Denmark	22.4	10	Italy	26.1	10
Belgium	30.9	11	BRITAIN	*31.7*	*11*	Belgium	22.1	11	BRITAIN	*22.6*	*11*
Italy	26.6	12	Finland	24.6	12	France 4	19.8	12	Finland	20.6	12
Finland	18.8	13	Italy	22.5	13	Finland	16.0	13	France 4	8.8	13
France 4	8.8	14	France 4	17.6	14	Italy	14.3	14			

TABLE 3.2 (continued)

Commonwealth countries

Interior			Finance			Agriculture			Education		
Australia	52.8	=1.5	Australia	52.8	1	Canada	53.0	1	New Zealand	52.8	1
New Zealand		=1.5	New Zealand	42.8	2	Australia	48.8	2	Ireland	35.8	2
BRITAIN	35.2	3	Ireland	40.8	3	BRITAIN	36.7	3	BRITAIN	24.5	3
			Canada	39.7	4	Ireland	35.8	4			
			BRITAIN	24.4	5	New Zealand	33.3	5			

European countries

Interior			Finance			Agriculture			Education		
Sweden	81.0	1	Luxembourg	151.0	1	Belgium	61.8	1	Luxembourg	53.0	1
Luxembourg	60.4	2	Sweden	69.5	2	Sweden	55.6	2	Austria	52.2	2
Austria	44.7	3	Iceland	49.7	3	Germany	53.4	3	Sweden	46.3	3
France 5	39.0	4	Holland	41.8	4	Austria	52.2	4	Norway	44.9	4
Germany	38.1	5	Germany	38.1	5	Holland	48.8	=5.5	Holland	41.8	5
BRITAIN	35.2	6	Norway	34.9	=6.5	Iceland	48.8	=5.5	Iceland	41.7	6
Italy	29.3	7	Denmark	34.9	=6.5	Luxembourg	37.7	7	Germany	38.8	7
Belgium	25.8	8	Austria	34.8	8	BRITAIN	36.7	8	Denmark	31.4	8
Holland	24.5	9	Belgium	34.3	9	Norway	34.9	9	Belgium	25.8	9
Denmark	22.4	10	France 5	26.0	10	Denmark	28.5	10	BRITAIN	24.5	10
Finland	14.5	11	BRITAIN	24.4	11	Italy	24.1	11	Finland	22.9	11
France 4	13.2	12	Italy	19.5	12	France 5	22.3	12	Italy	19.5	12
			Finland	14.5	13	Finland	20.0	13	France 5	17.3	13
			France 4	9.3	14	France 4	15.3	14	France 4	14.4	14

office in the Commonwealth countries, presented in Table 3.2, reveals that British ministers have experienced a high rate of turnover. In the postwar years Foreign Ministers have, for example, remained in office twice as long in Ireland and New Zealand as they have in Britain; Defence Ministers three times as long in New Zealand than in Britain, and about half as long again in the other three countries; Finance Ministers twice as long in Australia as in Britain, and three-quarters as long in the other countries. Britain has had more Prime Ministers and more Ministers of Foreign Affairs, Trade, Defence, Interior (Home Affairs), Finance and Education than the other Commonwealth countries; Britain's ranking is last on seven of the eight portfolios (Agriculture is the only exception). Her ministers come to, and leave, office at a considerably greater rate than those in the other four Commonwealth countries.

In comparison with the other Commonwealth countries, the pattern revealed is that British *ministers'* tenure in office is relatively short. They also remain in office for a relatively short amount of time compared to British *governments* (only holders of the Agriculture portfolio remain in office in Britain for more than thirty-six months). The average tenure of office of all of the British ministers is less than the average tenure of office of governments (forty-five months); this suggests a high incidence of ministerial reorganisation *within* governments, a point we take up in detail below. This pattern is mirrored in the remaining four Commonwealth countries, where the tenure of office of only a few ministers is greater than that of the governments of which they are a part.[10] British ministers not only remain in office for shorter periods of time than British governments, but their tenure of office is also shorter than their counterparts in Commonwealth countries. How does the British pattern of ministerial turnover compare with the European one?

(A.2) European comparisons

We noted earlier that in comparison with British governments European governments are generally shortlived: in three cases (the Fourth French Republic, Italy and Finland) governments lasted for less than twelve months, and in a further five cases (Belgium, the Fifth French Republic, Denmark, Holland and Iceland) they lasted between twenty-two and thirty months. On the basis of this we could, quite reasonably, expect that British ministers would enjoy longer periods in office than their European counterparts. But this is far from being the case. When compared to thirteen other European countries, British Ministers of Foreign Affairs, Defence and Finance rank eleventh, Education tenth, Trade ninth, Agriculture eighth and Interior sixth. Only in Finland, Italy and the Fourth Republic have there been more ministers of Foreign Affairs and Finance than in Britain; only Finland and the Fourth French Republic have had more Defence ministers than Britain; only in Finland, Italy and the Fourth and Fifth French Republics have there been more ministers of Education than in Britain. Once again, when viewed in a cross-national perspective, the British ministerial pattern is one of high turnover in office. Several countries (notably Iceland, Luxemburg, Germany and Austria) which have had less stable governments than Britain have also experienced less ministerial turnover; many ministers in these countries have remained in office for two or three times as long as their British counterparts.

Table 3.3 is of assistance in summarising our findings up to this point. In the first column the average duration in office of seven ministries (the Prime Minister has been excluded) is presented for each country; in the second a rank ordering of the duration in office for the eighteen countries, in the third a rank ordering for the five Commonwealth countries, and in the fourth a rank ordering for the fourteen European countries. Again, Britain has been included in each of the three sets of rankings. Table 3.3 illustrates the general pattern we have observed already. Britain ranks fifteenth out of the eighteen countries; only Italy, Finland and the Fourth French Republic — countries which have experienced chronically unstable governments in the postwar years — have, on average, experienced more ministerial turnover than Britain. Britain ranks fifth, and last, when she is compared with the other Commonwealth countries, in each of which ministers have remained in office half as long again as their British counterparts. Britain's ranking in Europe is eleventh

TABLE 3.3
Average ministerial turnover

	Duration in office (months)	Rank orders		
		All countries	Commonwealth countries	European countries
Sweden	70.8	1		1
Iceland	51.4	2		2
Luxembourg	51.1	3		3
New Zealand	46.8	4	1	
Germany	46.2	5		4
Austria	44.9	6		5
Australia	44.7	7	2	
Canada	40.8	8	3	
Ireland	39.9	9	4	
Holland	37.8	10		6
Norway	37.7	11		7
Belgium	32.3	12		8
Denmark	30.1	13		9
France 5	28.7	14		10
BRITAIN	27.5	15	5	11
Italy	21.2	16		12
Finland	18.2	17		13
France 4	12.9	18		14

out of fourteen. In Sweden, average ministerial duration in office has been almost three times as great as in Britain. Whether comparisons are made with either Commonwealth countries (whose party systems and constitutional orders are very similar to Britain's) or with European countries (whose party systems and constitutional orders are very different from Britain's), the picture is the same: holders of British ministries have remained in office for relatively short periods of time in the postwar years.

(B) Ministerial reorganisations

So far in our analysis we have equated both governmental stability and ministerial turnover with longevity, that is to say, with the amount of time that governments and certain selected ministers remained in office. As we were careful to point out earlier, however, duration is only one way of measuring the phenomena of stability and turnover. In this and the next section we consider two alternative conceptions of ministerial stability. In the present section we will examine patterns of turnover *within* governments: if these patterns are stable we should not expect to find ministers changing portfolios (or, alternatively, being reorganised or re-shuffled)[12] with any regularity, except where death, illness, or resignation from office for personal reasons brings about changes in personnel which cannot be attributed to political events. In the next section we examine patterns of ministerial stability *across* successive governments: if these patterns are stable we would expect to find that individuals held the same or different portfolios in successive governments where the party bases of these governments are identical and where ministers do not leave office for non-political reasons.

We turn our attention, first, to examine patterns of stability *within* governments. Are cabinet ministers in Britain subjected to more or less governmental reorganisation than ministers in other countries? The material presented in Table 3.4 allows us to answer the question. In the first column of the table is recorded the total number of times that the seven portfolios considered earlier (again the position of the Prime Minister is excluded) changed hands in the period under consideration. In the second is recorded the total number of these portfolio changes that took place within governments. The third column records the number of within-government ministerial changes as a percentage of the total number of changes: this percentage is the *'reorganisation score'* for each of the eighteen countries. The fourth, fifth and sixth columns present rank orderings on the reorganisation score for all the countries, the Commonwealth countries, and the European countries, respectively.

(B.1) Commonwealth comparisons

Are British ministers reorganised more than their Commonwealth counterparts? From the reorganisation score and rankings presented in Table 3.4 we can see that they are. A number of interesting features of the ministerial reorganisation phenomenon are worth drawing attention to at this stage. Firstly, it is noticeable that Britain has had more

TABLE 3.4
Ministerial reorganisation scores

	Total changes	Within-government changes	Rank orders			
			Reorganisation score (%)	All countries	Commonwealth countries	European countries
BRITAIN	77	42	55	=1.5	1	=1.5
Sweden	20	11	55	=1.5		=1.5
Canada	34	16	47	3	2	
Australia	36	14	39	4	3	
Austria	40	15	37	5		3
France 5	31	11	35	6		4
Norway	50	16	32	7		5
Germany	30	9	30	8		6
Ireland	42	12	28	9	4	
Denmark	74	20	27	10		7
Holland	50	10	20	11		8
New Zealand	35	6	17	12	5	
France 4	94	13	14	13		9
Belgium	71	6	8	14		10
Finland	148	9	6	15		11
Italy	105	5	5	16		12
Iceland	26	1	4	17		13
Luxembourg	38	1	3	18		14

within-government ministerial changes (forty-two of them) than any other country: the magnitude of ministerial reorganisation in Britain is not matched elsewhere. A ministerial appointee is less likely to serve for the lifetime of a government in Britain than in any of the other seventeen countries: his chances of being promoted or demoted to another ministry within the government are high; his chances of remaining in his original position are low. Secondly, it is clearly the case that within-government ministerial changes are experienced more in Commonwealth countries than in European countries: three of the four countries with the highest reshuffle rates are in the Commonwealth (we return to this point in a moment). Thirdly, it is important to note that in Britain *all* of the seven portfolios we are considering have experienced a high number of within-government ministerial changes in the postwar years: the Finance and Education portfolios have each been subjected to eight reorganisations, the Foreign Affairs, Trade and Defence portfolios to six, the Interior and Agriculture portfolios to four. Whereas all the ministerial positions we are considering have been reorganised with some frequency in Britain, this pattern has not been matched in the other Commonwealth countries. The Finance portfolio in Australia has never been subjected to a within-government change, the Trade portfolio there to only one such change. In Canada, the Finance and Agriculture portfolios have been reorganised much less than the Defence and Foreign Affairs portfolios. In New Zealand, the Foreign Affairs, Defence, Interior, and Education portfolios have never been reorganised.

When comparisons are made with four other Commonwealth countries it can be seen that Britain has the highest incidence of within-government ministerial changes, that all its ministerial posts are subjected to these changes, and that the British experience fits into a reshuffling pattern more typical of Commonwealth than of European countries.

(B.2) European comparisons

The number of Britain's within-government ministerial changes has not been matched by any other European country. (Sweden ranks equal highest with Britain on the ministerial reorganisation index but has experienced less than a quarter as many within-government ministerial changes.) The governments of most of these countries very rarely reorganise their ministers; when these reorganisations do take place they are never of the same magnitude that they are in Britain; none of the European governments has had more than two major reorganisations (or reshuffles) in the postwar years (several of them in fact have had none); when such reorganisations do take place a few individuals, rather than several as in Britain, are likely to alternate portfolios at any one time. Whereas in Britain reorganisations are relatively commonplace and are nearly always deliberately brought about by Prime Ministers, elsewhere in Europe they are relatively rare and are normally forced upon governments by the death, illness or resignation of ministers.

In a number of European countries (notably Finland, Italy and the Fourth French Republic) administrations have been shortlived, and governments have had little or no opportunity to periodically move ministers around different portfolios. In Britain and other countries which have had relatively stable governments, a certain amount of administrative change has been deliberately brought about by Prime Ministers moving individuals into and out of ministries within governments. In certain European countries which by contrast have had relatively unstable governments, such changes have been brought about by the formation of a *new* government rather than a *newly shaped* government. These governments, it must be pointed out, have typically been coalition and/or minority[13] governments where prime ministers' freedom of action in reorganising individual ministers has been limited. Many of Britain's government reorganisations have been, in terms of the movement of personnel, of the same magnitude as changes between successive administrations in certain of the European countries. Whereas in Britain (and other Commonwealth countries) administrative changes have resulted in ministers being moved to and from different portfolios while the party base of the government has remained the same, in Europe administrative changes have taken place just as frequently while involving different parties entering and leaving the government. In Britain, people rather than parties are frequently moved into and out of office; in Europe, both parties and people are moved frequently.

As we have seen, the phenomenon of within-government ministerial changes of any magnitude is most evident in the Commonwealth countries, and best exemplified by Britain; in Europe, within-government ministerial changes are rare, but changes in the party bases of coalition governments are more frequent. From this it does not follow that the rate of ministerial turnover is lower in Commonwealth countries than it is in Europe, even though, as we have seen, governments are more stable in Commonwealth than in European countries. Although the party bases of many European coalition governments[14] change with considerable regularity (and hence these governments are unstable), the personnel occupying ministries change less frequently. We examine why this is the case in the next section of this chapter when we examine patterns of ministerial turnover across, rather than within, governments.

(C) Structural and personnel continuity of ministries

Our analysis so far has concentrated on the tenure of office of Cabinet ministers and the frequency of within-government ministerial changes. We have shown that British ministers spend relatively short amounts of time in office and are subject to a high rate of government reorganisation. We have pointed to both these findings as illustrating different aspects of ministerial stability. In this section we approach the problem of ministerial stability in a different manner and consider patterns of structural and personnel continuity *across* successive governments.

By *structural continuity* we refer to a pattern of stability in which an individual minister (of Foreign Affairs, Finance, Defence, etc.) holds the same office in successive governments. We define an index of structural continuity as the percentage of ministers in government 1 who hold the same portfolios in government 2. Structural continuity represents one kind of ministerial stability. A minister can, however, hold different offices in successive governments (he can, for

TABLE 3.5
Structural and personnel continuity

Structural continuity

	Ministerial continuity (%)	Rank orders — All countries	Rank orders — Commonwealth countries	Rank orders — European countries
Sweden	90.0	1		1
Austria	73.5	2		2
France 5	66.5	3		3
Australia	65.5	4	1	
Canada	65.0	5	2	
New Zealand	56.0	6	3	
Luxembourg	52.5	7		4
Germany	50.5	8		5
Italy	50.0	9		6
Norway	49.5	10		7
BRITAIN	47.5	*11*	*4*	8
Holland	46.5	12		9
Denmark	45.5	13		10
Iceland	45.0	14		11
Ireland	37.5	15	5	
Belgium	34.0	16		12
France 4	23.5	17		13
Finland	23.0	18		14

Personnel continuity

	Ministerial turnover (%)	Rank orders — All countries	Rank orders — Commonwealth countries	Rank orders — European countries
Sweden	93.5	1		1
France 5	77.0	2		2
Australia	75.5	3	1	
Austria	74.0	4		3
Canada	67.5	5	2	
Germany	63.0	6		4
Luxembourg	61.5	7		5
New Zealand	60.5	8	3	
BRITAIN	*57.5*	9	*4*	6
Italy	56.0	10		7
Denmark	52.0	11		8
Holland	51.0	12		9
Norway	50.5	13		10
Iceland	49.5	14		11
Ireland	48.0	15	5	
Belgium	40.0	16		12
Finland	29.0	17		13
France 4	27.0	18		14

70

example, be moved from the Foreign Affairs portfolio to the Defence portfolio, or from the Ministry of Agriculture to the Ministry of Education), and we refer to this second kind of ministerial stability as *personnel continuity*. We define an index of personnel continuity as the percentage of ministers in government 1 who hold the same or different portfolios in government 2. The structural continuity index measures to what extent the composition of successive Cabinets is identical in the sense that the same individuals occupy the same offices. The personnel continuity index measures to what extent the composition of successive cabinets is identical in the sense that the same individuals occupy the same or different offices. In Table 3.5 we present structural and personnel continuity scores (and three sets of rank orderings) for the eighteen countries. These have been obtained by calculating the individual scores for successive governments on the basis of the seven portfolios we have been considering, summing these scores, and then dividing the sum by the number of changes of government in each country.

A brief comment on the relationship between the structural and personnel continuity indexes is necessary at this stage. Where the two indexes, either for individual governments or averaged for sequences of governments, equal zero per cent then the pattern of governments can be described as 'all change' (or extreme ministerial instability): a series of governments replace each other with no overlap of personnel occurring between successive administrations. Where the continuity scores both equal 100 per cent, then the pattern is of 'no change' (an absence of ministerial instability): successive governments are identical in terms of both their personnel and the portfolios which these personnel hold. In those cases where the structural and personnel continuity scores are the same and their values range between 1 per cent and 99 per cent, the pattern of ministerial stability lies between the 'all change' and 'no change' positions. Where the personnel continuity score is greater than the structural continuity score, then a different form of ministerial turnover, which we can describe as 'musical ministerial chairs' take place: ministers change jobs (hence low structural continuity scores) while still remaining in the Cabinet (hence high personnel continuity scores).

(C.1) Commonwealth comparisons

The ministerial pattern of 'no change' across successive governments is most closely approximated to by Australia and Canada. Britain lies almost exactly between the 'all change' and 'no change' positions of extreme stability and extreme instability. Britain obtains a ranking of fourth (out of five) on both the structural and personnel continuity measures: among the Commonwealth countries only Ireland experienced less ministerial continuity across governments than Britain. We have already illustrated two aspects of ministerial instability in Britain: on the one hand the relatively short periods of time that ministers remain in office, and on the other hand the fact that they are considerably more likely to be reorganised than their Commonwealth counterparts. Our measures of structural and personnel continuity and turnover reveal a third aspect of ministerial instability. Britain's structural continuity score (47.5 per cent) points to the fact that the number of ministers who remain in the same office in successive governments is low: Britain's personnel turnover score (57.5 per cent) points to the fact that there is a slightly greater tendency for the same set of ministers to appear in successive governments but in charge of different portfolios. Our index of within-government changes revealed that a Cabinet minister in Britain appointed at the beginning of a government is unlikely to remain in the same office for the duration of that government. Our continuity indexes across governments reveal that if a minister does remain in office to the end of a government his chances of being reappointed to the same ministry or to a different ministry in the next government are about fifty-fifty. These figures are not greatly affected by the alternation in office of the Labour and Conservative parties in the postwar years. All the other Commonwealth countries have experienced similar changes in the party composition of their governments, and all of them (with the exception of Ireland) have higher rates of across-government continuity. Britain's low continuity scores cannot, then, be explained away by different parties coming to office. The same (or a very similar) set of reasons which leads

Prime Ministers to reorganise their ministers within governments, most likely explains why these ministers occupy
different portfolios in successive governments.

(C.2) European comparisons

How do the British patterns of continuity compare with the
European patterns? From Table 3.5 it can be seen that, in the
European context, British ranks eighth out of fourteen on
the structural continuity index and sixth on the personnel
continuity index. Britain's patterns of across-government
ministerial changes lie midway between the 'no change'
pattern of Swedish governments, and the 'all change' pattern
of governments in Finland and the Fourth French Republic.
In Sweden, successive governments in the postwar years have
been almost identical in the sense that the same ministers
have retained the same portfolios across a number of
successive administrations; as we have seen earlier, Swedish
ministers have remained in office, on average, for almost six
years. In Finland and the Fourth French Republic, there has
been very little continuity of individuals across administrations and ministers have, on average, remained in office in
each country for eighteen and twelve months, respectively.
Britain has experienced less across-government continuity in
the postwar years than these two countries, but to a
considerable extent this has been offset by a high incidence
of within-government ministerial changes.

Conclusion

In this chapter we have undertaken a comparative analysis of
the stability of British Cabinet ministers in the postwar years.
Our major conclusions can be summarised as follows. (1)
Although British governments have remained in office for
relatively long periods of time, the same cannot be said for
the holders of key portfolios in these governments. Whether
comparisons are made with either Commonwealth or
European countries, the tenure of office of British ministers
has been noticeably short. One of the most distinctive

features of British Cabinets is the rate at which ministers come to and leave office, a rate which is matched by no other Commonwealth country and very few of the European ones. (2) The pattern of ministerial government in Britain is not only distinguished by the limited tenure of office of ministers, but also by the fact that these ministries are subjected to more governmental reorganisations than their counterparts in any other Commonwealth or European country. The high incidence of within-government changes experienced in Britain is not experienced elsewhere. (3) Although the British patterns of structural and personnel continuity across successive administrations compares unfavourably with those of other Commonwealth countries, they compare quite favourably with the European patterns. In Britain, ministers are both unlikely to remain in office for the duration of a government or (even if the party base of the government remains the same) to be in the same office at the formation of a new government.

At this stage in our analysis we must ask what, if any, are the consequences of the low tenure of office of British Cabinet ministers? It does not appear to be the case that ministerial instability has a detrimental effect on the policy-making process. By and large government policies are continuous and lasting and are not unduly affected, at least in the short and medium runs, by a high rate of ministerial turnover. Notwithstanding the comings and goings of Cabinet ministers, the fact that senior civil servants remain attached to specific ministries for lengthy periods ensures a large amount of policy continuity. Innovative policies are much more likely to be brought about by changing social and environmental conditions than by a particular minister entering or leaving a department. Given the whole variety of political, social and economic restraints on the policy-making process, it appears most unlikely that the formulation and implementation of policies in Britain would be different in nature if ministerial stability were greater. When comparisons are made with either Commonwealth or European countries, it seems that there are few, if any, major policy discontinuities of any consequence which can be attributed to the kinds of ministerial instability we have been focusing on in this chapter.

Notes

1. Robert Jackson and Michael Stein, 'The Issue of Political Stability', Jackson and Stein (eds), *Issues in Comparative Politics* (London: Macmillan, 1971) pp. 195–211.
2. The theme of 'instability' runs through much of the literature on French politics. See, for example, Roy Pierce, *French Politics and Political Institutions* (New York: Harpers, 1968), Chapter 1; Pierre Avril, *Politics in France*, (Harmondsworth: Penguin, 1969), Chapter 10. Britain's achievement of political stability as early as the eighteenth century is documented in J. H. Plumb's *The Growth of Political Stability in England, 1675–1725*, (London: Macmillan, 1967).
3. See, for example, Roy Macridis, 'Cabinet Instability in the Fourth Republic', *Journal of Politics*, Vol. 14 (1959) pp. 643–58. André Siegfried, 'Stable Instability in France', *Foreign Affairs* (1956) pp. 394–404. A detailed comparative study of ministerial instability in the two countries can be found in Mattei Dogan and Peter Campbell, 'Le personnel ministériel en France et en Grande-Bretagne', *Revue Française de Science Politique*, Vol. 7 (1957) pp. 313–45 and 793–824.
4. See Michael Taylor and Valentine Herman, 'Party Systems and Government Stability', *American Political Science Review*, Vol. 65 (1971) pp. 22-31.
5. The first comparative analysis of ministerial instability in a number of western democracies was Anthony King's 'Britain's Ministerial Turnover', *New Society*, 18 Aug 1966, pp. 157–8.
6. Jean Blondel, 'Party Systems and Patterns of Government in Western Democracies', *Canadian Journal of Political Science*, Vol. 1 (1968) pp. 180–203. For an alternative definition of a 'government' see Leon Hurwitz, 'An Index of Democratic Political Stability', *Comparative Political Studies*, vol. 4 (1971) pp. 41–68.
7. Our data are from *Keesings Contemporary Archives*.
8. Including Ireland.
9. These eight ministries are the only ones suitable for a comparative analysis which includes a large number of countries and a twenty-six-year time period.
10. Cf. King, 'Britain's Ministerial Turnover'.
11. The Ministers of Foreign Affairs and Defence in New Zealand, the Ministers of Trade, Interior, and Finance in Australia and the Minister of Foreign Affairs in Ireland.
12. A reorganisation which involves a sizeable proportion of the Government can be thought of as a reshuffle, a term which cannot

be correctly applied to a reorganisation which involves a small number of ministers.

13. See Valentine Herman and John Pope, 'Minority Governments in Western Democracies', *British Journal of Political Science*, Vol. 3 (1973) pp. 191—212.

14. See Michael Taylor and Michael Laver, 'Government Coalitions in Western Europe', *European Journal of Political Research*, Vol. 1 (1973) pp. 205—48.

4 Resignations

P. J. MADGWICK

One afternoon just before Christmas, in the year 1886, Lord Randolph Churchill journeyed by train to Windsor, in response to an invitation from the Queen. Lord Randolph was Chancellor of the Exchequer in Salisbury's Conservative Government. On the platform at Paddington he met one of his Cabinet colleagues. Lord George Hamilton, the First Lord of the Admiralty, also bound for Windsor, and the two travelled together. Churchill began the conversation in striking fashion by announcing his intention to resign — much to his companion's consternation. Arriving at the Castle, Hamilton joined Churchill in his room, where the Chancellor wrote to the Prime Minister requesting 'to be allowed to give up my office and retire from the Government'. Within two weeks Lord Randolph's political career was in ruins; he was out of office, never to return; the policy he had clung to was equally lost. And there would be no more invitations to Windsor.

The point at issue between Chancellor and Prime Minister was important but not fundamental. Lord Randolph aimed in his budget to reduce some taxes and at the same time increase grants to local government. He needed to cut expenditure by something over one million pounds (in a total budget of under a hundred millions), and he expected the squeeze to fall on the Admiralty and the War Office. The Cabinet was not inclined to accept these budget proposals, and Lord Randolph's letter of resignation was intended to squeeze the Cabinet. It failed: Salisbury replied courteously and firmly disagreeing with Churchill, but leaving the way open for Churchill to withdraw. Instead Churchill told the Editor of *The Times* of his resignation, thus confirming it. Salisbury's government survived the crisis — if such it was —

*Reprinted from *Parliamentary Affairs*, Vol. 20 (1966–7) pp. 59–76, with the permission of the Hansard Society for Parliamentary Government and the author.

and Lord Randolph by his resignation ruined his political career, a victim of the hallucination of indispensability.[1]

This is the most famous of political resignations in modern times, and justifiably so. But there are several other examples to set beside it, some of them equally dramatic. They raise important political and constitutional questions.

All such resignations are in obedience to the convention of collective responsibility. This was given Mosaic form by Lord Salisbury in 1878: 'For all that passes in Cabinet each member of it who does not resign is absolutely and irretrievably responsible, and has no right afterwards to say that he agreed in one case to a compromise, while in another he was persuaded by his colleagues . . .'[2] Gladstone, another judicial legislator in constitutional matters,[3] also gave the convention weight and precision. Commenting on a speech of Chamberlain's in 1883, which had, he thought, transgressed the limits of propriety for a Cabinet Minister, he wrote:

> . . . I should be as far as possible from asserting that under all circumstances speech must be confined within the exact limits to which action is tied down. But I think the dignity and authority, not to say the honour and integrity, of government require that the liberty of speaking beyond these limits should be exercised sparingly, reluctantly, and with much modesty and reserve.[4]

The convention, thus stated and supported, is a characteristic feature of the British Cabinet system and has no equivalent in the Cabinets of Presidential systems like France and the USA.

However, while the existence and form of the convention are clear, its actual operation has changed. There has, first, been a major change in the nature of Cabinets since the late nineteenth century. Once party lines had sharpened, there were few individuals in a Cabinet who carried substantial personal support. Thus, Disraeli felt he must carry Salisbury with him in 1877[5] (though he had survived his resignation ten years earlier). Gladstone had to take seriously Joseph Chamberlain's threats of resignation,[6] for Joe had the support of Dilke in the Cabinet, and a following outside. However, apart from the Coalition period, twentieth-century cabinets have been comparatively united bodies. Prime

Ministers threatened with resignation are faced with the loss of an individual not with the loss of an element in a coalition.

Apart from this change in the structure within which the convention works, the operation of resignation has been inconsistent. Thus Cabinets have sometimes included people notoriously in disagreement with major lines of policy; for example, the Free Trader Churchill sat in Baldwin's Cabinet of 1925–9, a supposedly protectionist Cabinet, and got much of his own way. Some matters of high policy have been left as 'open questions'; Women's Suffrage was such in the Asquith and Lloyd George Cabinet. This applies, of course, to matters on which action is not yet taken. But even when action has been completed, it has always been acceptable for a Minister to make private reservations, including recording his dissent in the Cabinet minutes.[7] It has sometimes even been acceptable for a dissentient Minister to make public reservations. Of this the most striking example is Lord Birkenhead. In commending the Equal Franchise Bill to the House of Lords in 1928 he cheerfully admitted he was opposed to the Bill:

> . . . I have been a member of the Cabinet with a very slight interruption for thirteen years, and I can hardly recall a single measure of first-class importance on which all members of the Cabinet had precisely the same views . . .
>
> Through my own attitude there runs a golden vein of consistency. I was against the extension of the franchise to women. I am against the extension of the franchise to women . . .
>
> I have spent nearly the whole of my political life in giving wise advice to my fellow-countrymen, which they have almost invariably disregarded, and if I had resigned everytime that my wise and advantageous advice was rejected I should seldom, indeed, during that critical period, have been in office.[8]

In addition to these cases of non-operation of the convention, there is the agreement to differ of 1931–2, when three liberal and Free Trading Ministers stayed in MacDonald's Cabinet, but with liberty to oppose (i.e. speak against) protectionist measures. This open breach of

the precedent was proposed on grounds of national crisis: 'an
exception to a very sound constitutional principle which can
only be justified by exceptional circumstances . . .' (Lord
Hailsham). The Lord Chancellor (Sankey) went a little
farther: with large Cabinets dealing with a great range of
subjects, 'the doctrine of collective responsibility remained as
an ideal to be aimed at, but not always one to be realised . . .'
He doubted whether 'it will ever be possible to get a large
Cabinet to be unanimous on every subject'.[9] And, of course,
it is true that Cabinets begin with disagreements and achieve
consensus sometimes by the submission rather than the
persuasion of a dissentient minority. So the question arises,
why does the convention sometimes lead to resignation, and
sometimes not?

This question of political explanation leads to a question
of political and constitutional values. What is a resignation
worth? Resignations are often well received — a resignation is
an act of integrity, courage, perception and so on. A timely
resignation was one of Eden's chief claims to the office of
Prime Minister. Resignation can be a mark of grace. John
Gregg, writing recently in *The Guardian,*[10] expressed the
belief that if Mrs Shirley Williams had been a Minister when
the government's Immigration White Paper was published,
'Labour might have been spared the disgrace that not a single
person was prepared to resign office in protest against that
singular betrayal'. Mr Cousins was criticised for not resigning
sooner because of his alleged opposition to the government's
Incomes Policy — now known to have been fundamental. Mr
Powell on the other hand has been taunted for resigning too
much. Resignations are reputed to shake and even break
governments.

All this suggests firmer views about the nature of resignation than the record justifies. The history of resignations is
patchy and somewhat inconclusive, but it illuminates the
conduct of British politics in one of its few public revelations
of relationships and policy-making at Cabinet level.

Resignations since 1900

Policy resignations are not very frequent and in the last sixty
or so years no more than half-a-dozen could be considered

politically signifcant: Joseph Chamberlain (1903), Trevelyan (1931) Eden and Duff-Cooper (1938), Bevan and Wilson (1951), Thorneycroft (1958). Some others are interesting cases — Carson (1915, 1918), Simon (1916), Montagu (1922), Cecil (1927) and Salisbury — it's in the blood perhaps — (1958). Mayhew and Cousins (1966) are but the latest of a distinguished line. A few others — Curzon, Amery, Elliot, Cripps — may be observed *contemplating* resignation. Of course, Ministers leave the Cabinet for other reasons, retirement, dismissal, and occasionally, as perhaps in the recent case of Mr Fraser, such withdrawals coincide with policy disagreements. The 'refusal to serve' of Mr Macleod and Mr Powell in 1963 is equivalent in some ways to a resignation, but politically — operationally — leaving an existing Cabinet is very different from not joining a Cabinet in process of formation.

Policy resignations are scattered fairly evenly through recent political history, with the 1950s a vintage decade to match the thirties. The 1960s are a little thin so far (politicians please note) unless we count in Mr Powell and Mr Macleod. But there are not sufficient grounds yet for seeing a decline in the custom. This is surprising in a way, for there are tendencies in British politics which might work against ministerial resignations. There are now more politicians who are professionals, in the sense that they need the money. Since 1945 there has been a sharp two-party conflict and commitment to this struggle would suggest a reluctance to resign in the face of the enemy. Again, the power of the Prime Minister is said to have grown, and Ministers have learned, dutifully, to submit. Despite these factors, resignations have still occurred.

Here is a brief catalogue of the major policy resignations of Cabinet ministers in this century:

1903 September. Joseph Chamberlain resigned as Colonial Secretary in Balfour's Cabinet on the issue of Free Trade. Balfour cleverly allowed Chamberlain to believe he had his blessing for resigning in order to 'pioneer' the cause of protection.[11] Four other Ministers including the Duke of Devonshire, resigned at the same time but only two were in sympathy with Chamberlain. This is the most numerous of the resignations apart from that of 1931. Chamberlain believed he could win public support for Tariff Reform and campaigned vigorously until his illness in 1906. Balfour's government survived a little shakily until the end of 1905. A. Gollin[12] claims the episode disproves the English prejudice that upstarts and outsiders like Lloyd George are the most devious politicians.

1914 August. Burns and Morley resigned when the Cabinet decided that the violation by Germany of Belgian neutrality (then imminent) must be resisted.

1915 October. Carson resigned as Attorney-General disagreeing with the running of the war generally and in particular the failure to support Serbia through Salonika. Walter Long said: 'Your resignation will be a fatal blow to the Government'.[13] This was not so.

1916 January. Simon resigned as Home Secretary over conscription. In May twenty-seven MPs voted with him against the Bill. Lloyd-George did not restore him to office but he became Foreign Secretary when the Liberal Party next had a share in power — over fifteen years later, in 1931.

1918 February. One example of a major threat of resignation by Derby, Cecil and Long against Lloyd George's move to deprive Robertson, CIGS, of power. Robertson and the resigners had the support of the King, but Lloyd George himself threatened resignation and won.[14] The resigners were not the most powerful group in the Cabinet. Derby dithered: Lloyd George said in (mock?) anxiety: 'Derby has been the chief difficulty; he has been resigning twice a day'.[15] Such threats of resignation were not infrequent in the coalition cabinets.

1922 March. Edwin Montagu resigned as Secretary of State for India. Montagu was opposed to Lloyd-George's pro-Greek policy, and generally out of sympathy with Lloyd George's methods of government. But the resignation came about after Montagu published a telegram from the Viceroy of India recommending pro-Turkish policies — a serious breach of propriety. The Cabinet held a discussion on collective responsibility,[16] viewed the other way round: how could the Prime Minister be made to conform to the collectivity? They reached no firm conclusion.

1927 August. Lord Robert Cecil resigned as Chancellor of the Duchy of Lancaster and representative at the League of Nations. '. . . On the broad policy of Disarmament', he wrote, 'the majority of the Cabinet and I are not really agreed.'[17] This had been true and, some thought, obvious, for the last two years: he should have resigned when the Geneva Protocol was dropped in 1925. Hence it is the longest delayed of our resignations. Cecil had resigned once previously in 1919 because he 'could not decently remain in a Cabinet pledged to the disendowment of the Church in Wales'.[18] He was not a strong party man and took a non-ministerial job in the Labour government of 1929.

1931 March. Sir Charles Trevelyan resigned as President of the Board of Education because his Education Bill (raising the school leaving age to 15) had been lost in the Lords and was not warmly supported by the Prime Minister and a section of his own party. The Bill was Trevelyan's third attempt. Trevelyan was also bitterly disappointed with the government's ineffectiveness in economic policy. There had been another resignation from the government — Oswald Mosley, May 1930, from the office of Chancellor of the Duchy. There followed some resignations from the Labour Party including that of W. J. Brown ('. . . continued membership has become irreconcilable with any kind of intellectual integrity')[19]

Trevelyan's resignation seems the most justified of all resignations before or since.

1931 August. The resignation of nine Ministers brought the government, but not the Prime Minister, down. Coalition politics transform the working of British government, and most of the rules are changed.

1932 September. Snowden and Samuel resigned, being Free Traders who could not, after all, stomach Baldwin's Protection policies. 'Having swallowed the camel of a general tariff (they) strained at the gnat of imperial preference'.[20] Thus the 'agreement to differ' broke down. Just as well, perhaps; it is roundly condemned by Jennings.

1935 December. Hoare resigned as Foreign Secretary after public outcry against the Hoare—Laval Plan to settle the Abyssinian crisis. Hoare resigned apparently under the doctrine of ministerial responsibility, in fact as a scapegoat for Cabinet policy. Thus the Cabinet decided that collective responsibility did not apply, since it did not suit them — a demonstration of the real nature of conventions in modern British government.[21]

1938 February. Eden resigned as Foreign Secretary, (and Cranborne, his under-Secretary with him) in protest against Chamberlain's conduct of foreign affairs — his policy of 'appeasement' and his method of managing without, and sometimes overriding, the Foreign Office. The specific occasion was a conciliatory move by Chamberlain towards Italy. An 'unnecessary quarrel', said Dawson of *The Times*[22] (a supporter of 'appeasement'). Chamberlain was adamant — it was his resignation or Eden's — and won but 'only with blood and tears'.[23] The Cabinet was shaken.

But Eden went at the wrong time ('There's more to come', wrote Vansittart, 'there's Austria'[24]), and did not attempt to win the support of other dissidents, e.g. Elliott and Stanley (the awkward group dubbed by Chamberlain contemptuously 'the Boys' Brigade'). Bevan said 'He could have ruined Chamberlain' and Foot comments with much justice: 'The most polite resignation of modern times'.[25] In some ways Eden almost put himself in the position of being dismissed.

It was characteristic of the feverish atmosphere of international relations at this time, that Cranborne's successor, R. A. Butler, should have called at the German Embassy to give reassurance: '. . . not a voice had been raised (in the Cabinet) in favour of Eden'.[26] The resignation became symbolic of the forces of righteousness and did much for Eden's reputation. Churchill wrote of hearing the news at Chartwell: 'I must confess that my heart sank, and for a while the dark waters of despair overwhelmed me . . .'[27] It has thus some claim to be an historic resignation.

1938 October. Duff-Cooper resigned as First Lord of the Admiralty in protest against the Munich settlement. Earlier, at the time of the Godesberg meeting, four or five members of the Cabinet had talked of resignation. Duff-Cooper had openly indicated to the Cabinet his own misgivings. His 'continued presence in the Cabinet was', he said, 'only a source of delay and annoyance to those who thought differently.'[28]

Munich — strangely enough — was a triumph for Chamberlain, and Duff-Cooper resigned in isolation, with all but a score of the party, most of the people, and his constituency all opposed to him. Stanley and Elliott stayed behind.

Duff-Cooper was a skilled politician as well as a man of principle and did not resign lightly. He had fought the Treasury over the Naval Estimates all that year and lost, but stayed to fight again. He knew what he was losing and his resignation ranks as the most courageous of modern times.

He returned to office under Winston Churchill in May 1940.

1951 April. Bevan (Minister of Labour), Wilson (President of the Board of Trade) and Freeman (Parliamentary Secretary, Ministry of Supply) resigned in protest against the rearmament programme and the imposition of charges under the National Health Service. The rearmament programme was regarded as impracticable rather than undesirable. Bevan's is the angriest resignation. His speech,[29] with its sharp cut at the newly promoted Chancellor, Gaitskell, put the resignation in the worst light.

The resignation is a more enigmatic episode in Wilson's career. But the economic point of the resignation was soon proved correct.

1956 October–November. Boyle (Economic Secretary to the Treasury) and Nutting (Minister of State, Foreign Office) resigned in protest against the Suez intervention. (No Cabinet Minister resigned.) The wonder is there were no others, to the right or the left — 'loyalty.' as Lord Kilmuir said, 'is the Tories' secret weapon'.[30] But once troops are engaged, resignation is difficult. Then the military operations were called off and the Prime Minister himself resigned. Perhaps it should be argued that resignations occur only when there is no danger of the Government's falling

Boyle accepted another office a few weeks later, a record for quick return to office. Nutting was rejected by his constituency (Melton Mowbray) and left politics.

1957 March. Salisbury resigned as Lord President of the Council and Leader of the Lords, in protest against the release of Archbishop Makarios. Salisbury (the Cranborne who resigned in 1938) was influential in the Conservative Party and had a part in the making of the Macmillan government. There was some unrest in the party. Salisbury's principles were near the heart of old-fashioned Toryism (as over Rhodesia at the Party Conference of 1965). But no one followed him. *The Economist*[31] aptly headed its comment, 'The Dog it was that died'. It is the most anti-climactic of resignations.

Salisbury did not recover his influence in the Party.

1958 January. Chancellor Thorneycroft and his Economic and Financial Secretaries, Nigel Birch and Enoch Powell, resigned in protest against the irresolution of the Government in its fight against inflation — in particular they wanted a further cut of £50 millions in the Estimates. In the subsequent debate Sir Toby Low, Chairman of the Conservative Members' Finance Committee, spoke in support of the resigners — but without opposing the Government. *The Times*, in its leader and correspondence columns, produced its high moral tone. One leading article was headed 'Flinching', and Mr Micawber was also quoted.

The situation was a considerable test for a Prime Minister, and there is no doubt Macmillan emerged triumphant. Giving an interview at London Airport, before flying off for a tour of Africa, he spoke of the departure of his distinguished colleagues as 'little local difficulties'.[32] True, he was comparing domestic politics with the problems of the Commonwealth he was about to face: nevertheless, the phrase is rightly remembered as a characteristic, lordly gesture.

No incident illustrates better that a resignation is by definition the occasion when the Prime Minister stands firm.

1966 February. Mr Mayhew resigned as Navy Minister, in protest against the cutting of the aircraft carrier programme, while retaining policy-commitments East of Suez. His junior Minister took his place.

Mr Mayhew was not a member of the Cabinet and was subordinate to the Minister of Defence. The Prime Minister, in an airport interview, said Mayhew was 'a passionate man'. Airport interviews seem to suit Prime Ministers with resignations on their hands.

Mayhew's views have some support in the Party, and in the long term, he is likely to win his point.

1966 July. Mr Cousins resigned as Minister of Technology,

because of disagreements over the Government's policy on prices and incomes. The disagreements were fundamental and of long standing: the imminence of legislation precipitated the resignation. Mr Cousins had held his Ministerial post on leave from the General Secretaryship of the Transport and General Workers' Union. On resigning he was tipped as a new leader of a Left opposition group, but this was to misread the normal consequences of resignations. Moreover, Mr Cousins' power-base was in the Trade Union movement, not in Parliament; he was not a professional parliamentary politician. For the proposed role of rebel leadership this is a serious, possibly disabling, disadvantage — and one highly significant for the assessment of power in British politics in general, and in the Labour party in particular.

Mr Cousins' resignation is also a case-study in the relations of Parliament and outside bodies — but that is another story.

The political context of resignation

Resignation is a matter of strategy and persuasion as well as honour and dissociation. A Minister resigns when he is in disagreement with his colleagues on a matter judged by him to be of high importance. This dissociates him from the policies he disapproves of, and it is usually regarded as the honourable course for a man of integrity. Since the resigner gains the right to proclaim the truth as he sees it, at the cost of both influence and career prospects, this is an acceptable judgement. There are two reservations however. First, 'honour' is a slightly stilted word, to do with duelling-pistols or village maidens. In politics, as in everyday life, honour appears as a concern not simply for principles, but for what is practicable and agreeable among colleagues in co-operation. Second, resignation is not the only path of honour. It may be equally honourable to stay and fight again.

Usually, however, resignations mean much more than honourable withdrawal; they are part of political strategy, the attempt to win over colleagues. In the Cabinet, the threat to resign secures consideration by the full Cabinet, under some pressure to make concessions. If this works, there is no resignation and incidentally no public knowledge of the

situation for several years. Most of the time Cabinets argue
and bargain for a consensus: this arises from their political
nature rather than from an implied threat of resignation. But
occasionally, an explicit threat lies, so to speak, on the table.
This seems to have been particularly true of the Lloyd-
George and Attlee Cabinets. But the threat of resignation is a
dangerous weapon, for the bluff may be called, as Randolph
Churchill discovered in 1886. Few men are indispensable, and
a Cabinet will not often be called to heel by a sudden threat
of resignation, even from a senior Minister. Like military
deterrents, resignation works only if it can inflict unacceptable
damage. Normally, this is beyond its capacity.

If the Cabinet is not persuaded by a threat of resignation,
the resignation itself may be no more than the result of
failure in this tactic. But it can be part of a further political
manoeuvre, an appeal beyond the Cabinet to party or people.
There have been times when such an appeal has not looked a
forlorn hope. For example, Joseph Chamberlain in 1903 and
Mosley in 1930 both expected to create new parties to
promote their policies. (These were not unreasonable calculations, for the party system was in flux at these dates. But
neither Chamberlain nor Mosley had much to do with the
reshaping.) Bevan was able to take the fight to the Labour
Party's National Executive Committee and to Conference.
Eden could see in the cheering crowds in Downing Street and
outside his house popular support for his cause.[33] But all this
is much to exaggerate the tactical opportunities of resignation. If the possibilities exist, they can rarely be developed. A
more likely sequel is Charles Trevelyan's meeting with the
Parliamentary Labour Party in 1931. His speech was 'received
in stony silence ... a silence maintained throughout.'
MacDonald, rising to reply, was cheered for 'a full two
minutes'.[34] However, Trevelyan was freed by his resignation
to take the issues to the Party Conference, and this he did
with effect next year.

In a constitutional monarchy resignation might also be a
means of appealing to the Crown. Some of those who
threatened resignation against Lloyd-George, e.g. in February
1918, were certainly in touch with George V, and the King
was by no means unswervingly loyal to his Prime Minister.[35]

If by resigning the dissidents could bring down the government, then the King would have been consitutionally activated (so to speak). But the fall of the government would still have been determined in the House of Commons, and hence that is where power lay. Thus resignation is not effectively an appeal to the Crown, because in normal circumstances, the Crown has no power to re-form a government having the confidence of the House of Commons. The 1931 crisis is not an exception to this rule. Of course in theory the Crown might seek to persuade a Prime Minister to make concessions to avoid a resignation. But in practice, the normal relationship between Crown and Prime Minister does not admit of political advice of this kind.

Thus far the political circumstances in which policy resignations occur have been described as including on the one hand, a Cabinet standing firm, in disagreement on the other with a Minister concerned with his honour and calculating his tactics. There fall now to be considered certain secondary features of the resigning situation.

First, *there is no characteristic resigning issue, but there are some common features of such issues.* Ministers have resigned most over financial and economic policy (Randolph Churchill, Joseph Chamberlain, Bevan and Thorneycroft). This is not surprising since so much policy depends on finance. Mr Mayhew's case illustrates the point again: the cutting of the carrier programme is a financial as much as a defence policy.

Resigning issues are of course regarded — by the resigner at least — as important. But they are often marginal aspects of important issues — a last straw, which is significant only in relation to many previous straws. Tactically this makes the position difficult for the resigner. Mr Mayhew can be told that it is absurd to resign over one aircraft carrier; Mr Thorneycroft over a mere £50 million; Mr Bevan over £13 million. Mr Eden in 1938 resigned over a comparatively unimportant diplomatic move with Italy. But for him as for the others, it is fair to say that the issues were bigger than the immediate occasion of resignation suggests. (Mr Mayhew seems particularly to be at a tactical disadvantage in that he resigned apparently for the sake of an additional aircraft-carrier, but in general, it seems he favours a reduction in British defence commitments.)

It does not help to define a resigning issue as an issue of principle or conscience. There is, it is true, the traditional association of conscience with pacifism, and this was the basis of the resignation of Burns and Morley in 1914 and of old John Bright and Forster and Argyll in 1882 (when old William Gladstone had bombarded Alexandria). But this is an unduly narrow definition of conscience. A politician may be allowed to have a conscience over the balance of payments or the Health Service. A resigning issue is simply an issue regarded by the resigner as important.

Second, most resignations go along with party instability, at once its consequence, its sympton, its reinforcement. But some resignations occur at times of party stability.

Many resignations are smothered by the need for party and governments solidarity. Most of those which are actually pressed through occur at times of tension and instability within the party, especially when the leadership is in doubt or dispute. When the front has lost its solidarity, there is little to lose by breaking away. This is clearly true in the period 1915–22, when coalition governments were much threatened with resignation. Dalton's account of Attlee's Cabinet suggest there were frequent thoughts of resignation,[36] by Cripps, Morrison and Bevin over the leadership, by Dalton himself over demobilisation, by Cripps again on exports. Cripps at one time had his proposals for a completely new government worked out in some detail. Then with the government not quite defeated in the Election of 1950, an acute succession problem and low morale lay behind the resignations of Bevan and Wilson in April 1951. Was such disarray a characteristic of the Labour Party alone? Not at all. In 1958 Thorneycroft's resignation as Chancellor in Macmillan's Conservative Government struggling still to establish itself after the Suez disaster, showed again the resigners are most active in troubled parties. They are a symptom of the sickness and the sickness afflicts both right and left.

However, Mr Mayhew's resignation, like Cecil's in 1927, does not fall into this pattern. In both cases the party leadership was not in doubt, and there was at least an air of calm and unison along the party front. So resignations do occur in stable party situations, and they have then to be explained in terms of policy or personality.

Third, certain personal characteristics seem to impel some politicians into resignation in circumstances and for issues which would leave others unmoved. Resigners are not always tough men, acting deliberately with the consequences accurately calculated. The politician is no more than anyone else an actor on his own, shaping his destiny. He is one of many players and he has been in the play a long time; his character takes hold of him and an accumulation of minor performances gives a set to his political character which perhaps he cannot break. It is not always easy to turn back, even for the sake of solidarity.

There is another personal factor which seems to count in some resignations, again a matter outside the actor's control. This is the failure of nerve and stamina, or the loss of balance, when the press of persons, arguments and events, tiredness, demoralization sweep the Minister into a decision for which cooler reflection might provide no justification. Salisbury explained Randolph Churchill's resignation in this way: '(his) conduct can only be accounted for on the theory that the work has upset his nerves — and when his nerves go, his judgment goes altogether...'[37] This could apply to several other resignations too; for many of our politicians are not, fortunately, entirely nerveless.

Ambition and particularly frustrated ambition, impels resignation. This is partly true of several of our resigners, but most sharply illustrated in Bevan's resignation in 1951. Prime Minister Attlee would obviously soon retire. Of his senior colleagues, Bevin had died and Cripps was seriously ill: they were out of the race. Of his likely rivals, Morrison had just been promoted Foreign Secretary and the young Hugh Gaitskell — comparatively a newcomer — was the new Chancellor. For Bevan, then Minister of Labour, the indications were clear: he was not to be the leader. Now this might look too facile an interpretation: but Bevan's resignation speech revealed his resentment. Bevan said: '. . . there are too many economists advising the Treasury, and now we have the added misfortune of having an economist in the Chancellor of the Exchequer himself'. Of this speech *The Economist*[38] wrote: 'No man has even done more to ensure that his own party will shortly be defeated in a general election. No Minister has on resigning attacked in more vehement and bitter fashion his own colleagues of the day before.'

This is an explanation, but not in itself a condemnation. For ambition is not a reprehensible quality in a politician (or anyone else). Power is desired for what you can do with it, and the ambitious politician may fairly claim that he seeks the triumph of his principles, not himself. Of course, an ill-judged resignation may still sink both.

Among the gallery of resigners there are a few who stand out as natural, predictable resigners. Cecil, Curzon and Salisbury (Cranborne) all managed two resignations during their careers. They are the type of Aristocratic Amateur, men whose antecedents and traditions gave them a taste for high principle, rather than for party, and for whom politics was not a trade but a way of life. Trevelyan also resigned twice (as his father had before him) and was later expelled from the Party too. He was typically the Man of Principle for whom politics meant the rapid promotion of the good life. Aneurin Bevan brought to his resigning both principles and a vision of social justice — but also a mercurial temperament. Attlee said of him he worked best in harness ('He'd had six years of it with Stafford Cripps ... He cut loose after Stafford went ...'[39]) He is a type of Radical Resigner. On the other side, Enoch Powell is a man of powerful intellect, reluctant to compromise and careless of established sensibilities. Such resigners may sometimes lay themselves open to the charge of arrogance.

Since the Aristocratic Amateur is a declining force in British Politics, Trevelyan, Bevan and Powell remain the typical resigners of left and right. If all resigners resembled these types they would make a splendid gallery of characters, and resignation would be a mark of personal eccentricity — an out-of-the-ordinary richness of character. But the truth is less appealing: for some resigners are simply Able Professionals like Thorneycroft, Mayhew, Eden: run-of-the-mill as top politicians go, and disappointing if you like your politics 'tuppence-coloured'.

Fourth, Ministers may, in resigning, act rather as Heads of Departments of State, than as Members of Cabinet or Party.
The Minister's connection with his Department is an important element in the resigning situation. The Minister quite properly identifies himself with the Department, seeks to protect its interests, catches the officials' sense of Departmental self-esteem — and is trapped between two loyalties. Mr Thorneycroft's departure in 1958 had some roots in the Treasury's feeling for power, and Mr Mayhew, in a non-Cabinet, subordinate Ministry, had surely caught something from the outraged Admirals. Eden in 1958 resigned partly because he had too little power as Foreign Secretary. With the Prime Minister's frequent interventions, and Hoare and Halifax in the Cabinet, the Foreign Office had been downgraded.

Resignations over finance are related to the power of the Treasury in British government, and the secrecy with which financial policy is prepared. The Chancellor, with the Treasury knights at his back, may feel the iron in his soul. 'It may shorten discussion on this matter, Mr Prime Minister, if I say there is no money for it'.[40] This is Snowden's rather brusque version of a Chancellor's regular Cabinet statement. In this situation a Chancellor and some economised-against Minister take up their resigning positions and the Prime Minister has to arbitrate. In the three major post-war resignations the Prime Minister and the rest of the Cabinet have had to choose which of their colleagues is to resign. Chancellor Thorneycroft, like Randolph Churchill, was sacrificed. Neither was a senior man politically; but nor was Chancellor Gaitskell in 1951 when Morrison (deputising for Attlee) chose to back him. In a similar dispute in 1925 Chancellor Winston Churchill, in dispute with Bridgeman, the First Lord of the Admiralty, was asked by the Prime Minister whether he, like the First Lord, thought the matter a resigning one.[41] Winston — son of Randolph — said no! and conceded the point.

The Admiralty, strangely enough, has some claim to be one of the great resigning Departments. It has lost its chief by resignation in 1938 (Duff Cooper) and again in 1966 (Mayhew). There is the case of Bridgeman in 1925 and of Lord

George Hamilton in 1886 — both resisting resignation. There is the Churchill—Fisher saga. The Sea-Lords themselves are inclined to be mutinous. The First Sea Lord resigned along with Mr Mayhew, and others stayed on only 'for the good of the Navy'.

Resignation as political strategy

Resignation has usually been regarded as an effective political action; not just a dissociation, a standing aside, but one way of fighting back. Nigel Birch said of his resignation in 1958: '. . . if we were to break with the old ways a shock had to be administered to the system . . .'[42] *The Times* thought the intention had been realised: the government was 'damaged . . . at an awkward time in subtle psychological as well as crude party ways . . .'[43] Amery wrote of his failure to resign over unemployment in 1928, '. . . if ever I made a mistake in not resigning . . .'[44] — as if it might have made a difference. Bevan wrote, at the time, of Eden's resignation: 'If Eden had been big enough he could have ruined Chamberlain'.[45] Churchill's comment on Eden in 1938 is revealing: 'I hoped he would not on any account resign without building up his case beforehand, and giving his many friends in Parliament a chance to draw out the issues.'[46]

Thus Churchill saw resignation properly managed, as an effective tactic, certainly in an unstable situation when profound disagreements were developing in both Cabinet and majority party. Proper management of resignation means resigning on a major issue, at the same time securing support from some substantial Party leaders, and doing this when the leadership is vulnerable. Thus, Vansittart thought Eden should have waited for a bigger issue so that other disaffected Ministers like Stanley and Elliott would have joined him. He wrote, 'There is worse to follow you know. There's Austria.' Randolph Churchill in a Cabinet devoted to the preservation of the Union, chose a marginal issue and then did not bother to secure any support at all; though simply by winning over the influential Hicks-Beach, he might have had his way.[47] Finding a moment of vulnerability is more difficult.

Macmillan's government looked vulnerable in 1958 — but proved resilient. Attlee's government was vulnerable in 1951 but resignation helped to bring the Cabinet down but not round. In 1931, MacDonald's Cabinet was impotent but not so easy to displace. Nine resignations brought it down. It is numbers not management which count.

Indeed for all the distinguished tributes to the Cabinet-shattering possibilities, *resignations by two or three Ministers do not in practice succeed.* Firm handling by the Prime Minister, a steady nerve, and the ranks are closed. The resigners, from Randolph Churchill to Cousins, have never won. Salisbury and Thorneycroft provide the most remarkable illustration. Lord Salisbury resigned in March 1957, in protest againt the release of Archbishop Makarios. Salisbury had been in the Cabinet since 1951, prominent and influential, especially in the making of the Macmillan government in 1957; not perhaps a king-maker, but almost so. He resigned and all breaths were, as they say, bated. Nothing happened: the man recovered of the bite — the dog it was that died. Ten months later, when Macmillan lost all three of his Treasury ministers, he flew off to Africa, unperturbed. When he returned the crisis was over — solved by ignoring it. Resignation has thus usually proved to be little more than dissociation from the Government's policies: it is not a political launching-pad. Winston Churchill, remembering his father's fall and ignoring his comments on Eden, had good reason to take this view of resignation; it is unlikely *he* would have resigned in 1938.

The record suggests indeed that the surmounting of a resignation does not require very great wisdom or skill on the part of the Prime Minister. If he plays it cool and firm in the Macmillan manner he will survive. The lesson is well illustrated in the exchange of letters between MacDonald and Baldwin in January 1932. The Free Traders were about to resign, MacDonald was ready to panic: 'What will the new Government be? Party. How can it be National? How can I remain?' To this Baldwin phlegmatically replied: '. . . First, don't worry. You are bound to carry on. The many questions arising can be discussed during the autumn, but your duty is straight and clear. You must stick to the ship till we are in calmer waters.'[48] Thus all a Prime Minister needs is a steady nerve.

If resignation is an ineffective political tactic, at least it does not seem to be totally disastrous to a political career. Here the classic case of Randolph Churchill is untypical. Resignation ended his ministerial career. For the six years of Salisbury's administration he was in the wilderness. Illness and premature death then supervened, but his career was already in ruins. There is no other comparable disaster, unless strangely enough we count the resignation of Lord Randolph's son, Winston, from the Conservative Opposition Front Bench in 1930. Only exceptional circumstances enabled him to regain office in 1939. The next year, of course, the son truly avenged his father. Other resigners have had an easier passage back. Eden returned to the humbler post of Dominions Secretary in September 1939 (18 months after his departure). Thorneycroft and his colleagues returned after the 1959 General Election (again about 18 months). The case of Bevan and Wilson is difficult to assess since Labour went out of office in October 1951. Bevan was then able to draw influence from his substantial support in the Party and his position as a leading member of the Party could not be denied. But he could not capture the leadership when Attlee retired at the end of 1955. For Bevan, resignation probably did no more than confirm his unsuitability for the leadership. Wilson, on the other hand, seems to have suffered more. Dalton slyly recalls in his memoirs that he *may* have called Wilson 'Nye's little dog',[49] and he implies he was not alone in his hostility. But if Wilson lost some friends, he had the time to work his passage back. Like Bevan, too, he had his supporters in the Party outside Parliament. The next year Wilson and Crossman replaced Morrison and Dalton on the (elected) National Executive Committee. This was not the same as geting back to office, but since the Party was then out of office, a seat on the NEC was a sufficient position of influence. The incident suggests that the elective elements in the Labour Party's constitution can be important though not in Mayhew's case, for it seems unlikely that NEC or a Labour Party conference will go overboard for another aircraft carrier.

Resignation, then, does not ruin a politician who is otherwise acceptable to his colleagues: but a period in the wilderness does least damage early in his career and when his party is soon to be out of office anyway. And it may be the Labour Party provides the easier passage back. Trouble-makers on the other hand may, as the careers of the two Churchills show, stay a long time in the wilderness.

In these considerations it may make a difference (and surely it ought to?) if the resignations are soon proved correct. This was certainly the case in 1951, when the incoming Churchill government virtually accepted the Bevan—Wilson view of the defence programme. Again Eden was soon vindicated in his views on Chamberlain's foreign policy in 1938. But Prime Ministers are no better than anyone else at enjoying I-told-you-so comments; so the ambitious resigner had best observe a modest (and impotent) silence.

Constitutional value of resignation

There is not much in the record to encourage a rising politician to resign (and they are all rising except the Prime Minister himself): it will not promote his cause, or his career. Yet the convention of collective responsibility is accepted. It is in the books, it certainly receives 'lip service' (and that is quite significant). It was given a firm and well-phrased reinforcement by Harold Wilson in 1951: '. . . the principle (of collective responsibility) requires from each Minister a full and wholehearted acceptance of the measures decided upon by the Cabinet and of the policies underlying them . . .'[50] The resigner is given a privileged and respectful hearing in the House, and even Cabinet secrecy is mildly waived. Junior Ministers may also resign but they are expected to slip away unheard: the convention allows a senior Minister a kind of ceremonial resignation.

Thus the convention of collective responsibility with its corollary of resignation holds firm: it may be regarded as part of the constitution. But the convention operates in changed political circumstances. The Cabinet is no longer the corporate entity it was. Salisbury spoke in 1890 of the difficulty of dismissing a Cabinet Minister except for 'some open and palpable error'.[51] This was perhaps to exaggerate the collective nature of the Cabinet. Even so it has been changed since then by the development of the committee system, by the inflation of the office of Prime Minister and by the development and enforcement of party doctrinal unity. The modern Cabinet has been, so to speak, pre-processed in unity before its formation; then its decision-making is compartmentalised. The individual member of the Cabinet does not feel so intimately involved, so operationally committed to every decision of the Cabinet. In consequence, the convention, in so far as it may lead to resignation, hardly now applies in practice for any member of the Cabinet over the full range of Cabinet policy. And when resignation does happen, it is no longer a fundamental breach, and the Cabinet suffers no organic damage.

Moreover, the convention is an optional convention. It is supported by the sanction of opinion; but, if a Minister who does not want to resign chooses to hold his tongue in public, the sanction and the convention are invalidated. Indeed, conventions work only if they serve a political purpose; and the overriding political purpose of the modern British Constitution is the preservation of government and party solidarity in face of a potentially critical public. Resignation does not help and Prime Ministers are seldom enthusiastic supporters of this particular consequence of the convention.

But constitutions are not made only for the convenience and preservation of governments. So the question arises: is resignation on grounds of policy a valuable element in the constitution from the point of view of the governed?

The principle of resignation on grounds of policy-disagreements seems to be worth preserving. It provides an open, public check on the Government — particularly on the Prime Minister, the Cabinet committees, the great Departments, all those parts of government which might, left alone, take us for an uncovenanted ride. It enhances the importance of the Cabinet as a whole. The resignation with full ceremony is the individual member's weapon of last resort against an arrogant or heedless majority.

The device of resignation encourages government based on principle rather than persons. The 'agreement-to-differ' of 1931–2 showed what this means in practice. By abandoning collective responsibility, the elector's choice was depoliticised and degraded. 'Emancipation from machine-made caucus-ridden politics', giving 'men of independence and character more of a chance' — these (phrases of Milner to Curtis, November 1915[52]) remove government from the arena of genuine public debate. Parties based on policies and a collectively responsible cabinet are democratic devices, and of this democracy, resignation is a small but essential prop.

Further, the convention makes for effective government in that it provides a recognised (and indeed respected) way out of deadlock. A Cabinet trying to contain within itself too wide or too deep a disagreement may evade decisions for too long, or attempt the execution of policy with a fatal lack of conviction.

There are other advantages in the convention of collective responsibility when it leads — as it should from time to time — to resignation. It modifies the impenetrable secrecy of government; it highlights disagreements, an essential element in public political education. It persuades politicians to behave, and to be seen behaving, in a human fashion. These are considerable advantages. Democracy thrives on political drama. For a comparatively literate and sophisticated public, resignations provide dramatic insight into politics. Their history is part of political culture.

Thus there are grounds for approving of Mr Mayhew's resignation as evidence of the continuing validity of the tradition; and for disapproving of Mr Cousins' long delay in resigning when he was so fundamentally opposed to the government's incomes policy. On the other hand, we should regard resignation as one way of registering serious disagreement; and not necessarily the path of superior honour. We should accept that the personal motivation and the political context will be complicated, and the outcome insignificant. But all in all, we should look forward to one or two more resignations before the decade is out.[53]

Notes

1. The best account is R. R. James, *Lord Randolph Churchill* (London: Weidenfeld, 1959) pp. 281 ff. James does not accept the 'hallucination of indispensability' theory (p. 310), because

Churchill 'in his own eyes did not resign'. But, in fact, he did resign, in order to be taken back on his own terms — thus gambling on his indispensability.

2. Lady G. Cecil, *Life of Robert, Marquis of Salisbury*, 4 vols. (London: Hodder & Stoughton, 1921—31).

3. Of Gladstone in this role, Labourchere wrote: '. . . he will deliver so many essays on the Constitution to his colleagues that there will be no time for anything else.' Letter to Akers-Douglas, May 1892, quoted in E. A. A. Chilston, 3rd Viscount, *Chief Whip; the political life and times of Aretas Akers-Douglas, 1st Viscount Chilston* (London: Routledge, 1961).

4. Letter to Lord Granville, 1 Jul 1893, quoted in J. Morley, *The Life of William Ewart Gladstone*, Vol. 3 (London: Macmillan, 1903) pp. 113.

5. J. Mackintosh, *The British Cabinet* (London: Stevens, 1962) p. 297.

6. Ibid., 298.

7. For examples see Mackintosh, ibid., pp. 445—6. Harcourt's position in the Rosebery Cabinet of 1894—5 is not of much significance here, or at other points, because of the peculiar political circumstances of the Rosebery interregnum. Harcourt wrote to Lord Spencer: 'As you know, I am not a supporter of the present Government . . .' Harcourt was at the time Chancellor of the Exchequer and Leader of the House! The letter is quoted in Chilston, *Chief Whip*, p. 257.

8. 71 H.L. Deb 5s, Cols 252—3 (22 May 1928).

9. 83 H.L. Deb 5s, Cols 543—6 (10 Feb 1932).

10. 14 Apr 1966.

11. A. Gollin, *Balfour's Burden; Arthur Balfour and Imperial Preference* (London: Blond, 1965) Ch. VIII.

12. Ibid., p. 116.

13. I. Colvin, *The Life of Lord Carson*, Vol. 3 (London: Gollancz, Vols. 2 and 3, 1932—6).

14. See W. M. Aitken Beaverbrook, 1st Baron, *Men and Power 1917—18* (London: Hutchinson, 1956) p. 412.

15. G. A. Riddell, Baron, *Lord Riddell's War Diary 1914—18* (London: Nicholson & Watson, 1933) p. 313.

16. Mackintosh, *The British Cabinet*, p. 363.

17. *The Times*, 30 Aug 1927.

18. E. A. R. G. Cecil, Viscount Cecil of Chelwood, *All the Way* (London: Hodder & Stoughton, 1949) p. 174.

19. *The Times*, 6 Mar 1931.

20. I. Jennings, *Cabinet Government* 3rd ed. (Cambridge: CUP, 1959) p. 281.

21. See Mackintosh, *The British Cabinet*, p. 16.

22. From an entry in Dawson's diary at the time; quoted in Sir J. E. L. Wrench, *Geoffrey Dawson and our Times* (London: Hutchinson, 1955) p. 367.

23. K. Feiling, *The Life of Neville Chamberlain* (London: Macmillan, 1946) p. 338.

24. I. G. Colvin, *Vansittart in Office; an historical survey of the origins of the 2nd World War based on the papers of Sir Robert Vansittart* (London: Gollancz, 1965) p. 193.

25. M. Foot, *Aneurin Bevan: A Biography*, Vol. 1, 1897—1945 (London: MacGibbon, 1962) p. 272.

26. M. Gilbert and R. Gott, *The Appeasers* (London: Houghton, 1963) pp. 86—7.

27. W. S. Churchill, *The Gathering Storm* (Harmondsworth: Penguin, 1960) pp. 232—3.

28. A. Duff Cooper, Viscount Norwich, *Old Men Forget: An Autobiography of Duff Cooper* (London: Rupert Hart-Davis, 1953) p. 236.

29. 487 H.C. Deb 5s, Cols 34—43 (23 Apr 1951). The whole incident is covered in Joan Mitchell, *Crisis in Britain 1951* (London: Secker & Warburg, 1963).

30. D. P. M. Fife Kilmuir, 1st Earl of Kilmuir, *Political Adventure; the memoirs of the Earl of Kilmuir* (London: Weidenfeld, 1964) p. 324.

31. 6 Apr 1957.

32. *The Times*, 8 Jan 1958.

33. A. Eden, *Facing the Dictators* (London: Houghton, 1962) pp. 592, 598—9.

34. *Manchester Guardian*, 4 Mar 1931, quoted in R. T. McKenzie, *British Political Parties* (London: Heinemann, 1963). See also L. MacNeill Weir, *The Tragedy of Ramsay McDonald: a political biography* (London: Secker & Warburg, 1938) pp. 252 ff.

35. Sir H. G. Nicolson, *King George the Fifth: His Life and Reign* (London: Constable, 1952) pp. 320—2, and Lord Beaverbrook, *Men and Power, 1917—18* (London: Hutchinson, 1956) esp. p. 412.

36. H. Dalton, *High Tide and After: Memoirs 1945—60* (London: Frederick Muller, 1962) p. 241; Dalton also talked of resignation from Churchill's coalition at the end of 1944: H. Dalton, *The Fateful Years: Memoirs 1931—45* (London: Frederick Muller, 1957).

37. Chilston, *Chief Whip*, p. 99.

38. 28 Apr 1951.

39. F. Williams, *A Prime Minister Remembers* (London: Heinemann, 1960).

40. Mackintosh, *The British Cabinet*, p. 401.

41. Ibid., p. 394. The Naval Estimates went up by nearly £5 million; but the question of certain replacements was referred to a Committee.

42. *The Times*, 16 Jan 1958.

43. Ibid., 20 Jan 1958.

44. L. S. Amery, *My Political Life*, Vol. 2 (London: Hutchinson, 1953) p. 496.

45. M. Foot, *Aneurin Bevan*, Vol. 1, p. 272.
46. W. Churchill, *The Gathering Storm*, p. 232.
47. R. R. James, *Lord Randolph Churchill*, pp. 290, 310.
48. The correspondence is quoted in G. M. Young, *Stanley Baldwin* (London: Hart-Davis, 1952) pp. 171–2.
49. H. Dalton, *High Tide and After*, p. 369.
50. 487 H.C. Deb 5s, Cols 228–31 (24 Apr 1951).
51. *Letters of Queen Victoria*, Third Series, Vol. 1 (London: John Murray, 1930–2).
52. Quoted in A. Gollin, *Proconsul in Politics; A Study of Lord Milner in Opposition and in Power, 1854–1905* (London: Blond, 1964) p. 314.
53. See George Brown, 'Why I Resigned From The Cabinet', in Chapter 5 below.

5 Personal Views of Ministerial Resignation

Why I Resigned from the Cabinet*

LORD GEORGE-BROWN

I resigned on a matter of fundamental principle, because it seemed to me that the Prime Minister was not only introducing a 'presidential' system into the running of the government that is wholly alien to the British constitutional system — others have been tempted to do it that way too — but was so operating it that decisions were being taken over the heads and without the knowledge of ministers, and far too often outsiders in his entourage seemed to be almost the only effective 'Cabinet'. I put this plainly in my letter of resignation, written to Mr Wilson on 15 March:

> The events of last night and the long hours of this morning have brought to a head a really serious issue which has, as you know, been troubling me for some time.
>
> It is, in short, the way this Government is run, and the manner in which we reach our decisions. You and I have discussed this more than once. I regard this general issue as much more fundamental than any particular item of policy.

The particular incident which brought things to a head was the Prime Minister's decision to ask the Queen, at a hurriedly called meeting of the Privy Council late at night, to proclaim a Bank Holiday in order to meet a request from America which had to do with arrangements being made internationally to steady the chaotic gold situation which then existed. No announcement of this had been discussed among Ministers and no statement had been made to the House of

*Reprinted from Lord George-Brown's *In My Way* (London: Gollancz, 1971) Chapter 9, with the permission of the author and publisher.

Commons. The statement that was subsequently made at 3.20 am on the following morning was only made because of the events of that night leading to my declared intention to resign. Whatever may be said as afterthought, there had been no intention to make a statement and there would not have been any announcement that night to the House of Commons. There have of course been attempts since by quite sincere people to say that this really was a very technical matter — simply a question of whether you have a Bank Holiday on a particular day in order to be able to shut the banks and stop financial manoeuvring. But the 'technicality', if that's what it was, cloaked two very serious issues: the first one was what it was all about, who asked for it or authorized it, and were we in fact doing something which the Americans wanted which nobody else over here in authority knew very much about; and the second was this grave, as I saw it, departure from constitutional practice which allowed the Prime Minister and two other Ministers to act as though a decision which should have been that of the Cabinet as a whole had in fact been taken. The proclamation was reasonable enough — had the Cabinet been consulted in the ordinary way it may well be that we would have supported it. The point was that the Cabinet was not consulted. Although I was Deputy Prime Minister, Foreign Secretary and a member of the Economic Committee of the Cabinet, I for one knew nothing about it. Other Cabinet Ministers learned by chance that Mr Wilson, Mr Jenkins and Mr Peter Shore had gone to the Palace to attend a Privy Council to have the holiday proclaimed. We had no idea what was happening, whether another devaluation was imminent, what on earth was afoot. It was a decision taken by Mr Wilson in the 'presidential' manner, without consulting us, without even informing us. That was what made it so important. It was the *way* in which the decision was taken, not the decision itself, which seemed to me then — and seems now — to mark a clear breach in constitutional practice.

But the events of the night of 14/15 March cannot be considered in isolation. In order really to understand the impact this particular issue had on me it is necessary to look back a little in time to other occasions when I had found myself in difficulties which seemed to me seriously disquieting as a result of the Prime Minister's method of running the government. One of the more serious of these — but I must emphasize there were a number — was the way in which the ultimate decision was reached not to accede to the South African Government's request for further deliveries of certain categories of arms which we had previously been supplying. [Here the author reviews events transpiring while he was out of the country, leading up to his surprise on returning to find himself very much in a minority on the issue.] And so there it was. Mr Healey and myself, who had jointly submitted the original memorandum and recommendation and those others who were originally in favour of supplying these limited arms, had become a pretty small minority, and we were no longer able to carry our colleagues with us.

There is one other thing that I remember very clearly about this period, and that is that all attempts, by those in favour of supplying, to take it to the Parliamentary Labour Party were resisted and refused. After hearing about the emotion which was said to have arisen at a previous meeting which none of us had attended, I volunteered to put the case to the Parliamentary Party to test whether the feeling in the Party was as strong as we were being told, and I had colleagues who were willing to support me in order that the issue could be tested. This was never done and we had no more to go on so far as the Party was concerned than the stories of the atmosphere and the emotion about an issue on which they were never genuinely consulted and never properly informed.

I now learned in much more detail from colleagues in the government and members of the Parliamentary Party of the extraordinary lengths to which they said the Prime Minister had gone in the House of Commons, not merely to *bow* to the feeling of the Party on the arms issue but, as they saw it, to *organize* the feeling of the Party. . .

From then on, a whole series of issues arose on which I found myself increasingly unhappy about the decisions which were taken and again, almost without exception, at the manner of their taking. One of these came, for example, in the next phase of the financial squeeze, when the question of going back on our decision to raise the school leaving age from fifteen to sixteen came up. The decision to do so for a ludicrously small and highly dubious saving of money made me exceedingly angry — I thought it was one of the greatest betrayals a Labour government, so overwhelmingly composed of university graduates, could make of the less privileged people who, after all, had elected it. At the same time there was the question of the reintroduction of the Health Service charges which we had abolished in 1965, and with one thing and another I found myself more and more in a minority in the Cabinet.

So we come back to the events of that night, 14/15 March 1968, to which I referred earlier. . . Around 11 o'clock or so I got a note from one of the Prime Minister's secretaries saying, 'My master has asked me to give you a message. Can I see you?' So I left the bench, went outside, accompanied him to my room and said, 'Now what is it?' He then told me that the Prime Minister wished me to know that he was on his way to the Palace to arrange for a Privy Council meeting to declare tomorrow as a Bank Holiday, so that the banks would be closed. I said, 'What's it all about?' He said, 'Well, I don't know any more than that: this is what I have been asked to tell you.'

I telephoned No. 10 and asked to speak to the Prime Minister, and there was one of those long lulls which led me to believe, rightly or wrongly, that the Prime Minister was, in fact, still at No. 10. After this long pause I was finally told that he had left for the Palace or was in his car on the way there.

About this time my brother Ronald (the Member for Finsbury and Shoreditch) came to tell me that he had heard rumours that something was going on. Another division was called while I was talking with him, and I went again to vote. As I went into the division lobby I met some members of the Cabinet and said, 'By the way, do you know that there is a Privy Council going on at this minute? Do you know that there is going to be a proclamation issued? Do you know that tomorrow is going to be a Bank Holiday? Have *you* heard anything about it?' One was Tony Crosland, then President of the Board of Trade, and he said, 'No, certainly not.' Another was Michael Stewart, the Secretary of State for Economic Affairs. He said, 'Of course not, I would know about it.' I said, 'Well, my dear friend, I'm awfully sorry, but I've just been told.'

We walked down the Lobby, each of us talking, and I said, 'Look, come back to my room and we'll have a chat about this. . .'

We gathered in my room and discussed among ourselves what had happened — not one of us knew *what* was supposed to be happening, nor *why* anything was happening at all. We thought of the most dreadful things, like a sudden new devaluation.

It was then about 1 o'clock in the morning. I decided to telephone No. 10 again to try to find out what was happening. I got hold of the Prime Minister and asked, 'What the hell is going on?' A somewhat angry exchange took place, and finally I said, 'I've got a number of our colleagues here, who are interested to know.' At this point Mr Wilson started to accuse me of trying to engineer a palace revolution behind his back. I said, 'Well, why don't you talk to Michael Stewart?' having it in mind that he would be hardly likely to harbour such a suspicion of him. Stewart took the telephone from me, and said in his precise and very careful way, 'But Prime Minister, you can't do it like this. I wouldn't have known anything about it if George hadn't seen me. Other colleagues wouldn't have known anything if they hadn't met Members in the House who had got it from the tape. Really, we can't do it like this.'

Subsequently I spoke again to the Prime Minister and said, 'Look, I think it would be better if we had a proper meeting. Shall we come to your room here?'

. . . But a few minutes later — presumably having discussed things with other advisers — he rang back and returned to the accusation of being summoned by an irregularly called Cabinet meeting, called by me. He said that he wasn't going to have it, and that if we wanted a meeting we must all go over to his house.

So over we all went, taking such care as we could to avoid

drawing attention to ourselves. I walked and went round the back way, and my recollection is that this was what most other people did. But once there the conversation again went right off-beam. Instead of our dealing with the questions in all our minds, the Prime Minister simply went on and on about my having tried to engineer his dismissal, about my calling an irregular 'Cabinet' meeting, and so on, until I was sick of it. Finally, I said to him, 'Look, it's pretty obvious that you want my resignation, and, brother, if this is the way you are going to run affairs, you can have it.'

The final outcome of the evening's events was that the Chancellor of the Exchequer at 3.20 am made his statement to the House about the gold situation and the decision to proclaim a Bank Holiday. What we were not told, and have not been told to this day, is who took the decision. The Cabinet didn't and wasn't told. The Economic Committee of the Cabinet didn't take it, because I was a member of that Committee and would have known. A number of us suspected that the decision had simply been dictated to the Prime Minister from across the Atlantic. And this is in part why I felt so strongly about the way in which a British Government had apparently been committed to a major decision affecting Britain without the British Cabinet being given any inkling of what was happening.

I felt — and feel still — that this was a major constitutional issue. Government simply mustn't be conducted in this way if the British democratic system is to be maintained. I had already that evening drawn a parallel between Wilson's going to the Palace with Roy Jenkins and Peter Shore, and Ramsay MacDonald's conduct of affairs almost alone with Snowden and Thomas in 1931. I said, 'You know, we've all read this history, and we've repeatedly said that if only the Party or the government had stopped Ramsay, Snowden and Thomas from behaving on their own, the events of 1931 and the subsequent Labour disaster need never have happened.' The particular issue in 1968 may not have been of critical importance, but that did not matter. What *was* of critical importance was that decisions — which might have been decisions of appalling gravity — had been taken without the knowledge of the Cabinet. What had happened once in breach of constitutional practice might happen again.

You must have effective Cabinet government if democracy is to survive. If you don't have it, and you have instead all the powers of patronage, of 'leaking', of manipulating the Parliamentary Party against whichever of your colleagues is for the moment out of favour, it doesn't seem to me that you have effective democracy.

I came to feel that Mr Wilson preferred something akin to the presidential system, that he really did prefer to have his own outfit at No. 10, rather like the way in which the President of the United States had his own outfit in the White House. In my view, one of the arguments against the White House system, and I speak as one who has been allowed to see it operate under more than one President and who has many friends who have served in it and suffered from it, is that it places too much power in the hands of one man. It also places power where it shouldn't be, in the hands of friends or unofficial advisers to the President or Prime Minister, who are not accountable to Congress or Parliament while reducing the real Cabinet to the level the others should occupy. And indeed, the greater the pressures – quite apart from the temperament of the man – the greater the chances are that the effective decisions will be taken by these friends or unofficial advisers.

I suppose it could be argued – and no doubt some people would argue – that concentrating things in this way at No. 10, in these modern rather hectic times when events move so fast, may well be better than our traditional system, just so long as the man at No. 10 runs things well. And it may be said that, whatever the constitutional niceties, no great damage has been done. But what if he doesn't run things well? – after all, the more hectic the pace the greater the chance that one man, with a handful of irresponsible advisers around him (using the word 'irresponsible' in its proper meaning) will go wrong. Look at what we have been allowed to know of Mr Eden's actions and relations with his then Ministers and, in consequence, the way Britain got into the Suez disaster. If you look into this, even with our limited information, it seems uncannily reminiscent of the events that culminated in my resignation. How many members of the Cabinet at the time of Suez knew that Mr Selwyn Lloyd was outside Paris with the Israeli Foreign Minister of the day and Monsieur Mollet, the French Prime Minister, presumably arranging the implementation of the ultimatum given to Israel and Egypt? The relevant document which was effectively a declaration of war against Egypt, wasn't even signed by Selwyn Lloyd as Foreign Minister — a Civil Servant was left behind to sign it. I am not even now at all clear on whose say-so he did sign it, apart from the Prime Minister and Selwyn Lloyd. This seems pretty analogous with the events of 1931 and 1968. For it isn't the merit of the particular decision that matters. What matters is the way in which you do things. You can do enormous damage or you can do little damage, but once allow the British constitutional system to be flouted in this way, and we may end by finding that system has been irrevocably breached.

Why I Resigned from the Cabinet*

LORD THORNEYCROFT

I have called this meeting for one purpose only: to explain to my constituents my reasons for resigning the high office of Chancellor of the Exchequer. The reasons are not at all complicated. They are contained in the letter which I wrote to the Prime Minister on January 6. I will quote from it:

> I am not prepared to approve estimates for the Government's current expenditure next year at a total higher than the sum that will be spent this year. . .
>
> Your proposed departure from this country on January 7 has made it essential that a decision of principle upon this matter be taken now. It is clear that in this proposal I do not have your support or that of a number of our colleagues. In the circumstances, and since the level of Government expenditure is central to my responsibilities as Chancellor of the Exchequer, resignation is the only course open to me.
>
> In the sterling crisis of last summer restrictions were placed in money terms upon the level of public investment

*Reprinted from *The Times*, 15 Jan 1958, by permission.

and of bank advances. The Government itself must in my view accept the same measure of financial discipline as it seeks to impose on others. I recognize that in order to achieve my aim some combination of politically unpopular courses would have been necessary. I nevertheless regard the limitation of Government expenditure as a prerequisite to the stability of the pound, the stabilization of prices, and the prestige and standing of our country in the world.

It was one of the hardest letters I have ever had to write. The Prime Minister replied, and much has been said and written on the subject since, but I have preferred to keep my counsel. I have neither added to, nor detracted from, the statement contained in the letter which I have just read.

I was not prepared to support expenditure by the government next year at a level higher than that of this year. I regarded that and still regard it as a matter of principle. I stand by it. Nevertheless, to you who returned me to Parliament and, I hope, will go on returning me to Parliament I will give some elaboration of the problem. I emphasize that it is to you that I speak and for your support that I ask. My words may perhaps reach a wider audience, but I must exphasize that it is not my purpose to engage in fractious criticism of my late colleagues. It is certainly not my purpose to gather to me some body of revolt within the Conservative Party. If I were the only man in England who holds my views I would still have acted as I did.

I see some Conservative members of Parliament are being asked whether they are for me or for the Prime Minister. I would remind those who ask that question that I am a back-bench member of the Conservative Party and a supporter of the government. Anyone asked that question would, I hope, reply that they find themselves in precisely the same position.

Now, as to the background. For 12 years sterling has been under pressure. Crisis has followed crisis. Prices have steadily, inexorably gone up. These are the facts. They face all parties, they are incontrovertible.

There are sincere differences of view among many men as to how this problem should be dealt with. There are some who sincerely believe that a solution is to be found in still more government expenditure and still higher levels of investment. There are others, among whom I count myself, who see no future for this country in constantly attempting to do more than our resources can achieve.

One must make up one's mind which of these views one accepts. One must decide whether one is trying to beat an inflation or a slump. For my part, I regard inflation as the danger. I am clear that if we show restraint, our economic difficulties are not insoluble, and we can remain with profit and with honour the centre and heart of a prosperous sterling area, to the great good not only of ourselves but of the world.

But I believe something more. I believe that the condition of our survival, or of our survival as a great Power, rests not upon luck, not upon the whims of fortune, but in the last resort upon ourselves.

When I first went to the Treasury, I heard a lot about the Zürich bankers, and no doubt such worthy men exist and are important. But the decisive factor in our future is our own faith and our own absolute determination to put and keep our own house in order. Last summer all the signs of inflation were upon us. It was evident that not simply the world outside but the British people were themselves losing faith in their own currency. Against that background, certain events abroad touched off another exchange crisis for sterling.

Let no one be under any illusions as to the gravity of that position. Had it not been checked, it could have resulted in irreparable injury to the economy of these islands and all who live here. It could have done more. It could have led to the economic disintegration of the Commonwealth.

The measures the government took were in line with instructions I had given earlier to the Treasury. They were harsh, they were unpopular, but they were necessary. The essence of those measures was set out in the statement which I made on September 19:

> There can be no remedy for inflation and the steadily rising prices which go with it which does not include and indeed is not founded upon a control of the money supply. So long as it is generally believed that the Government are prepared to see the necessary finance

produced to match the upward spiral of costs, inflation will continue and prices will go up.

I made that statement with the full approval of my colleagues. I took many and difficult steps to implement it. The bankers had to be persuaded to hold the level of bank advances for the next 12 months and at the same level as the last 12 months. Those concerned with public investment, the nationalized industries, the public authorities were told to hold investment over the next two years in money terms at the same level as last year.

The railways were told that if wages went up no more money would be made available, and thus fewer men would have to be employed, or services reduced. Civil servants were told that if higher wages were asked and given, government services would be reduced and fewer Civil servants might be employed. Civil servants to-day are being dismissed upon this principle.

Finally, in the world outside, to the International Monetary Fund, in front of the bankers and Finance Ministers of the free world, I was, in the last weeks of September defending our position, and if I may say so, not altogether unsuccessfully. I said to them:

If inflationary pressure grows inside the economy, other things may alter, other aspects of policy may have to be adjusted, but the strain will not be placed upon the value of the pound sterling.

In all this period I was often asked by the Press, by the Conservative Party, by all concerned, what about the government's own expenditure. We said that steps were being taken and would be taken to limit that expenditure, but that such limitation was not in itself sufficient.

Then we come to the Estimates for this year. Of course, the cost of some items will go up. That happens in any family if more children arrive or as they grow older. But in a family it is not an unanswerable reason for the *total* of expenditure to grow. If some things cost more, economies are needed elsewhere. Families cannot print banknotes, and Governments can only do so with danger to the economy.

Many figures have been bandied about in recent days, and

some of them are hard to recognize, but as they were either referred to in the Cabinet or are not yet published, I do not propose to quote them.

Let me say this, however. The figures which matter are the following: first, what we estimated we could spend this year; second, the substantially larger sum we will have spent this year; thirdly, what we plan to spend next year.

At no time have I pressed my colleagues to reduce expenditure to last year's original estimate. What I have said is: 'Take last year's estimate; add to it the substantial supplementary sums which Parliament will be asked to vote because we spent more than we planned; and then next year do not plan to spend more than that very large total.' I have, if you like, taken the measure of our failure this year as the base-line for attempting success next year. If open to criticism at all, it is that I have been too lax and not too strict.

Various figures have been given. Some mention has been made of £50m. I do not comment on that, but I do say bluntly that I do not approve of the terms, 'a mere £50m.', 'mere chickenfeed'. In some circles there is a tendency to talk of £50m. as though it were a triviality. That is, if I may say so, an attitude of mind which is part of the evil of our times.

Nor am I at all impressed by the argument that such sums are marginal in our affairs. The lesson must be learnt in every business, that it is the margin that matters. If it is on the right side, we are solvent; if it is on the wrong side, we are in the red. Margins are not irrelevant but vital to stability.

Finally, I would say that if £50m. is the figure and is a triviality, could it not be found somewhere out of the £5,000m. to keep us straight?

But let us leave aside the arithmetic. I have always said, and I repeated it in my letter to the Prime Minister, that I recognize that some combination of unpopular measures would have been necessary to achieve my aim. I stand by that. I in no way flinch from it. Great aims are not achieved without pain and effort, and this is no exception.

What could be done? It is said by some that you must not touch the welfare state, though some men in recent years must have seen drawbacks in benefits clawed back each year in a constantly depreciating currency. Nevertheless, it is said that if we touch it, it will automatically mean higher wage demands. I would say this at once. It is not the making of wage claims but the printing of the money to grant them which feeds the wage-price spiral. The welfare state covers a wide field, from family allowances to welfare milk, from the National Health Service to school meals. Powerful arguments can be adduced against touching any of it, but is it all sacrosanct? Or, if it is to be sacrosanct, can we do all the other things we seek to do or do them to the same extent?

Let us consider defence expenditure. We spend vastly on the conventional and unconventional field. We develop missiles and anti-missiles; we develop conventional arms as well. At the same time we also want to press ahead with research and development for civil aviation.

I recognize the importance of all these. I recognize the sincerity of those who wish to go forward with them. It means that between £200m. and £250m. year by year is being spent by the Ministry of Supply on military and civil projects. The costs of these projects climb year by year. Projects estimated at one figure are rapidly found to cost double, treble or more. Projects which, early on, cost thousands rapidly soar into the millions class.

Don't misunderstand me. Of course tentative efforts are made to check it. Of course a substantial cut in this field would hurt. Of course it would mean stopping some projects already started or deferring work of value to the nation. But is all this to be regarded as sacrosanct?

Or again, it was said by the Minister of Defence in November that we want a volunteer Army and for that purpose conditions of service must be improved. The political prizes of a volunteer Army are certainly great and in the long run the economic prizes, too. Opinions vary as to how far improvements in pay and allowances affect recruiting, but how much additional expenditure can we afford here?

Now, I respect the view of those who say that heavy expenditure in all these things must have priority. I speak in no spirit of bitterness or of recrimination. I do not pretend the reduction of any of the plans for any of these things would be painless or would not mean sacrifices; but if it is said that the welfare state is sacrosanct and that you cannot touch that, if it is said that you must make pay and conditions for the Forces more attractive and pay more for them, if at the same time the vast expenditure of the Ministry of Supply is not susceptible to any substantial reduction, then there is a residuary legatee. There is someone left at the end of the queue and that someone is the pound sterling.

Whatever others have said, I have put the pound sterling˙ and the stability of prices first, not last. I could not change my policy upon that matter. It just is not true to say that over this vast field such reductions as are necessary in order to stand on this year's level of expenditure would have disastrous consequences.

The government's current account could have been held, and it still could be held, at last year's high level of spending. I regarded it as a matter of principle to hold that line as the limit. I could not accept for the government, in their own house-keeping, a standard of financial stringency different from that which I was seeking to impose and was, in fact, imposing upon others.

My colleagues would not agree, either upon the object of containing next year's expenditure at a level no higher than this or upon a broad pattern for obtaining it in the fields which I have mentioned.

It is possible to be wrong on issues of this kind, but I am bound to say that it would be a remarkable thing if three men with backgrounds and approaches as different as myself, Enoch Powell, and Nigel Birch arrived at the same clear conclusion and were wrong at the same moment.

At the end of the day, none of us had any doubts whatever as to where our clear duty lay. Every Treasury Minister was united in the action we should take. I would say now how notably I have been sustained in these difficult weeks and days by their unfailing and unflinching courage and good sense in the struggle in which we have been engaged.

The Times put it simply and well: 'If ever there was an issue upon which the Treasury team should stand, it was this.'

For my part, I have been much moved by the wealth of sympathy, understanding, and support which has flowed in to me from rich and poor, from employer and worker, from friends and strangers, in all walks of life.

I recognize that different views can be honourably held about these matters and I respect those who hold a different view from my own; but they are not small matters. They turn in the last resort upon a determination of the question where greatness lies. I am firmly convinced that true greatness does not lie in constantly attempting a range of projects in total beyond the resources at our command.

Our greatness depends on demonstrating that we are masters in our own house, that we are in control of our own currency, that we can meet our liabilities, honour our debts, and sustain the value of our money.

It is for this reason that I have taken the action that I did. It was hard, but I believe a right decision, and I stand before you as a man content. I do not know what the future may hold for me, but I thank God I found the strength to make the decision I did.

Part Two

THE ENVIRONMENT
OF THE CABINET

6 Cabinet Ministers and Senior Civil Servants: Mutual Requirements and Expectations[*]

BRUCE HEADEY

In the 1950s complacent native and Anglophile American political scientists held up the British political system and culture for general admiration. The political system, it was said, had proved adaptable and stable, and a significant feature of the political culture was mass public deference and trust in the ability and integrity of political elites.[1] By the mid-1960s, however, under the impact of domestic and external policy failures, the performance of governmental institutions and office holders was being stringently criticised in books and articles with such titles as *Crisis in British Government* and *The System: The Misgovernment of Modern Britain.*[2] Cabinet ministers and senior civil servants — top politicians and top officials — have inevitably come in for their share of criticism. The Fulton and Duncan committees, appointed by the government itself to review the Home and Diplomatic civil services, respectively, drew attention to deficiencies of departmental organisation, staff training and skills, and career planning.[3] For obvious reasons attacks on ministers have lacked the same official sanction but specific policy mistakes have been carefully analysed and survey data suggest that public cynicism about politicians and politics, which is always said to be on the increase, may at the present time actually be so.[4] The purpose of this article is to examine

*The author wishes to thank the Nuffield Foundation for financial assistance to support a study of the roles of Cabinet Ministers. This research is reported more fully in 'The Job of the Cabinet Minister, (University of Strathclyde, Ph.D, 1973) and in *British Cabinet Ministers: The Roles of Politicians in Executive Office* (London: Allen & Unwin, 1974).

121

politicians' and officials' expectations and criticisms of each others' performance in office and review some key aspects of the minister/civil servant relationship. What abilities do ministers require in civil servants, and are Whitehall departments so organised as to supply politicians with the range and quality of advice they require? Conversely, what tasks do civil servants want ministers to be able to perform adequately in order to expedite the business and protect the interests of departments?[5]

I. What ministers want from civil servants

Individual ministers approach their jobs differently and hence have different advisory requirements and look for different attributes in their civil servants.[6] A minister who is mainly concerned to win the plaudits of his fellow Parliamentarians by bravura performances at the despatch box may value most highly civil servants who are effective at preparing answers to Parliamentary (including supplementary) Questions and drafting speeches for delivery in the House of Commons. Similarly, a minister who cared primarily for his public reputation (rather than his 'insider' Whitehall and Westminster reputation) and who wished to attract a great deal of media attention would presumably set much store by having a few advisers with a shrewd sense of publicity and a knack for assisting him in headline catching. Most ministers, however, whatever their other priorities, attach considerable importance to their constitutional responsibility for policy decisions and wish to make a significant contribution to policy either by imposing their own or their party's objectives on their departments or (a less activist role) by reviewing a range of programme options before finally taking decisions.[7] They therefore require the following from their civil service advisers:

(1) Loyal implementation of ministerial or party objectives and programmes in cases in which these have been publicly stated and reasonably clearly specified;

(2) Advice on a *range* of alternative objectives, priorities and programmes in cases in which firm commitments have not been made in advance of taking office;

(3) Expert advice (i.e. advice based on up-to-date specialised knowledge) on the probable and possible problems and consequences of implementing alternative
policy programmes.

*Loyal implementation of ministerial objectives
and programmes: a non-problem*

Ministers, especially those appointed in mid-term rather than
immediately after a general election, rarely come to their
departments armed with policy programmes (as distinct from
broad objectives) which have been worked out in advance
and which can more or less immediately be translated into
legislation or some other type of binding enactment. However, in instances in which such programmes have been
prepared — the most clearcut recent example is the Conservative industrial relations package set out in 'Fair Deal At Work'
and translated wholesale into the Industrial Relations Act of
1971 — there seems little doubt that ministers can loyally
rely on civil servants to attempt full implementation. Even
when only broad objectives have been stated and the means
of achieving them have not been specified, civil servants
appear generally to follow the wishes of their political
masters. Thus both postwar Labour Prime Ministers, Attlee
and Wilson, have paid tribute in their memoirs to the loyalty
with which officials sought to implement reform programmes, and Mr Wilson relates that in 1964 Whitehall had
already worked out proposals to implement some of the
commitments made in Labour's manifesto before the result
of the election was known.[8]

Other Labour Ministers have also praised the willingness
and capacity with which officials have sought to implement
their objectives and, indeed, to this author's knowledge, the
only Labour ex-Cabinet Minister who has recorded experi-
encing Civil Service obstruction is Mrs Barbara Castle who
apparently ran into difficulty at the Ministry of Transport
(1965—68) in winning acceptance for the concept of 'inte-
grated transport planning'.[9] The Conservative party tends not
to include many specific pledges in its election manifestos, but
this is not to say that its Ministers lack policy commitments.
Again there is little or no evidence in ministerial memoirs of

obstruction in Whitehall. It is worth noting that the present government appears to have obtained a reasonably rapid response from Civil Servants in working out proposals (originally outlined in opposition) for simplifying the tax system and introducing a negative income tax, for replacing farm price supports by import levies on farm products, for introducing greater selectivity in the social services and for giving higher priority to primary and nursery school education.

The range of objectives and programme options presented to ministers

We may accept, then, that the civil service is at its best in implementing publicly stated ministerial objectives, 'the soul of the Service is the loyalty with which we execute ordained error'.[10] What happens, though, in situations in which ministerial intentions are unclear — is there then a tendency for civil servants to monopolise policy formulation, agree among themselves and present ministers with too restricted a statement of alternative policy objectives and priorities or too narrow a range of programme options? It is convenient to consider separately the risk that this may happen at departmental level (within a single Whitehall department) and interdepartmentally in informal discussions between officials, or on interdepartmental committees.

Some ministers believe that officials are too keen to arrive at a 'united departmental view' before submitting proposals to each other. This is particularly likely to happen if a permanent secretary sees it as his task to co-ordinate all advice. Mr Harold Macmillan reports in his memoirs that the permanent secretary at the Ministry of Housing in the early 1950s told him that it was 'unconstitutional' for him to consult anyone but the permanent secretary.[11] More recently, Mr Roy Jenkins has described the dangers, as he saw them, in the procedure employed in the Home Office until 1965.

All advice to the Secretary of State was submitted in the form of a single co-ordinated Minute under the initials of the Permanent Secretary. I admired the speed of comprehension and decisiveness of expression on the part of the Permanent Secretary which made the system possible, but feared that the system effectively removed the point of decision from the Home Secretary. It also produced a certain reluctance, on the part of officials, to disagree with each other at meetings within the department. Coordinated views on paper tended to produce co-ordinated silence round the table.[1][2]

Stories are still current in Whitehall of permanent secretaries who vetted all papers submitted to ministers and who even habitually rewrote answers to Parliamentary Questions. There is no doubt that a few permanent secretaries still prefer to remain the principal if not the sole adviser of ministers. Two points should be noted in mitigation, however. First, it may be that for less able ministers there are advantages in having a permanent secretary as centraliser. If a minister lacks the capacity to evaluate complicated policy options, the existence of such a permanent secretary may at least prevent a bottleneck and increase the probability that decisions will be taken reasonably promptly and the department's business despatched. As Sir Edward Playfair, former permanent secretary of the Ministry of Defence once remarked, 'many a Minister needs to have one man at his side, whom he knows thoroughly, whose reactions he can gauge and to get his views on everything.'[13] Secondly, it has to be recognised that in some departments the hierarchy, with the permanent secretary at the top alone in his eminence, is now definitely considered outmoded. These departments have adopted what is sometimes referred to as the 'management team' type of organisation.[14] A clear example is the Ministry of Defence in which the chief scientific adviser and the chief of defence staff sit alongside the permanent under-secretary in the Defence Council. The Ministry of Technology (founded in 1964 and in 1970 absorbed into the Department of Trade and Industry) was also working towards a management team concept with its system of 'controllers' in charge of segments of the department's work.[15] Even in departments in which no formal steps have been taken, it is increasingly common for permanent secretaries to meet with their senior colleagues once a month, or even once a week, for a review of current business. Of course, a minister can himself create an open advisory structure by holding 'office meetings' at which middle or even junior officials are present alongside their senior colleagues and by arranging that several advisers, besides the permanent secretary, have direct access to him.

Despite recent changes it is hard to feel entirely reassured about the role of permanent secretaries. In most European countries and the USA the heads of various sections or bureaus of departments are equal in rank.[16] The pre-eminence of the British permanent secretary's position and the fact that officials below the rank of deputy secretary are mainly dependent on him for promotion may, to some extent, make the latter hesitate about pressing hard for proposals their boss is known to disagree with. Permanent secretaries are not normally petty tyrants, although the civil service does contain some 'high fliers' who are marked out for promotion and could survive a row with their boss. Even so, it seems quite likely that the position permanent secretaries hold tips the balance somewhat away from officials seeking to preserve ministerial options and towards their being loyal to their department in uniting behind 'agreed' sets of proposals. Officials are bound, on occasion, to experience tension between loyalty to the department and loyalty to the minister, but from a ministerial point of view it may well be worth taking steps to modify the role of permanent secretaries.

A second possibility is that ministerial options may be foreclosed not only through the formation of a 'united departmental view' but also through the operation of the inter-departmental civil service network. It is not widely realised that almost all committees of the Cabinet are serviced by parallel official committees (i.e. committees of civil servants) which are also registered with the Cabinet Office.[17] To take one example, the main economic policy committee of the Cabinet is SEP (the Steering Committee on Economic Policy). Parallel to it and including officials (in this case permanent secretaries) of all the departmental ministers concerned is SEPO, the equivalent official committee. Official committees are supposed only to reach agreement on matters not considered intrinsically important or politically sensitive enough to refer to ministers. The agenda prepared for a ministerial committee should therefore set out the options in relation to all issues that ministers might wish to decide themselves. However, official committees normally meet far more frequently than ministerial committees and, not untypically, might take up to a year preparing proposals before submitting them to ministers, who might then pass them in a single meeting. The time factor alone means that there is a *prima facie* risk that options may be foreclosed.

The Labour Party in its evidence to Fulton was in no doubt that ministerial options are foreclosed.

> Inter-departmental committees of officials are a particularly effective way of undermining the authority of Ministers. The Minister may not be consulted until the officials have arrived at an agreed compromise: and if he then wants to disagree, he can only do so at the cost of telling the officials to go back and put forward a different view from the one they have been arguing for against other departments.[18]

Another proponent of this line of analysis is the American political scientist, Richard E. Neustadt, better known as a President-watcher, but also a shrewd observer of Whitehall. Neustadt believes that the 'real separation of power in the British system' is between ministers and civil servants and that the influence of the latter is largely maintained through inter-departmental official committees which give officials the capacity for 'taking considerable steps to make sure their masters don't agree on things they very seriously disapprove of'![19] Neustadt evidently takes the view that the influence of civil servants over ministers is likely, as a general rule, to be greater if matters are decided inter-departmentally than if ministers tend each to rule their own empire. Civil servants therefore have an interest in preserving the doctrine of collective Cabinet responsibility and in trying to prevent ministers deciding issues unilaterally, or presenting the Cabinet with virtual *faits accomplis*.

Against this view, however, many ministers believe that

official committees, apart from being inevitable corollaries of
the increase in the scope of governmental and hence
inter-departmental business, in fact assist politicians to have
greater influence on policy by enabling them to concentrate
on making value judgements about major objectives and
priorities. Impractical or over-costly proposals can be weeded
out by official committees, purely technical judgements can
be made and ministers enabled to perform the normative role
which, as elected representatives, it is their primary duty to
perform. This assessment of official committees assumes, of
course, that civil servants are genuinely anxious not to
foreclose ministerial options and adhere strictly to the norm
of always trying to decide matters as they expect their
minister would if he were in their seat. It is also perhaps too
readily assumed that the distinction between technical or
administrative judgements and value judgements is readily
recognisable, and that technical judgements do not embody
implicit and, on the part of some advisers, sub-conscious
value judgements. Possibly the fairest conclusion to reach is
that most civil servants most of the time strive not to
foreclose ministerial options — they have been socialised
since entering the service not to do so and their careers would
be jeopardised if they were plausibly accused by a minister of
overstepping their remit — but that there is much to be said
for accepting the widely canvassed proposal that junior
ministers should sit on official committees which are dealing
with major issues. The latters' task would be to ensure that
realistic options were preserved for top level political
consideration and, in general, that party values and objectives
were fully taken into account in the process of policy
formulation.

Are officials expert enough?

Ministers want to be assured that the advice they receive is
based on up-to-date and, where relevant, specialised or
technical knowledge of the subjects under review. Historically, the civil service has not taken the view that its top
officials (the now abolished Administrative Class) should
themselves be subject-matter/policy-area specialists but rather
that they should predigest the assessments of specialists

within and outside the civil service before submitting advice to ministers. Their final advice, it was held, should also take account of administrative, political and other non-quantifiable considerations. In recent years, however, the argument has been put forward that top level officials should themselves receive more specialised training and should specialise more in the course of their careers. The Fulton Committee on the civil service took this line and its analysis may be briefly summarised.

First, Fulton noted that civil servants are recruited on the basis of general academic ability rather than specialised knowledge relevant to the tasks they are destined to perform. The largest number of successful candidates in the entry examination continue to be classics and history graduates. Fulton believed that more weight should be attached to the subject in which the first degree was taken (social science preferred) and that, in any case, all entrants to the service should take courses lasting 'up to a year' in management and in subjects appropriate for either 'economic' or 'social' administrators. None of these recommendations has been fully implemented. The government rejected the idea of giving preference to social science graduates and the distinction between social and economic administrators has been found too blurred to apply.[20] The standard period of training for assistant principals has been increased; but only to twenty-eight weeks, not a year. Furthermore the core subject, taken for twenty-two weeks, is not management but economics, with additional six week courses in one of the following: project appraisal and control, international economics, industrial growth, environmental planning and social administration.[21]

As well as criticising training deficiencies Fulton argued that Whitehall promotion practices prevent specialisation:

> The ideal administrator is still too often seen as the gifted layman who, moving frequently from job to job within the Service, can take a practical view of any problem, irrespective of the subject matter, in the light of his experience and knowledge of the government machine. . . The cult (of the generalist) is obsolete at all levels and in all parts of the Service.[22]

Research commissioned by the Committee itself does not fully support this picture of civil service career planning. Job rotation was found to be quite rapid – the average official spent 2.8 years in each posting – but transfers were mainly within a single department. Career patterns in three departments (the Home Office, the Ministry of Housing and Local Government, and the Ministry of Power) were analysed and it was found that only one-third of all officials had ever changed departments.[23] However, the picture Fulton projected *does* fit the so-called 'high fliers' of the service – future permanent and deputy secretaries – who do generally serve in a number of different departments, and who could not conceivably be regarded as subject-matter experts.[24]

Fulton made several recommendations intended to ensure that, in future, ministers would receive more expert advice. Members of the specialist classes – engineers, accountants, lawyers, etc. – should no longer automatically have their advice vetted and perhaps modified by administrative class officials. It was recommended that specialists and administrators – indeed all civil servants – should be graded in a single hierarchy with the same opportunity to reach the top.[25] As implemented, this recommendation has not eliminated 'high fliers' but it has meant that specialists can now get direct access to ministers if they reach sufficiently senior posts.

Another important Fulton recommendation in this area was that all senior posts in the civil service should be advertised, and hence be open to outside applicants instead of being filled by career officials as a matter of course.[26] Also the practice adopted by Mr Wilson's government of having outside experts as temporary civil servants was commended. Most of Labour's 'irregulars' were economists – there were about 150 of them by 1970 – with a high concentration in the Ministry of Transport, the Ministry of Overseas Development and the Board of Trade, as well as the Treasury.[27] After 1970, under the Conservatives, the preference for economists gave way to a preference for businessmen.[28] The position of 'irregulars' in Whitehall can be difficult. Some of the 1964–5 imports felt that career officials had tried to freeze them out and deny them access to vital information and to ministers.[29] However, when it is realised that outsiders are going to continue to be appointed in significant numbers, opposition to them will presumably diminish and the civil service may cease to regard them with suspicion.

II. What civil servants want from ministers

Inevitably civil servants evaluate ministers primarily from a departmental point of view, in terms of how their performance affects the department rather than in terms of, say, their achievement of party policy objectives or their capacity to advance their own careers. From a departmental perspective there are three tasks which officials hope their ministers will perform satisfactorily.[30] These tasks are:

(1) The taking of decisions reasonably rapidly; the department's business must be despatched;
(2) The winning of Cabinet battles;
(3) The defence of the department from Parliamentary criticism.

Regarding the first requirement, the *bête noire* of the civil service is the minister who delays decisions, or persistently modifies his position on issues submitted to him. 'Decisiveness', as M. J. Barnett has written, 'might almost be regarded as the ideology of the Service.'[31] A minister who is indecisive is a critical bottleneck and poses problems both intra- and inter-departmentally. Intra-departmentally, delay forces officials either to do nothing about a problem and run the risk that it will reach crisis proportions, or else to continue to work on proposals while remaining uncertain that they will ever receive the necessary political endorsement. Inter-departmentally, officials representing a minister who has not made up his mind on an issue are bound to be seriously hampered. It is only after a minister has 'taken a view' that the department can prepare briefs and press points home with conviction. This applies whether proposals under review originate from one's own department or from another department.

Clearly, a minister is more likely to display the quality of

decisiveness if he is capable of reading and rapidly compre-
hending complicated submissions prepared by civil servants.
The consequence of inability to master written advice can be
serious; a minister who cannot 'move paper' is likely to have
limited impact on policy formulation and implementation.
Officials will try to assist him by preparing précis of essential
documents and some ministers, of whom Ernest Bevin was
one, have relied largely on oral communication with officials.[32] Bevin and a few others excepted, though, it remains
true as a general rule that ministers who cannot do
paperwork rapidly are bound to find their options seriously
curtailed. Speed-reading, which the late President Kennedy
practised, may be the most valuable of all ministerial skills.

In addition to taking decisions and despatching business,
civil servants also hope that their minister will be able to win
Cabinet battles. It is frustrating for a department to spend up
to a year preparing proposals only to see them hopelessly
compromised in Cabinet or Cabinet committee, when other
ministers representing the interests of other departments
attack them. A special case of this is defeat at the hands of
the Treasury; proposals for which adequate finance is refused
almost inevitably have to be modified and made less
ambitious. Worst of all, for those departments which introduce a great deal of legislation, is ministerial failure in the
Future Legislation Committee of the Cabinet to get a bill
accorded sufficiently high priority to be enacted in the next
Parliamentary session.[33] Far more bills are proposed each
January, when the Cabinet Office asks for legislation for the
next session, than can possibly be enacted. Inter-
departmental competition is intense and the minister who is
an effective battle-axe in Cabinet is a godsend to his officials
who have the opportunity to press for measures which they
have long thought worthwhile but have hitherto regarded as
not top priority or as politically unmarketable. Conversely,
civil servants in a department headed by a minister who lacks
weight in Cabinet sometimes lose heart and simply cease to
put up proposals which are innovative, or which at any rate
are likely to be opposed. This appeared to happen at the
Department of Economic Affairs after the departure of Mr
George Brown in 1966.[34]

A final ministerial task which civil servants want their
minister to perform well is that of managing relations with
Parliament and particularly with members of his own party.
This is partly a matter of the minister acting as trouble
spotter, discovering in advance from gossip in the tea room
and smoking room of the House of Commons what issues are
troubling MPs and trying to prevent their being raised in the
Chamber. It helps a good deal, though, if a minister is an
effective performer at the despatch box. If he is not, he is
likely to be baited with an exceptional number of Parliamentary Questions and debates on his subjects. This places an
extra burden on the department. As it is, senior civil servants
spend 20 to 25 per cent of their time on Parliamentary
business; any further addition to this is unwelcome. It should
be noted, though, that Parliamentary ability is more important in some departments than others.[35] The Chancellor of
the Exchequer and the Home Secretary have to be particularly adroit, whereas, at the other end of the spectrum, the
Minister of Defence and ministers dealing with highly
technical subjects like fuel and power are less subject to
Parliamentary scrutiny and hence less in need of despatch-
box skills.

In addition to reviewing the tasks civil servants require
ministers to perform satisfactorily, it may also be useful to
comment on some common Whitehall criticisms of politicians
in office. The two most common criticisms relate to the
consequences of ministers' career ambitions and their lack of
experience as organisation men and hence their failure to
appreciate how large complex organisations – and specifically Whitehall departments – function.[36] On the first matter,
civil servants recognise that ministers are bound to be anxious
not to alienate important sections of their own party or
provoke a public outcry against their actions. They claim to
be not unsympathetic if a minister tells them that, though a
measure may be administratively sound, it is too politically
risky for him to take responsibility for. Civil servants do,
though, sometimes express anxiety about the tendency of
career-minded ministers to seek short-term political kudos at
the expense of the longer-term public interest. Sir Edward
Playfair has put the point this way:

They [civil servants] are growingly — to an extent that is hardly realised — the guardians of some form of public interest ... But do not forget that Ministers are all men interested in power and they will tend, whatever their party, to what I might call interventionist solutions ... When I was concerned with overseas finance I found that ministers of all parties were terribly ready and willing to break the letter or the spirit of international agreements; it was our job to say: 'You cannot do that — the country's good name counts'.[37]

Drawing firm conclusions from such statements about the consequences of ministerial ambitions is not easy. Motives are hard to interpret and observers rarely agree in the assessments of where the public interest lies. Civil servants are perhaps making a more significant point when they criticise ministers for not fully recognising the implications of the fact that Whitehall departments are large complex organisations. One task that the heads of such organisations need to perform is that of ensuring that policy programmes are not based on contradictory goals. Inevitably, sub-units of organisations adopt different priorities and hence put forward conflicting proposals to superiors.[38] In the Treasury, for example, some divisions are primarily occupied with international economic relations, the balance of payments and the parity of the pound sterling. Other divisions accord high priority to the full utilisation of resources and economic growth. Ideally, the Chancellor of the Exchequer, as head of the Treasury, needs to resolve contradictory policy recommendations coming up from these divisions not merely by arbitrating or splitting the difference but in such a way as to produce a coherent economic strategy. Andrew Shonfield, Samuel Brittan and other economists have, of course, argued that this is what successive Chancellors have conspicuously failed to do.[39]

Another point, which officials tend to make quite vehemently about ministers, relates again to the Service 'ideology' of decisiveness. Decisions are often urgent and ministerial delay may have worse consequences than several alternative sub-optimal decisions. Apart from simply failing to get through paper work rapidly, there are a number of ways in which ministers can cause delay. An overconscientious or over-suspicious minister, anxious to be aware of all available policy options, may intervene too early in the policy formulation process, instead of being content just to be kept informed of developments. The result of such interventions, so some civil servants believe, is that the usual filtering process, by which unsatisfactory options are eliminated as proposals and passed up the organisational hierarchy, is delayed and disrupted. Discarded options have to be resurrected and old arguments uselessly gone over in response to the minister's requests and suggestions. Another way in which ministers may cause delay is by insisting on numerous meetings with officials to review decisional alternatives. Some ministers appear to enjoy large meetings at which middle-level officials (principals and assistant secretaries) as well as senior officials are present. Large meetings tend to be time consuming and most senior officials probably prefer ministers who, if they wish to unravel the options, rely on reading through the files rather than on oral communication. Ministers who ask to see middle level or junior officials alone are even more unpopular with their senior advisers, who naturally feel that they are being by-passed and may be handicapped in implementing decisions by not knowing the arguments which preceded them.

Finally, civil servants sometimes complain that ministers cause problems in implementing programmes by being unwilling to rely on departmental experience and precedents. Large organisations are inevitably precedent-bound and rely, as a former Head of the Civil Service put it, on their 'storehouse of wisdom and experience'.[40] A minister who frequently disagrees with advice on policy implementation and casework — on individual immigration cases or on planning appeals, for instance — and is inclined to overturn precedents not only delays matters but may also provoke appeals against decisions which would otherwise have been accepted.

Conclusion

Despite strident criticisms from outsiders, it would be mistaken to suppose that the insiders — Cabinet ministers and senior civil servants — regard each other's performance in office as seriously deficient. Memoirs, occasional newspaper articles and interviews conducted by the author, indicate that they have some criticisms and doubts about the appropriateness of each others' skills, career patterns and organisations, but, by and large, these doubts are muted. Why should this be so? In part, it may be because they share similar social and educational backgrounds — predominantly upper middle class and Oxbridge — and there is no doubt that in their official lives they shape each others' views both on policy and machinery of government questions. Further, ministers and civil servants are mutually dependent. As Neustadt writes:

> Your Civil Service has a tradition of loyal execution of government decisions. By our standards it is astonishing. In return for loyal execution, the governing politicians in your system, the Cabinet Ministers, have a tradition, rarely violated, of consulting civil servants, of protecting their anonymity, of respecting their co-optative system, and of assuring their honorific status in society. Now that is quite a reasonable treaty, a good trade.[41]

Are ministers and civil servants justified in being tolerably satisfied with each other? This observer believes that both sides bring to their jobs important attributes and skills but that it is a weakness of British government that their assets are duplicatory rather than complementary. Both Westminster and Whitehall careers, with their rapid job rotation deriving from an intelligent layman tradition,[42] develop general knowledge of a broad range of subjects, political sensitivity and committee, verbal and inter-personal skills. They do not develop specialised knowledge, or managerial expertise — attributes which, arguably, are increasingly required in modern government.

Notes

1. See, for example, the works of Sir W. Ivor Jennings including *Parliament* (Cambridge: CUP, 1957) and *Party Politics*, 3 vols. (Cambridge: CUP, 1960–2,). American political scientists who commented favourably on the British political system and culture included Richard Rose, *Politics in England* (Boston: Little, Brown, 1964) and Samuel H. Beer, *Modern British Politics* (London: Faber & Faber, 1965).

2. W. J. Stankiewicz (ed.), *Crisis in British Government* (London: Collier—Macmillan, 1967); Max Nicholson, *The System: The Misgovernment of Modern Britain* (London: Hodder & Stoughton, 1967).

3. *The Civil Service* (Fulton Report) Cmnd 3638, 1968; *Committee on Overseas Representation* (Duncan Report) Cmnd 4107, 1969.

4. For a discussion of the determinants of government popularity which includes evidence which can be interpreted as indicating a current decline in public respect for politicians and parties, if not the political system, see W. L. Miller and M. Mackie, 'The Electoral Cycle and the Assymetry of Government & Opposition Popularity: An Alternative Model of the Relationship Between Economic Conditions and Government Popularity', *Political Studies*, Vol. 21, (1973) pp. 263—79.

5. Background information for answering these questions comes from interviews with fifty Ministers (twenty-seven Labour, twenty-three Conservatives) and twenty-five senior civil servants contacted by the author in 1969—70. The interview data are analysed in detail and a much fuller treatment of the roles of ministers and their relations with civil servants is presented in Bruce Headey, *British Cabinet Ministers: The Roles of Politicians in Executive Office* (London: Allen & Unwin, 1974).

6. A typology of ministers based on their different job priorities is presented in Ibid., Chapter 3.

7. The distinction being drawn here is between policy objectives (5 per cent per annum economic growth, the building of 500,000 homes a year, greater selectivity in the social services, etc.) and policy programmes (legislation, statutory instruments, circulars, etc.) designed to achieve objectives.

8. F. Williams, *A Prime Minister Remembers* (London: Heinemann, 1960) p. 91; Harold Wilson, *The Labour Government 1964—70* (London: Weidenfeld & Nicholson and Michael Joseph, 1971) pp. 4, 20.

9. Barbara Castle, 'Mandarin Power', *Sunday Times*, 10 June 1973.

10. A former permanent secretary, quoted in Ian Gilmour, *The Body Politic* (London: Hutchinson, 1969) p. 198

11. Harold Macmillan, *Tides of Fortune 1945—55* (London: Macmillan, 1969) p. 401.

12. Roy Jenkins, 'The Reality of Political Power', *Sunday Times,* 17 Jan 1971. (Below, Chapter 11.)

13. 'Who are the Policy Makers?', *Public Administration*, Vol. 43, (1965) pp. 251—87.

14. For a full discussion of these themes see L. Gunn, 'Ministers and Civil Servants: Changes in Whitehall', *Public Administration* (Australia, 1967) pp. 78—94.

15. Ibid.

16. For a comparison of British, French, Swedish, Australian and American departmental organisations, see F. F. Ridley (ed.), *Specialists and Generalists* (London: Allen & Unwin, 1968).

17. Lord Gordon Walker, *The Cabinet* (London: Cape, 1972) gives an incomplete list of Cabinet standing committees in the appendix to his book.
18. *The Civil Service* (Fulton Report) Vol. 5(2), para. 655.
19. Richard E. Neustadt, '10 Downing St', in Anthony King (ed.), *The British Prime Minister* (London: Macmillan, 1969) p. 129.
20. *First Report of the Civil Service Department* (London: HMSO, 1970).
21. Curiously, in view of the rejection of the distinction for the purposes of training and career specialisation, the title of the twenty-two week course is economic *and* social administration. In substance, however, the course is mainly economics.
22. *The Civil Service* Vol. 1, para. 15.
23. Ibid., Vol. X, paras. 582—91.
24. Most permanent secretaries of domestic departments have served in the Treasury for a period. See John S. Harris and Thomas V. Garcia, 'The Permanent Secretaries: Britain's Top Administrators', *Public Administration Review*, Vol. 26 (1966) pp. 31—44.
25. The Administrative, Executive and Clerical Classes were merged on 1 January 1971. The Specialist Classes remain separate but promotion to the higher posts was open to their members.
26. *The Civil Service* (Fulton Report) Vol. 1, paras. 125—7.
27. Samuel Brittan, *Steering The Economy* (London: Secker & Warburg, 1969) p. 16.
28. See *The Re-organisation of Central Government*, Cmnd 4506 (1970) pp. 13—14.
29. *The Civil Service* (Fulton Report), Vol. 5(2), paras. 559—68. Evidence about the use of 'irregulars' under Labour and their perceptions of how they were treated was presented by the Fabian Society.
30. See Headey, *British Cabinet Ministers*, Chapter 6.
31. M. J. Barnett, *The Politics of Legislation: The Rent Act 1957* (London: Weidenfeld & Nicholson, 1969) p. 29.
32. Alan Bullock, *The Life and Times of Ernest Bevin*, Vol. 2 (London: Heinemann, 1967) Chapter 4.
33. See Headey, *British Cabinet Ministers*, Chapter 7, for a comparison of the amount of legislation and also the number of Parliamentary Questions and debates relating to their subjects handled by different Whitehall departments.
34. Mr Harold Wilson in his memoirs states that he moved Mr George Brown and handed the department over to Mr Michael Stewart so that the DEA could enjoy 'a period of quiet and orderly administration' following 'the late night explosions' which 'its creating genius' went in for. See Wilson, *The Labour Government*, p. 272. In fact the DEA was so quiet and orderly after 1966 that it lost almost all influence in Whitehall and was abolished in 1969.
35. Headey, *British Cabinet Ministers*, Chapter 7.
36. Ibid., Chapter 6.

37. Sir E. Playfair, 'Who are the Policy Makers', *Public Administration* Vol. 43 (1965) pp. 251–87.
38. On this aspect of organisational pathology see James G. March and Herbert Simon, *Organisations* (New York: John Wiley, 1958) Chapter 5.
39. Andrew Shonfield, *Modern Capitalism* (London: OUP, 1966); Samuel Brittan, *Steering The Economy* (London: Secker & Warburg, 1969) Part 2.
40. Lord Bridges, *Portrait of a Profession* (Cambridge: CUP, 1965).
41. Neustadt, '10 Downing St', ed. King, *The British Prime Minister*, p. 128.
42. It is worth repeating, though, that most job rotation in the Civil Service involves movement within departments and not between departments.

7 Her Majesty's Shadow Government: Its Evolution and Modern Role*

R. M. PUNNETT

In clear contrast to the situation before 1955, the leaders of Her Majesty's Opposition today are organised in a highly formalised team of 'shadow ministers'. Both major parties when in opposition now create not merely a 'shadow Cabinet', in the sense of a committee of twenty or so party leaders meeting on a regular basis to co-ordinate the activities of the opposition, but also a 'shadow government'. This comprises the members of the shadow Cabinet and other prominent members of the opposition, appointed to specific posts as opposition spokesman for particular subjects. These spokesmen are recognised as the party's 'experts' in their assigned areas, leading the attack upon the government, playing a prominent part in the formulation of party policy in their subject, and generally acting as a link between the Parliamentary leadership, the backbench MPs, and the party outside Parliament. When Labour is in opposition the shadow Cabinet, or 'Parliamentary Committee', has a fixed membership of nineteen members. The leader and deputy leader, the chief whip, the chairman of the Parliamentary Labour Party, and the leader and deputy leader of the Labour peers are ex-officio members. Twelve others are elected by the Labour members of the Commons, and one by the Labour peers. After these elections, which take place at the beginning of each session, the leader appoints the Parliamentary Committee members, and other leading MPs, to posts as spokesmen. In the first session of the 1970 Parliament, Labour's team in the Commons consisted of the sixteen Commons members of the Parliamentary Committee, seven senior spokesmen out-

*For an expansion of the themes covered in this paper, see R. M. Punnett, *Front Bench Opposition: the Role of the Leader of the Opposition, the Shadow Cabinet and Opposition Spokesmen in British Politics* (London: Heinemann, 1973).

side the Parliamentary Committee, and forty assistant or deputy spokesmen.[1] There were also eleven assistant whips in the Commons, and a team of twenty-two spokesmen and whips in the Lords. This was a larger opposition team than had been appointed at any time previously. Indeed, so large was it that in the Commons there were more Labour spokesmen than there were Conservative ministers, and more than a quarter of Labour MPs held posts as spokesmen or whips.

When the Conservatives are in opposition the members of the shadow Cabinet (more properly known as the 'Leader's Consultative Committee'), and all lesser members of the shadow government, are appointed by the party leader. In the last session of the 1966—70 Parliament the Conservative opposition team consisted of a Consultative Committee of sixteen members (two of them peers), seven senior spokesmen outside the Consultative Committee, and twenty-three assistant spokesmen.[2] In addition there were eleven assistant whips. Including these, the team accounted for between a fifth and a quarter of Conservative MPs. When the Conservatives returned to opposition in March 1974, a Consultative Committee of twenty-one members was appointed, with an additional fourteen spokemen outside the Committee.[3] The party leader made all of these appointments, while the leader of the Conservative peers appointed a House of Lords team.

Thus each of the two parties when in opposition creates a large and complex shadow government, which broadly reflects the ministerial structure that it faces across the floor of the House. When and why did this modern organisational pattern emerge, and what does it contribute to the effectiveness of Her Majesty's Opposition, both in its role as a critic of the government and in its role as a potential government? In particular, does the shadow government system enhance the opposition's chances of achieving office, and does service in the shadow government provide any real preparation for life as a Minister of the Crown?

Origins of the shadow Cabinet and shadow government

The practice of appointing a shadow government, and announcing its structure and composition to the press and the public, dates only from 1955. The history of the shadow Cabinet, however, is much longer, and can be traced back even to the eighteenth century, when two distinct types of 'shadow Cabinet' can be identified.[4] Firstly, it was the practice in the eighteenth century for groups of leaders of out-of-office factions to meet together in order to organise and co-ordinate opposition to the ministers of the day. The Rockinghamites' 'Conciliabulum' in the 1760s was one of the most formally organised of such bodies,[5] but even earlier in the eighteenth century there are examples of 'directing councils', 'cabals' and 'anti-ministerial Cabinets' being formed to enable the out-of-office factions to organise their Parliamentary strategies more effectively.[6] Secondly, it was also often the practice in the eighteenth and early nineteenth centuries for a 'shadow Cabinet', in the sense of a list of possible ministerial appointments, to be formed by the out-of-office groups when the fall of a ministry seemed imminent. Such a 'potential ministry' was named by the Tories in 1741, and by the Whigs in 1788, 1809, and 1811.[7] These two distinct practices reflect the modern shadow Cabinet's twin functions of, on the one hand, managing the opposition party's Parliamentary affairs, and, on the other, posing as an alternative team of ministers.

With the development of the party system in the nineteenth century, and particularly with the regular movement of parties between office and opposition around the middle of the century, the practice developed of former ministers continuing to meet in opposition, as the 'ex-Cabinet' or 'late Cabinet', in order to manage their party's Parliamentary business.[8] For the most part such gatherings were irregular, and even late in the nineteenth century the ex-Cabinet was not universally recognised as an 'institution of opposition'. In this period, as much, or more, business was transacted in informal social contacts as in formal gatherings of ex-ministers in committee. Nevertheless, the need for such an institution increased towards the end of the century as the Parliamentary parties became more cohesive. Further, by the turn of the century it was becoming misleading to refer to these gatherings of opposition leaders as meetings of the 'ex-Cabinet'. During the long periods of Liberal opposition in the 1880s and 1890s, and in the decade of Conservative opposition after 1905, it became necessary for the party leader to dispense with the services of some of the older former ministers, and replace them with MPs who had not served in the previous period in office, but who had achieved prominence during the extended period in opposition.[9] As a consequence, references to the 'ex-Cabinet' became less appropriate, and the term came to be replaced by that of 'shadow Cabinet'.

Thus in the 1905—15 period of Conservative opposition, and in the four other periods of Conservative opposition this century, the shadow Cabinet consisted of some twenty senior figures selected by the party leader on the basis either of their seniority and experience, or their potential for the future.[10] When Labour became the main opposition party in 1922 it also created a shadow Cabinet, although it departed dramatically from Conservative and Liberal practice by introducing the principle of the election of the shadow Cabinet by the party's MPs.[11] Labour has retained this method of choosing a shadow Cabinet in each of its subsequent periods in opposition, although, of course, unlike the Australian and New Zealand Labour parties, it has not extended the elective principle to the selection of the Cabinet when the party is in office.

Thus by the 1950s a pattern had emerged on the opposition front bench of an elected shadow Cabinet when Labour was in opposition, or an appointed shadow Cabinet when the Conservatives were in opposition, usually meeting once or twice each week during the session. Through these meetings the party leaders would manage the day-to-day affairs of the Parliamentary party, plan the opposition's tactics and attitudes with regard to the immediate Parliamentary business, and consider longer-term aspects of party strategy and policy. Before 1955, however, there was no shadow government, in that there was no formal allocation of shadow Cabinet members and other MPs to specific posts as opposition spokesmen for particular subjects. Inevitably, of course, shadow Cabinet members, and other leading MPs, would tend to take special interest in particular subjects, and become recognised as being particularly competent in these areas. An ex-minister, for example, might concern himself particularly with the affairs of his former department, while another MP might use the time in opposition to develop a new area of interest with a view to a subsequent ministerial appointment in that subject. Again, the shadow Cabinet might ask particular MPs to organise the opposition's attack on a particular bill or in a specific debate. In these ways some MPs would become associated, in the eyes of the party and of the public, with particular subjects. Before 1955, however, the involvement of opposition leaders with particular subjects was essentially informal, un-official, and un-announced. The significance of the practice of appointing official spokesmen that Clement Attlee introduced in 1955, was that MPs were asked to take on a specific and continuing responsibility for a particular subject, with these arrangements being announced to the party and the public. In this way the opposition acquired an official front bench team which, like the government, had a clearly defined composition, with each subject area being covered by one or two MPs.

The 1955 change to the formal system of official, publicly named Parliamentary spokesmen came in response to demands from a section of the Parliamentary Labour Party for greater clarity in the allocation of responsibilities among the party's leaders. These demands had been stimulated particularly by an incident in a foreign affairs debate in the Commons in April 1954. In this debate Attlee expressed the official Labour policy of supporting the Conservative government's search for collective security in South East Asia, but Aneurin Bevan, also speaking from the opposition front bench, vigorously condemned his party's support for the government's policy.[1][2] Many Labour MPs felt that Bevan's action had weakened the party's credibility in that it had raised doubts as to what was the official Labour policy on the issue, and who was empowered to 'speak for the party'. Many felt that the embarrassment caused to the leadership contributed to Labour's defeat in the general election of May 1955. Consequently there were demands that in future it should be made clear, and made public, which MPs had responsibility for particular subject areas. Thus at the beginning of the new Parliament Attlee announced a list of thirty-nine Labour MPs who would serve as official Parliamentary spokesmen and assistant spokesmen for the various subject areas. The shadow Cabinet had evolved into a shadow government.

The modern shadow government system

Since 1955 all leaders of the opposition have followed Attlee's precedent and have named teams of spokesmen, so that the concept of a publicly announced shadow government is now a well established feature of opposition party organisation in Britain. It may also be noted that the members of the shadow government tend to concentrate on their assigned subjects in their contributions in Parliamentary debates and questions. Unlike ministers, few spokesmen confine themselves *exclusively* to their assigned area, but over the last twenty years or so there has been a tendency for opposition leaders to become increasingly specialised in their Parliamentary contributions. Some evidence of this is given in Figure 7.1, which shows, for one session drawn from each Parliament over the last fifty years, the level of subject specialisation achieved by shadow Cabinet members in their contributions in Parliamentary debates and questions. (The specialisation levels recorded in the figure represent the *average* for the several members of the shadow Cabinet in the session in question.)[13]

Figure 7.1 indicates that shadow Cabinet members in the 1960s and 1970s have achieved much higher levels of subject specialisation, at least in their Parliamentary contributions, than did shadow Cabinet members in the 1940s and before. In the pre-1950 sessions, the level of specialisation achieved by shadow Cabinet members was invariably well below 50 per cent. In all of the post-1950 sessions, on the other hand, the level of specialisation has been greater than 50 per cent, and has been in the region of 80 per cent in the period since 1964. In other words, today, on average, about four-fifths of a shadow Cabinet member's contributions on the floor of the House will be concentrated in one subject area, and, with perhaps an occasional expectation, this subject will be the one for which he carries responsibility as a spokesman. Not

FIGURE 7.1

Level of subject specialisation achieved by members of the shadow Cabinet* in selected sessions†

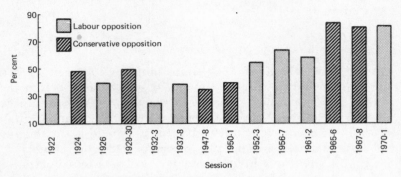

Source: Index to Hansard for the sessions in question.

*The level of specialisation shown represents the average for the several members of the Shadow Cabinet.

†One session from each Parliament since Labour replaced the Liberals as the main opposition party. Where practical, the middle session of the Parliament was chosen.

only is the opposition team today more highly organised than it was in the past, but its leaders are now much more specialised in their Parliamentary contributions.[14]

What benefits accrue to the opposition from the existence of a highly organised, and highly specialised, team of spokesmen?[15] For the leader of the opposition, the creation of a shadow government has the advantage of giving him a certain amount of patronage power. A place in a team that is widely regarded as a potential government, with an acknowledged role as the party's Parliamentary expert in a particular subject, and with a formal title of spokesman or shadow minister, gives an MP a certain status in the eyes of backbenchers and of his constituents. Posts in opposition, of course, can never be adequate compensation for the loss of ministerial power, and an appointment as spokesman is likely to be received less enthusiastically by an ex-minister than by an eager young backbencher looking for some advancement in his Parliamentary career. Nevertheless, even with former ministers, appointment to opposition portfolios can do something to satisfy MPs' desire for status, and can help to brighten the years in opposition. Control over these rewards can thus be valuable to a leader of the opposition, especially as he is often in a vulnerable position, either as an election loser (such as Harold Wilson after 1970 and Edward Heath after 1974) or as a new boy to the role of party leader (such as Harold Wilson after 1963 and Edward Heath after 1965). There is a danger, of course, that in dispensing this patronage in opposition the party leader creates among his colleagues 'great expectations' of subsequent ministerial rewards, which may not be fulfilled when the party does come to power. Thus Lord Morrison criticised Attlee's introduction of official spokesmen, arguing that a leader was foolish to anticipate in opposition the patronage powers that are his when the party comes to office.[16] (The precise extent to which spokesmen did receive ministerial posts in the transfers from opposition to office in 1964 and 1970 is looked at later in this chapter.)

The shadow government system, then, has rewards for the leader of the opposition and for the individual members of the team. More than this, however, the system almost certainly increases the overall efficiency of the opposition. The Labour opposition in the mid-1950s was plagued with particular problems of party disunity, but the desirability of a clear demarcation of responsibilities among opposition leaders remains even in less troubled times. This is especially so in the context of modern mass communications, when press, radio, and television demand from the opposition instant and authoritative reactions on current issues. The existence of recognised specialist spokesmen for various subjects provides a ready source of authoritative statements of party attitudes, and helps the opposition to achieve the kind of news coverage that it desires. As well as this, the system provides pressure groups and the party outside Parliament with a distinct point of contact with the opposition in each subject area. Further, by appointing senior and assistant spokesmen to cover each subject, and by giving them direct responsibility for organising and leading the attack upon the government in that subject, the opposition can make best use of its own resources in the Parliamentary battle.

In various respects the task of the Parliamentary opposition today is considerably more difficult than it was even twenty years ago. Government activities have increased in scope and technicality in the post-war period, and inevitably this is reflected in the nature and extent of the legislation and general issues considered in Parliament. By appointing senior and assistant spokesmen to cover each subject, and by giving them direct responsibility for organising and leading the attack in that area, the opposition can make best use of its own resources. There are no satisfactory objective measures of the 'effectiveness' of Parliamentary opposition in different time periods, but it can at least be argued with confidence that without the degree of organisation that is represented by the contemporary shadow government system, the opposition would perform its role much less adequately than it does. Because of the postwar changes in the nature of the business before Parliament, the comparatively relaxed and haphazard manner in which responsibilities were allocated, and performed, before 1955 would hardly be practical today.

Thus the opposition's effectiveness as an informed critic, and consequently its chances of destroying the government's credibility and thereby replacing it in office, are considerably enhanced by the shadow government system. In addition, the existence of a shadow government is electorally advantageous to the opposition to the extent that it emphasises the opposition's status as an alternative government. Window dressing and image-building undoubtedly are of vital importance to the opposition in its search for electoral success, and in general the more formal its front bench arrangements, and the more publicity they are given, the more credible will be the opposition's claim that it is fit and ready for office. This, however, raises the much broader question of whether service as opposition spokesmen in a shadow government is any real preparation for ministerial office: the rest of the article will be devoted to the consideration of this question.

Preparing for office

Experience as an opposition spokesman provides an MP with an opportunity to acquire a degree of expertise in the subject matter of the topic to he is assigned. No matter how deep a knowledge of a subject an MP may acquire on the back-benches, once he becomes a spokesman his knowledge is likely to be refined by his need to master legislative and administrative details for his front bench confrontations with the minister. As well as leading the attack upon the government, the spokesman has an opportunity to prepare, in outline or in detail, the policies that he and his colleagues will seek to implement when they come to power. In these respects an idealised picture can be presented of a party using its time in opposition to build up a team of budding ministers, all becoming experts in their respective spheres, and developing clear and detailed ideas of the policies they wish to implement when in power; in due course the electorate becomes so impressed by the opposition's positive appeal that it elects it to office; the new ministers then proceed to implement with few modifications and with outstanding success, all of the policies that they had so carefully worked out in opposition.

Clearly, however, the realities of the situation are hidden by so idealised an interpretation of the use to which time in opposition can be put. In first place, the wisdom of policy making in opposition is open to question. An alternative government, of course, has to consider its broad strategy for office, and in some instances there may be advantages in having draft legislation that can be implemented as soon as office is achieved. In general, however, the preparation of detailed plans for office probably involves as many pitfalls as rewards. Major debates over policy can seriously divide a party in opposition and can weaken its credibility as an alternative government, as Labour found to its cost in the 1950s and early 1960s. In revealing plans for office the opposition provides targets for the government to attack, while if it prepares policies but attempts to keep them secret, it risks being discovered and being accused of preparing sinister schemes that it is afraid to make public. Thus in the build-up to the 1970 general election Labour was able to capitalise on the reactionary image of 'Selsdon Man' that emerged from the Conservative opposition's policy session at Selsdon Park early in 1970. A party that announces new policies soon after leaving office, as did the Conservatives in the 1964—6 Parliament, is liable to be asked why it did not implement these schemes when in office; conversely, policies made by a party that has spent a number of years in opposition are likely to be condemned as being far removed from governmental realities (as with Labour's 'Santa Claus' plans in 1959 for increased public expenditure without increased taxation). Undoubtedly, policies made without the benefit of civil service advice can prove to be impractical, and once in office a party may have difficulty in implementing firm and detailed plans that it made in the innocence of opposition. The more such commitments a party has made, the greater the likelihood that it will be accused of inconsistency and of breaking its promises; the 1964—70 Wilson government and the 1970—74 Heath government both suffered in this respect.

Further, just as the wisdom of policy making in opposition is arguable, so it may be questioned just how practical it is for a new Prime Minister to base his ministerial appointments on the front bench team with which the opposition faced the electorate. It is clear from the transfers from opposition to office in 1964, 1970 and 1974 that (a) those who had held posts as opposition spokesmen did not necessarily receive ministerial posts; (b) former spokesmen who *were* included in the government did not necessarily receive posts in departments they covered while in opposition; and (c) ministerial career patterns meant that those who did receive posts in departments that they had covered in opposition did not necessarily retain those posts for long.[17]

In 1964 a fifth of the Labour opposition team at the dissolution was left out of the new Labour government, even though the government contained many more posts than had the opposition team. Forty-two of the ministers appointed in 1964 did have experience as opposition spokesmen, but less than half of these forty-two went to departments that they had covered at any time as opposition spokesmen. Within eighteen months, ten of the forty-two had been dropped entirely from the government, and only eleven of the rest were in posts they had covered in opposition. By the end of Labour's six years in office, over half of the original forty-two former spokesmen had been dropped from the government, and only five were in departments that they had covered at some time in opposition.

In June 1970 and March 1974 there was a more pronounced carry-over of personnel and of reponsibilities from Opposition to office, with only eight of the opposition team at the dissolution being omitted from the government on each occasion. Of the forty-eight Conservative spokesmen who did get posts in the Heath government in June 1970, thirty went to departments they had covered while in opposition. Nevertheless, by the end of the Heath government's period in office, ten of the forty-eight had been dropped, and only sixteen of those remaining were in departments that they had covered in opposition. It remains to be seen whether a similar pattern will emerge during the lifetime of the Wilson government.

Thus the Wilson and Heath governments were far from being carbon copies of the opposition teams that had evolved by the end of their periods in opposition. There are clearly a number of very good reasons why there should be this change in personnel in the transition from opposition to office. The front bench team with which the opposition faces a general election may not represent *in detail* the leader's notion of the party's best ministerial team. As an election approaches, a leader of the opposition may choose to leave his team of spokesmen intact in the interests of stability, postponing any changes he may wish to make until after the election, when he will be either beginning a spell as Prime Minister, or preparing for a further period in opposition. Thus when Harold Wilson became party leader in February 1963, at a time when an election seemed close, he made few changes in the team of spokesmen that he inherited from Hugh Gaitskell. Further, some MPs, after long service in opposition, may be too old to be considered as ministerial prospects when the party comes to power, and others may have to be overlooked because the Prime Minister wishes to give particular ministerial posts to MPs who declined to serve in opposition, or who entered Parliament only when the party came to power.

More important than these factors, however, is the consideration that the person who led the attack upon a department while in opposition is not necessarily the person best equipped to head that department when his party comes to power. There are two points here. Firstly, a former spokesman who receives a ministerial post in the department he covered in opposition may well be haunted by the speeches he made in opposition, as he faces in office the very problems that he criticised his political opponents for failing to solve. This is a general problem that faces the whole party when it moves from opposition to office, but the problem is emphasised if each minister brings with him a record of promises and controversial statements made in the specific subject area for which he has acquired ministerial responsibility. Secondly, regardless of 'ghosts from the past', it is at least arguable whether an 'expert', who has mastered a topic in opposition, necessarily makes the best minister. The respective merits of the 'generalist' and the 'specialist' have been well debated in the ministerial context, as in other contexts, and the arguments do not have to be rehearsed here. To some extent the merits of the case will vary from department to department, with the need for the expert being greater in a technical department, like the Ministry of Defence, than in a general department, like the Home Office. As is indicated in another chapter in this Reader,[18] ministers themselves are divided over the issue, and it is clear that even in a technical age the case for the generalist minister remains sufficiently strong for doubts to be cast on the value of ministers coming to office with an in-depth knowledge of the subject matter dealt with by their department.

The acquisition of 'front bench skills'

Ther are then, distinct limits to the value of experience in opposition as a preparation for service in a specific ministerial post. More generally, however, can an opposition spokesman acquire any broad skills which will prove valuable to him in office regardless of the particular minsterial post that is held? A party often uses a period in opposition to recruit young newcomers to the front bench. In October 1964, for example, after thirteen years in opposition, only a third of the Labour opposition spokesmen were former ministers.

Even after short spells in opposition just over half of the Conservative spokesmen in June 1970, and just under half of the Labour spokesmen in February 1974, were without ministerial experience. For MPs lacking ministerial experience, service in the opposition team can provide some training in general front bench techniques. In the first place, spokesmen who serve in the shadow Cabinet gain some experience of top-level committee work. The pressure of time is considerably less for the shadow Cabinet than for the Cabinet, and the type of business dealt with by the two bodies is somewhat different. Clearly, the shadow Cabinet does not have the Cabinet's direct responsibility for national policy, and its meetings are concerned primarily with Parliamentary strategy, short-term policy attitudes, and the affairs of the Parliamentary party. Nevertheless, for those who have not previously served in the Cabinet, the weekly deliberations of the shadow Cabinet provide some preparation for Cabinet routines.

Further, shadow Cabinet members in particular, but all spokesmen to some extent, will be made aware of the pressures involved in being members of a front bench team, and will learn at first hand of the attitudes, strengths and weaknesses of their colleagues. Such self-knowledge is important for any team, but is especially valuable for a group of party leaders who hope eventually to form the nucleus of a government that will be required to present a collective face to Parliament, party, and public. All spokesmen will experience the discipline necessary in accepting collective responsibility for the policies enunciated by the several members of the team. They will learn something of front bench techniques, which are not necessarily the same as those required by backbenchers or platform speakers at conferences or other party gatherings outside Parliament. They will acquire some training in defending and explaining to their backbenchers outside Parliament the decisions and activities for which they have become collectively responsible, and will learn something of the techniques required for facing the mass media as official party representatives. In particular, they will acquire a degree of responsibility and circumspection in making policy statements. In an attempt to achieve financial responsibility, for example, all Conservative spokesmen in the 1966—70 Parliament were required to obtain the approval of Iain Macleod, the Treasury spokesman, for any policy statements they wished to make that implied expenditure by a future Conservative government.

In these several ways new MPs and former backbenchers can be 'blooded' in the requirements of front bench politics. Even in the case of former ministers, for whom service in an opposition team can add little to the general front bench training they have acquired in office, elevation to the shadow Cabinet can broaden the experience of those who had not previously reached Cabinet rank. Nevertheless, it is easy to exaggerate the importance of the benefits that ministers can receive from prior front bench experience in opposition. While in such Parliamentary and 'public relations' aspects of the minister's role as have been mentioned above, former spokesmen will have initial advantages over those who move into ministerial posts directly from the backbenches, most of these advantages will disappear as new ministers settle into their role. Those who are thrown into the ministerial pool at the deep end, without the benefit of prior front bench experience gained in opposition, must rapidly learn to swim or else make way for others. What is more, there are many other vital aspects of the minister's role for which service as an opposition spokesman provides no experience at all. In particular, a spokesman's job gives no training in the administrative skills required by a minister. The spokesman does not preside over a department of state and cannot experience a minister's daily departmental routine. He is not served by a team of civil servants and acquires no experience of sifting information provided by departmental advisers. A spokesman does not face the same time pressures as a minister and does not have to deal with the masses of paper work that confront a minister each day. Thus he cannot gain experience of the important ministerial skill of working quickly through memoranda.

For these important aspects of a minister's job, then, service as an opposition spokesman provides no preparation. Earlier it was also argued that there are distinct limitations to the practicality of policy making in opposition, and to the value of expertise gained in opposition as a preparation for a specific ministerial post. In face of this, it is probably fair to say that the main practical significance of the post-1945 shadow government system lies not so much in the extent to which it prepares potential ministers for office, but rather in the two very real contributions, noted earlier in the chapter that it makes to the opposition's attempts to achieve office in the first place: that is the way in which the clear division of responsibilities among a front bench team adds to the efficiency of the opposition as a critic and scrutineer of the government's activities, and also the way in which the public presence of shadow ministers enhances the opposition party's image as an alternative government, waiting in the wings, primed for office with a team of potential ministers. In short, the shadow government system can contribute quite considerably to the opposition's chances of electoral victory, but can contribute less to the success of a period in office once it is achieved.

Notes

1. A list of the appointments is given in F. W. S. Craig, *The Political Companion*, No. 6 (London, 1971) p. 87.
2. *The Political Companion*, No. 3 (London, 1970) p. 87.
3. *The Times*, 11 and 21 Mar 1974.
4. A general history of the shadow Cabinet is to be found in D. R. Turner, *The Shadow Cabinet in British Politics* (London: Routledge & Kegan Paul, 1969).
5. A. S. Foord, *His Majesty's Opposition 1740–1830* (London: OUP, 1964) pp. 339–43.
6. Ibid., pp. 92, 164, 200, 240–2.
7. K. Feiling, *The Second Tory Party 1715–1832* (London: Macmillan, 1938) p. 36; J. W. Derry, *The Regency Crisis and the Whigs 1788–9* (London: C.U.P., 1964); M. M. Roberts, *The Whig Party 1807–12* (London: Cassell, 1965) pp. 317, 324.
8. References to meetings of the ex-Cabinet are to be found in, for example, Earl of Malmesbury, *Memoirs of an ex-Minister* (London: Longmans, 1884) pp. 317, 396–8; Lord Edmond Fitzmaurice, *Life of Lord Granville 1815–91*, 2 Vols (London: Longmans, 1905) Vol. 1, p. 516, Vol. 2, pp. 138, 141, 160; T. Wemyss Reid, *Life of W. E. Forster*, 2 Vols (London: Chapman & Hall, 1888) Vol. 1 pp. 165, 192–5, 401; R. A. J. Walling (ed.), *The Diaries of John Bright* (London: Cassell, 1930) pp. 315–6, 320–2, 362, 377, 388–91, 402, 406.

9. For examples see Lord Morley, *Recollections*, 2 Vols (London: Macmillan, 1917) Vol. 1, p. 259, Vol. 2, p. 70; Lord Oxford and Asquith, *Fifty Years of Parliament*, 2 Vols (London: Cassell, 1926) Vol. 1, p. 265, Vol. 2, p. 30; G. M. Trevelyan, *Grey of Falloden* (London: Longmans, 1937) p. 75.

10. For references to the shadow Cabinet in the 1905—15 period see Blanche E. C. Dugdale, *Arthur James Balfour*, 2 Vols (London: Hutchinson, 1936) Vol. 2 p. 49; Sir Austen Chamberlain, *Politics from the Inside* (London: Cassell, 1936) p. 368; R. Blake, *The Unknown Prime Minister* (London: Eyre & Spottiswoode, 1955) pp. 69, 102—3. For Baldwin's shadow Cabinet see K. Middlemas and J. Barnes, *Baldwin* (London: Weidenfeld, 1969) pp. 264, 533, 538, 541; Viscount Templewood, *Nine Troubled Years* (London: Collins, 1954) p. 48.

11. See M. Cole (ed.), *Beatrice Webb's Diaries*, 2 Vols (London: Longmans, 1952—6 Vol. 1, p. 237, Vol. 2, pp. 52—4.

12. 526 H. C. Debs., Cols 969—75.

13. The level of specialisation of each member of the shadow Cabinet was measured by calculating the extent to which his contributions in debates and questions, as recorded in the sessional index of Hansard, were concentrated in one subject area. For example, in the 1967—8 session, Sir Edward Boyle made a total of ninety-four contributions in debates and questions: seventy-six of these were in education, and eighteen were in other subject areas, so that his level of specialisation was 81 per cent (seventy-six as a percentage of ninety-four). A figure for the shadow Cabinet as a unit was obtained by averaging the figure for the individual shadow Cabinet members.

14. For a detailed discussion of causes and consequences, see Punnett, *Front Bench Opposition.*, Chapter 10.

15. These comments on the modern system are based on information gathered in a series of fifty-four interviews with Labour and Conservative shadow government members. I am grateful to the Nuffield Foundation for financing this research. For details see Punnett, *ibid.*

16. Lord Morrison, *Government and Parliament*, 2nd ed. (London: OUP, 1959), p. 350.

17. Punnett, *Front Bench Opposition.*, Chapter 11.

18. See Bruce Headey, 'Cabinet Ministers and Senior Civil Servants: Mutual Requirements and Expectations', Chapter 6 above.

8 The Cabinet and the Lobby*

COLIN SEYMOUR-URE

Ministers do not communicate with the public only through official pronouncements: parliamentary representatives of the media — the Lobby — are an important and sensitive channel of communication. How do Ministers use the Lobby? How are public relations institutionalised at the centre of government? How has the relationship between principal Ministers and the Lobby developed over the last thirty years? And what impact has the Lobby itself had on ministerial politics?

The uses of the Lobby

Backbenchers are of interest to Lobby men mainly as sources of information about their reactions to policy developments and to parliamentary or political events, and about their attitudes towards the party leadership. Reports of party meetings and generalised comment about backbench opinion are the product of their interest. The Lobby's interest in party leaders follows naturally from wanting to look at these developments from the other end. But primarily it is as members of the government that the majority party leaders are of interest to the Lobby, and the interest here emerges in reports of Cabinet affairs, the contents of White Papers and other documents, and stories about the interplay of personalities in the government and the trend of policies. The important machinery for these purposes is not so much the Lobby itself as the meetings. Of tremendous importance too is the Prime Minister's Public Relations Adviser; and such contact as the Lobby have with Civil Servants is also for this purpose.

Lobby meetings are frequent. The Prime Minister's PRO has two a day; the Minister in charge of Information Services (when there is one) will have at least one a week. So will the

*Reprinted, with minor alterations, from Colin Seymour-Ure, *Politics, The Press, & The Public* (London: Methuen, 1968) pp. 226—40, 289—300, with the permission of the author.

Leader of the House, to talk mainly about forthcoming parliamentary business but also about his Department if he has one and anything else topical; and the Leader of the Opposition will have at least one. At the beginning of the Session, with perhaps a dozen major Bills published in a week, there will be meetings with various Ministers; and these will continue whenever some departmental decision or policy statement or report of significance is announced. Without these conferences the Lobby's life would be even harder than it is. Take, as an extreme example, the Budget. How could Lobby Correspondents conceivably make sense out of it in the time available unless they were thoroughly briefed? What happens is that the Chancellor's Speech is divided into a number of sections released to the Press Gallery and the Lobby immediately they have been delivered. Then copies of the whole speech and of the White Paper giving details of the effects of any new fiscal changes are issued to the Lobby, and a conference is held attended by relevant Ministers and senior officials of the Treasury and Inland Revenue. The Budget procedure is streamlined because it is an annual event. Also it is complicated because of the high priority attached to the Budget not leaking in advance. Other documents may be extremely complicated even if they can be given to the Lobby 'embargoed' a few days beforehand. The Labour Government's Defence Review in 1965, for instance, or the Conservative's Industrial Relations Bill in 1971, were formidable pieces of work.

In that kind of case the value of a Lobby meeting is to ease the Lobby man's job of reporting and interpreting a document to his readers; and since these are 'Government' meetings not 'party political' ones a civil servant's presence may be both possible and desirable, for his familiarity with the details of the subject may exceed the Minister's. There have indeed been occasions, say, when a Minister has replied 'No' to a question and a civil servant has interrupted to say 'What the Minister has in mind, I think, when he says "No" is . . .' and proceeded to give an explanation amounting to the answer 'Yes'. Occasionally there may even be conferences where the Minister takes second place: not to a civil servant but to the Chairman of a Committee or Commission which is making its report on some important subject like Broad-

casting, a new London airport or Education. On all these
occasions the circumstances of the meeting — the fact that it
is subject to the Lobby rules, particularly the ones relating to
non-attribution — mean that as well as getting help about
details Lobby men get 'background' information too. Lord
Hill, writing from experience, comments that a Minister 'can
talk in the plainest of plain English. The information he gives
can be used, but not how he gives it — or the fact that he has
given it. What the spokesman is really doing is to help a
journalist to write his story more accurately with more
background and more supporting detail, at the same time
neither giving away secrets nor anticipating what Parliament
should be first to learn'.[1] All that is particularly true of the
majority of Lobby meeings, when nothing as concrete as a
Bill or Report is being discussed, but rather trends in policy,
ministerial decisions, or reactions to events.

Just as there was a 'two-way flow of communication'
between the Lobby and backbenchers, so there is between
the Lobby and Ministers. The only difference is in the type
of usefulness the Lobby man has. To backbenchers he could
be a valuable source of information of much the same kind as
they give him. But to Ministers he is useful overwhelmingly as
a channel to the public. The process has been succinctly
described in his autobiography by Paul Einzig, one-time
Financial Times Lobby man.[2] If a Minister has to take a
decision which could be unpopular he may let it 'leak out'
gradually to lessen the shock of the formal public announcement. First, therefore, he drops a hint to a Lobby man who
will write a story about it. The idea is then planted in the
readers' minds. Other Lobby correspondents may follow the
story up. Next the Minister goes to a Lobby meeting, gives
some definite information about his proposed decision and
answers questions. All the papers now carry the story, in
much the same terms but on their own responsibility. When
the official announcement is made in Parliament, therefore,
the public find it less of a shock. Finally, the Minister
probably has another Lobby meeting also attended by his civil
servants, at which he gives the full background and the
details, so that the formal announcement is accompanied by
well-informed interpretation and comment. 'Very often',
Einzig concludes, 'Ministers add a great deal to their public

statements at these Lobby meeings, facts or explanations which they do not care to give in the form of official public statements'.[3] Much the same kind of technique was used by the Labour government to let out news of its decision to apply for Common Market membership in 1967. There are many variations on the theme. For instance, a Minister may use the Lobby to 'fly kites'; that is, before reaching a decision he will drop a hint in some direction to see what the Press and public reaction is, and then he will use the reaction as a guide to making the actual decision. In any of these examples the party complexion of a paper may make a difference. Conservative Ministers naturally prefer to leak to Conservative papers – the *Daily Telegraph,* for example. Mr Wilson too was apt to distinguish 'sympathetic' or 'reliable' papers for favoured treatment.[4]

Although Ministers 'use' the Lobby in this way, they do also find Lobby men useful in the same 'direct' way as the backbenchers. For instance, Lobby men ask the kind of questions which a Minister sponsoring a Bill can expect to hear from his own backbenchers or the Opposition. He therefore gets a foretaste of the points that will arouse curiosity or criticism at the Second Reading and when he pilots the Bill through Committee. Secondly if a Minister is still chewing over the pros and cons of a policy problem he may be glad to hear the reactions of a group which, unlike his own backbenchers, is politically detached and without a vested interest in making the decision go one way. For the same reason the Lobby can be an early guide to general public opinion. On a simpler plane, the Lobby have made helpful suggestions about slogans or catch phrases. It was a Lobby man who thought of the name Belisha Beacon.

The third way in which Ministers find Lobby meetings useful is for putting across their own private views, perhaps indicating allusively where they differ from their Cabinet colleagues. After the devaluation of sterling in 1967, for example, several Ministers put across a very different point of view from that which emerged in the Downing Street briefings.[5] This, of course, is the opposite pole to the meetings civil servants may attend. Those concern putting across policy; these, so to speak, putting across politicians. A

Minister who cultivates the Lobby can presumably hope that not only will the area of his administrative responsibility be more sympathetically covered but also that his position in the Cabinet (and that of his rivals) may be affected to his advantage by the kind of impression the Lobby get and give of him. There can be no doubt that R. A. Butler's work as Home Secretary benefited, in the Public Relations sense, from the fact that, being Leader of the House for part of the time, he saw the Lobby more frequently than he would otherwise have done (and than his successor, Henry Brooke). At the same time, the Lobby's familiarity with him led them, one theory has it, to overrate his popularity in the party — an error which back in 1957 may have contributed to their failure to tip Mr Macmillan as Sir Anthony Eden's successor as Prime Minister. For all those reasons most Ministers attach considerable importance to the Lobby meetings and may even ponder at length whether and when to see the Lobby and may worry about what the Lobby are thinking.

But Ministers naturally do not confide in the Lobby only collectively. They also develop contacts with individual Lobby men. These follow the pattern of Lobby relationships with backbenchers, up to a point. Provincial Lobby men, for example, may be close to a Minister from their region, partly as a carryover from Opposition days. It is no accident that Mr Wilson's first Public Relations Adviser, Trevor Lloyd-Hughes, used to be Lobby man of the *Liverpool Daily Post*. The political colour of a newspaper, again, doubtless makes a difference, and also the personality of the Minister. The development of these contacts can obviously take place in a large number of informal ways that have no direct relation to the Lobby machinery but rather to the general environment of political life. But certainly the Lobby machinery helps. There are one or two lunch clubs frequented by the Lobby to which Ministers are invited off the record. Ministers can occasionally be contacted in the Lobby itself; or they can be reached by note, or through their Departments, or in their rooms at Westminster. Parliamentary Private Secretaries, too, do a good deal of Press liaison work; before the war and the expansion of Lobby meetings they did even more. More than this is difficult to say. Particular Ministers *do* establish close relations with particular Lobby men; but the logic of the Lobby conventions makes it tricky to discover examples and even trickier to quote them. Even Dr Hill, as Minister co-ordinating Information Services, took time to sort out the 'private lines' of some of his colleagues. 'As time went on', he writes in his memoirs, 'I came to identify the Ministerial sources of some of the published stories and even the puffs which the sources enjoyed in the papers which were re-positories of their confidence ... "Did you see that story about what I am supposed to be going to do? I don't know where these Fleet Street chaps get their stuff", said a colleague to me one Monday morning, referring to a story in a Sunday newspaper. I was unimpressed, for I knew that the Minister had spent two hours with the author of the pieces on the previous Saturday',[6] The desirability to the Lobby man of this closeness of contact raises the question, as with backbenchers, whether it inhibits criticism. The answer, as before, seems to be 'No'. A Minister has plenty to lose by getting on bad terms with the Lobby and although disputes inevitably occur there is a mutual interest in their being shortlived.[7]

Prime ministerial public relations

In discussing the government's relations with the Lobby the Prime Minister has to be considered entirely in a category by himself. Indeed the machinery of public relations involving the Prime Minister is regarded as a symptom of the existence of Prime Ministerial government by those who hold that this is what Britain has rather than Cabinet government.

Prime Ministers have never been at all close to the Lobby, in the sense of seeing them frequently either in groups or individually; though Harold Wilson certainly went much further than his predecessors (at least until 1966). There have always been intermediaries. But this limited area of contact has left plenty of scope for variations of closeness; and the types of intermediary have varied too. Until the First World War Prime Ministers, if they wanted to use the Press, confided in favoured editors; they certainly would not have stooped to using a Lobby man. Gladstone was almost never seen in the Lobby, for example: but his son Herbert — the one who leaked his father's conversion to Irish Home Rule in 1885 — was helpful to journalists. Asquith never went into the Lobby except on rare occasions to post a letter. Lloyd George preferred 'the use of intimates with personal connections in the higher reaches of journalism', as Francis Williams has put it.[8] Baldwin was probably the first Prime Minister to see the Lobby — initially on an individual basis — and he grew cautious after being let down by a Sunday paper. Ramsay MacDonald is said to have been eager and helpful: there was at least one Lobby man, for instance, at 10 Downing Street all through the Sunday evening in 1931 during which MacDonald went to the Palace to resign as Labour Prime Minister and came back again as the Head of a National Government. For a time during the 1929 Labour government MacDonald actually had a Press Officer to maintain links with the Lobby. Neville Chamberlain got on very well with the Lobby. Churchill, allegedly, had almost nothing to do with them until his black swans flew away from Chartwell and he wanted the Press to publicise the fact widely. In his post-war premiership, though, he was persuaded to see the Lobby now and again.

During most of the inter-war period, with Lobby meetings few or non-existent, Lobby men supplemented rare individual contacts with Prime Ministers in whatever ways they could. Parliamentary Private Secretaries were useful. Occasionally a civil servant in the Cabinet Office might give a Conference on the Prime Minister's behalf and from the early 1920s there was a Chief Press Relations Officer attached to the Prime Minister's staff. His function, though, was 'negative' — to keep the Press away from busy Ministers as much as possible. If a Press statement was needed from Downing Street the Chief Information Officer in the Treasury would probably issue it. He was also a help in the parliamentary recess. It was only during the Second World War that the system of 'intermediaries' became more firmly established; and the business of Government since then has made a permanent Public Relations Adviser to the Prime Minister indispensable. Sometimes there has been an appointee at ministerial level, acting as a spokesman on general government policy – an obvious example being William Deedes, who was brought into the Cabinet in the last two years of the Macmillan administration for that sole purpose. Always there has been an appointee at 'official' level: that is, a temporary or permanent civil servant attached to the Prime Minister's Private Office at 10 Downing Street. Whether there are these two levels and what the relationship is between them and between the Prime Minister and them, are questions that depend on the disposition of the Prime Minister. By the end of thirteen years of continuous rule – with nearly seven of them under one Prime Minister – the Conservatives had evolved an efficient system.[9] Arrangements under the Wilson government in 1964–70 varied; and Mr Heath adopted a modified form of the Macmillan arrangements.

The first of the 'modern' Public Relations Advisers to the Prime Minister (the name of the job has varied) was Francis Williams. His appointment by Mr Attlee, which was quite explicitly political, was, by his own account, to smooth any difficulties caused by the new government operating a distinctive political philosophy which was not the business of civil servants to expound. Williams was a Labour Party supporter, a personal friend of Attlee and a career journalist of authority (he edited the *Daily Herald* from 1937–40 and was made a Life Peer in 1962). During the War he had been Controller of News and Censorship at Brendan Bracken's Ministry of Information and then Chief Press Officer to the British Delegation to the San Francisco conference about the UN. He was thus very well suited to be a responsible source near the Government, explaining the broad purpose behind government actions and their place in the general pattern of Labour policy. He saw his job as a combination of Press Secretary, Chairman of various departmental committees dealing with particular information issues, and overseer of Government Public Relations as a whole. He was appointed first of all for one year, at his own request, but stayed for two and then went back into journalism. His successor, from 1947 till his death in 1951, was Philip Jordan. Jordan had also been a journalist with public relations experience; but the fact that he was on the *News Chronicle* typified his looser connection with the Labour Party. At his death the Lobby and Fleet Street editors alike indicated, when approached informally, that they would prefer a civil servant in the job. For the last four months of the Labour government the Public Relations Adviser was Mr Reg Bacon, a former journalist by then established as a civil servant in the Treasury Information Division. All this time at ministerial level the co-ordination of Information Services was regarded as a part-time job, which Herbert Morrison mostly handled, and although he came into contact a good deal with the Lobby it was not specially in this capacity.

When the Conservatives came into office the importance of a Prime Minister's personality showed. Mr Churchill did not find a Public Relations adviser necessary. Mr Bacon continued in office for a few months but, it seems, without much to do. He was not encouraged to talk to the Lobby. Churchill made no appointment at ministerial level either. The result was a number of protests from the Press — particularly the Lobby, who liked having a spokesman on general government affairs, as well as for the Prime Minister more specifically — and after little more than six months Lord Swinton, Chancellor of the Duchy of Lancaster and later Commonwealth Secretary, was given responsibility for co-ordinating Home Services. At the same time Mr Fife Clark, a civil servant from the Central Office of Information, who later went back as the Head of it, became Lord Swinton's adviser and later Mr Churchill's as well. Links with the Lobby were re-established. Lord Swinton and Mr Clark regularly saw the Lobby; and other Ministers, including Churchill, were persauded to go to meetings too.

The situation changed again when Churchill retired. Sir Anthony Eden abolished the ministerial job and, when Fife Clark moved back to the COI, made a personal appointment to the Public Relations Adviser post — Mr William Clark, later Director of the Overseas Development Institute and Director of Information at the World Bank. William Clark was more in Jordan's mould: not an established civil servant (though with Press attaché experience in Washington) but politically fairly 'neutral' — he was the *Observer's* Diplomatic Correspondent. (Eden, characteristically, was more at home with

Diplomatic Correspondents than the Lobby.) Since there was no co-ordinating Minister and yet William Clark was not a political appointment, his position must have been somewhat uneasy. There was no politician whom the Lobby could ask about government policy in general, since the Prime Minister was obviously too busy for the kind of regular meeting that developed under Lord Swinton; and for his part Clark must inevitably have performed some of the co-ordinating functions hitherto done at ministerial level but without, of course, having ministerial authority. The prolonged Suez crisis made the lack of a ministerial spokesman glaring. Added to that, Clark resigned because he evidently disagreed with the Government's handling of information matters in the crisis. After emergency arrangements Dr Hill, Postmaster-General, was given charge of all government information and Fife Clark was temporarily recalled to help reorganise the services. When Macmillan became Prime Minister in January 1957 he made Hill Chancellor of the Duchy of Lancaster, with a seat in the Cabinet and with full-time responsibility for the information services. At the same time the principle which the Lobby preferred was readopted, and a civil servant, Mr Harold Evans (not to be confused with Harold Evans, the editor of the *Sunday Times* from 1967) was appointed Public Relations Adviser to the Prime Minister and to Dr Hill.

Hill thought his choice of Harold Evans was 'the best thing I did for the government information services and the Parliamentary Lobby'.[10] Partly this was because of his personal qualities. But also Hill was convinced of the rightness of having a civil servant in the job. The Lobby men he consulted, apparently, felt that a civil servant would be more likely to give them what they wanted. Francis Williams, a political appointee, was all right because he was 'a spokesman on the same political wavelength as his masters'. But William Clark's views, Hill suggests, did not always coincide: 'So intelligent a man he could not fail to have his own views on current issues — and he expressed them. At times the Lobby, while enjoying his lively and independent mind, could not be sure whether he was expressing his masters' view or his own'.[11]

It seems, thus, that liaison with the Press worked best in

the years up to 1964 either when there was virtually a single spokesman, operating at the official level and, as Francis Williams has himself described it, 'in general and indeed in obvious symathy with the political views and philosophy of the Prime Minister he serves';[1][2] or else when there was a ministerial spokesman with a civil servant responsible both to him and the Prime Minister. The latter arrangement, Mr Macmillan's, evidently satisfied the Lobby well. Evans continued in the same job until he left government service (as Sir Harold Evans, Bart.) soon after Macmillan's retirement; and his Deputy, John Groves, held the fort under Sir Alec Douglas-Home till the General Election in 1964. At ministerial level, Hill latterly combined his information duties with being Minister of Housing and Local Government. His head fell in the Cabinet changes of July 1962 (see below); but co-ordination of information services became a full-time job again under William Deedes, who was promoted straight from the backbenches into the Cabinet and was presumably chosen because of his long journalistic experience (which included a spell in the Lobby). Both Deedes and Hill used to go to Lobby meetings at least once a week and were generally available for questions. Each developed close relations with the Lobby. Many of their functions were concerned basically with co-ordinating the work of the separate information services of each Department, so that the government spoke with one voice. In this way, too, 'clashes' could be avoided: for example two important committee reports — Pilkington on Broadcasting and Jenkins on Company Law — were originally scheduled to appear on the same day in 1962, which obviously would have been silly. These and other similar tasks (including encouraging good relations between other Ministers and the Lobby) made the job much more than just an intermediary between the Prime Minister and the Lobby; and the 'terms of reference' went beyond the Lobby as well as beyond the Prime Minister, for both Ministers naturally kept in touch as well with other journalists — in particular editors. But in the sense that the government is the Prime Minister's government all its business is his business, and the Minister's connection with the Lobby was therefore probably the kind that a Prime Minister would have had if time allowed. In each case Hill and Deedes kept the Lobby informally in touch with the government's news, the problems under review and so on, and therefore answered questions over the whole range of government activities. Hill has given a fascinating account in his memoirs of how his relations with the Lobby developed.[13] It is, inevitably, highly generalised and anonymous, and the substance of questions and discussions does not emerge; but it gives a rare and revealing impression of a Minister's reactions to regular face to face contact with the Lobby and is worth quoting at length.

It took me some time to learn the Lobby technique. At first I was inclined to view a piece of information that I believed to be important as something the Lobby was bound to welcome, only to discover that the interest it aroused was only because of some incidental answer I had given to a seemingly trivial question. What I wanted them to know excited them much less than what they really wanted to know. I forgot too that *how* I said something, the kind of expression I wore, could be seen to have a meaning I had no intention of conveying. At times I failed to anticipate the line of questioning which would follow an apparently innocuous announcement, underestimating the shrewdness and persistence of a good Lobby man. But as I gained experience, I got more wary, and mastered many more facts in preparation. I never consciously lied to the Lobby or tried to put over party politics. The few references they or I made to the party battle were light-hearted — and known by both of us to be irrelevant. If I could not reply to a question, either because I did not know the answer or because I could not properly give the information wanted, I said so — and the Lobby invariably accepted the refusal. Almost without exception, the Lobby as such has no politics, despite the political colour of the newspapers which employed its members, and any attempt on my part to take a party line would have been resented and criticised. My job was to see the members of the Lobby, together or separately, and give the information they wanted, whenever it was possible to give it.

The main change in these arrangements when the Labour government took office in 1964 was that the role of Hill and Deedes was in effect assumed by Harold Wilson himself. At the official level he appointed Trevor Lloyd-Hughes in place of Evans' successor Groves; and George Wigg, Postmaster-General, took over the routine job of answering parliamentary questions about the co-ordination of Home Information Services. Wilson saw the Lobby Correspondents frequently and on far closer terms of intimacy than any previous Prime Minister. It quickly became apparent, however, that there was a gap in this system. Lloyd-Hughes was not a member of the Labour Party. Like Evans and Groves he dealt only with 'Government' not 'party-political' work: he would not give details, for example, about a party speech as opposed to an official one. There was no one to direct the political side of Press relations in day-to-day detail. In May 1965, Gerald Kaufman, a Labour journalist on the *New Statesman,* was appointed to fill the gap.[14] Styled Parliamentary Press Liaison Officer, his job was perhaps more similar to that of Francis Williams than to any other of the variations since 1945. He was close to the Prime Minister, liaised with Lloyd-Hughes and the publicity spokesman at Transport House and was informally accessible to the Lobby.

The broad outline of those arrangements remained the same until 1970. Richard Crossman, Judith Hart and Peter Shore successively replaced George Wigg; and in 1969 Lloyd-Hughes moved across to the Cabinet Office and became co-ordinator of Home Information Services at the official level, being succeeded as Public Relations Adviser by his Deputy, Joe Haines (formerly the *Sun's* number two Lobby Correspondent). The practical changes felt by the Lobby, more than those changes of personnel, were caused by differences in the behaviour of the Prime Minister. Labour's 'honeymoon' with the Press ended in 1966, and Wilson stopped giving the Loby regular briefings. But he then experimented with what became known as the 'White Commonwealth' — discursive sessions with selected senior Lobby Correspondents at Number 10 (chosen apparently from among those he got on well with), sometimes as often as every fortnight and lasting three or four hours. These were

not altogether a success, partly because of doubts in Fleet
Street about the basis on which invitations were issued and
the dangers of 'news management'; and partly because of the
Lobby's concern with 'hard news', which the occasions were
not primarily intended by the Prime Minister for conveying.[15] In 1968 these meetings ceased, and thereafter
Wilson's contact with the Lobby diminished.

Under the Heath government there was a partial — but far
from complete — reversion to the Macmillan system. In
particular, the chief Public Relations Adviser, Donald
Maitland, and his deputies were career Civil Servants.
Maitland was Ambassador to Libya and formerly head of the
important Foreign Office News Department; and he was
known to be close to Heath. Unlike Macmillan, but like
Wilson, Heath did not appoint a spokesman at ministerial
level.

The conferment of a baronetcy on Harold Evans when Mr
Macmillan retired had measured the value attached to his
services. It was an unusual honour, being an hereditary one,
for a career civil servant to be given; and it illustrated well
the fact that his Public Relations Adviser can be immensely
helpful to a Prime Minister.[16] The exact relationship
between them is bound to depend upon their respective
personalities, and when there has been a co-ordinating
Minister or an extra intermediary like Kaufman the relationship between the three of them has obviously varied too. Dr
Hill and Harold Evans, for example, met every day. To the
Lobby, though, the arrangements have had more continuity.
The Adviser has long had a Deputy — it was William Clark's
Deputy, Alfred Richardson, who filled the gap temporarily
when Clark resigned. Evans's Deputy, John Groves, was an
established civil servant who for four years had been a
Treasury Press Officer and before that Assistant Lobby
Correspondent on *The Times*. Maitland greatly expanded the
office and appointed no less than three deputies (the first of
whom, Tom MacCaffrey, had been in charge of Home Office
information). The Advisers have a small secretarial staff in
their office at Number 10 and, by word of mouth and access
to various government documents, become thoroughly
steeped in the Prime Minister's affairs. Significantly, the

Adviser is always in the Prime Minister's retinue when he goes abroad. One or other of the Advisers goes to a Lobby meeting as a matter of course twice a day to answer questions and make announcements — for example of the names of Cabinet Ministers absent from a Cabinet meeting that day or of non-Cabinet Ministers who attended. The evening papers are specially interested in the morning conference and the others in the afternoon. At least one of them, again, will be at the House whenever the Prime Minister is up for Questions or to make a statement. One of them must also be available at weekends and all night: whoever it is will quite likely get rung up when the first editions appear. During the ordinary working day (say till 7.00 p.m.) they are naturally available for continual individual inquiries from journalists — not all of them Lobby men. In the parliamentary recess the Advisers become specially important to the Lobby since they are almost the only link the Lobby has left with the government. Any meetings then are in Downing Street, not Westminster.

There seems little doubt that the most satisfactory working relationship between the Advisers and the Lobby has been when the Advisers place full confidence in the Lobby's integrity. In this way mutual trust can develop. If an Adviser is dishonest and consciously misleads them, they will sooner or later discover and are bound to become always suspicious if not hostile. In the case study below of Mr Macmillan's Cabinet changes in 1962, we shall see that on Thursday 12 July the *Daily Mail* exclusively forecast changes sooner than the autumn — which was when they were expected. It is inconceivable that the Adviser was not asked at his Lobby Conference that day whether there was anything in the story; and it is impossible to believe that, given the relationship that had by then been built up, he categorically denied it; rather, he surely made some such comment as that the changes would not be in the autumn after all — but without indicating when they would be (at this stage, it is said, they were planned for the following Monday: they were eventually made before the weekend). In other words Advisers tell nothing but the truth, but not always the whole truth.

Post-war Prime Ministers have thus been effectively shielded from the Lobby, yet without the flow of information on all the multifarious activities of government stopping. But Prime Ministers have not been utterly remote. Churchill and Eden did not see the Lobby much, but Macmillan used to see individual Lobby men occasionally and come to Lobby meetings a few times a year. Wilson was undoubtedly closer to the Lobby at first than any of the others; so much so that the Lobby used to decamp with him abroad — for example to Rhodesia to handle the pre-UDI discussions with Ian Smith. Selected parties of political correspondents were also invited down to Chequers for chats about the Common Market when the Labour government was deciding on its application to join. The result was a series of inspired stories which prepared the public for the formal announcement and cushioned its impact.

The impact of the press

The Profumo Affair and its consequences happened only as a result of the action of the Opposition and the Press. An example of a type of 'unintentional' impact by newspapers on political events — impact on events which would have happened anyway, but in a different way or with different results — is provided by Mr Macmillan's major reconstruction of his government on what became the most famous Friday-the-thirteenth in recent British political history, 13 July 1962. The *Daily Mail* called the changes 'The Biggest Wave of Political Executions in Peacetime Memory'. They, as will be seen, had a vested interest in making the most of it. But their judgement was fair. Seven out of twenty-one Ministers in the Cabinet lost their jobs. Others remained in the Cabinet, but with new jobs. Seven new men were promoted to the Cabinet — one of them, Mr. William Deedes, straight from the backbenches. Three days later nine other members of the government (not in the Cabinet) resigned. Eleven more backbenchers took office. Altogether thirty-six appointments were involved.

The most important head to roll (even in retrospect one slips naturally into the language of the scaffold) belonged to Mr Selwyn Lloyd, Chancellor of the Exchequer. Others leaving the Cabinet were Lord Kilmuir, Lord Chancellor since 1954, Mr John Maclay, Secretary of State for Scotland, Dr Charles Hill, Minister of Housing, Mr Harold Watkinson, Minister of Defence, Lord Mills, Minister without Portfolio, and Sir David Eccles, Minister of Education. All had been appointed to Mr Macmillan's first Cabinet in 1957. New members of the Cabinet were Sir Reginald Manningham-Buller as Lord Chancellor, Mr Michael Noble, Secretary of State for Scotland, Mr John Boyd-Carpenter, Chief Secretary to the Treasury, Sir Keith Joseph, Minister of Housing, Sir Edward Boyle, Minister of Education, Mr William Deedes, Minister without Portfolio (to co-ordinate Information Services) and Mr Enoch Powell, who kept his job as Minister of Health. Mr Maudling, already in the Cabinet as Colonial Secretary, became Chancellor of the Exchequer.

The conception was grand as well as the scale. William Rees-Mogg, in a sympathetic analysis in the *Sunday Times* (15 July), saw the change as 'a decisive act in the history of the Conservative Party', comparable to the shift of attitudes induced by R. A. Butler in the late 1940s. 'With its dismissal or retirement of seven Cabinet Ministers it goes far beyond any ordinary reshuffle; it is the deliberate creation of a new government. And even more significantly it is a reconstruction with a consistent pattern. There is a great shift in power towards the men who are most aware of the issues and needs of the 1960s, and who most strongly believe in active policies of national development.' There was perhaps some wishful thinking here, and Mr Macmillan did not (then, at any rate) describe the change in quite these terms. But the general principle was right. Writing to Sir David Eccles in the usual (though belated) exchange of letters celebrating a resignation, the Prime Minister began: 'Yesterday you placed your office at my disposal in order to meet my wishes to introduce some younger men into the Government.' Lord Hill, who comments on the whole affair very acutely in his memoirs, records that the Prime Minister 'had decided, he told me, on a major reshuffle in order to bring in new and younger men'.[17] Mr Macmillan's purpose was, then, horticultural; to prune out the old wood and make room for and strengthen the new. Mr Powell, coming into the Cabinet at

49, was the eldest; the youngest, Sir Edward Boyle, was only 38. Outside the Cabinet the new appointees, few yet 50, included young men like Edward Du Cann, 38, Basil de Ferranti, 32, and Christopher Chataway, 31.

Shedding a third of the Cabinet would in any circumstances require a delicate touch. Since the aim was, as the *Mail* described it, 'to give the Government a new look and infuse it with fresh energy', it was all the more desirable that the manner of Mr Macmillan's change should be appropriately fresh and 'clean'. Specially was this true because the Ministers were all 'old friends' ('We have now worked together', the Prime Minister wrote to Lord Mills, 'for over 22 years — since the old days of machine-tools at the Ministry of Supply . . .'). One further fact made tact essential. Five of the Ministers — Lord Kilmuir, Mr Watkinson, Lord Mills, Dr Hill and Mr Maclay — had intimated months previously that they would be ready to retire from the government at a convenient time. To attach a stigma of being sacked to men who had already offered to make way for others would be wounding. 'There are times when the way a thing is done is so much more important than what is actually done', reflected Lord Hill.[18] This was pre-eminently such a time and it was precisely the way the thing was done which the Press affected so directly. What should have been a dignified valedictory occasion generated not warmth but heat. It was hasty and, largely for that reason, clumsy and embarrassing. Instead of a reshuffle it was dubbed a purge by the Press and nicknamed 'the night of the long knives'; and even *The Times'* leading article made play with axe-swinging metaphors. 'I was kicked out as though I was an office boy caught with a half-crown from the petty cash', one Minister was reported as saying. Another was said to have called it 'the most brutal humiliation of my life'. Mr Selwyn Lloyd, 'speaking out' in a *Sunday Telegraph* article the following 23 January, reflected soberly: 'No one likes to be asked to give up high office. It is even more unpleasant to be asked to do so at short notice. It would be humbug for me to pretend to feel otherwise.' Commenting some ten days after the event, the *Sunday Times* Political Correspondent, James Margach, wrote (22 July): 'The trouble from Mr Macmillan's point of view is that the hostile reactions to what has been termed the "shabby and disreputable treatment" of senior colleagues have blurred the excellent effect of about 90 per cent of the vast reconstruction . . .' The 'shabbiness' was undoubtedly a function of haste, and for this the Press were directly responsible. They forced the Prime Minister's hand by revealing his intentions before his detailed plans were complete. Exposing the Prime Minister to these criticisms was in itself significant and a source of capital for the Opposition. But to taste the full flavour the story needs to be traced more carefully.

It was 'common knowledge', the Lobby Correspondents wrote knowingly in their post-mortems, that Cabinet changes would be made some time in 1962. But nobody expected them until the autumn, in time for the Party Conference at Llandudno. The grounds for change had much to do with the government's flamboyantly bad performance in by-elections from the winter of 1961 onwards. Four by-elections in November produced an average drop of nearly 20 per cent in the Tory vote. The Labour vote did not move much: the trend was to the Liberals. In three Spring by-elections the Tory vote plummeted. Orpington was the nadir, where in a solid suburban stronghold there was an enormous swing from Tory to Liberal of nearly 27 per cent. It was almost regarded as a triumph when the government narrowly avoided coming third at Stockton-on-Tees (held by Labour) in April. The anti-government trend continued in the Local government elections in May and in three more by-elections at West Derbyshire, Montgomery and Middlesbrough West (which Labour won from the Tories, whose share of the poll dropped over 20 per cent). Obviously such disasters bred discontent. The *Evening Standard* wrote of the Montgomery result, for example (16 May): 'It can only encourage renewed behind-the-scenes pressure for a Cabinet reshuffle to give the Tory team a fresher look.' The discontent grew. *The Times* could refer at the beginning of July to 'regular meetings of the party vigilantes, who are now said to be calling for two new "F's" — new facets and new faces' (6 July).

Such pressure clearly was one reason for bringing forward the changes of July. Derek Marks in the *Daily Express* reported one dismissed Minister as saying that 'Mr Macmillan told him when he was sacked that the Chief Whip had reported that there was grave unrest among the backbenchers and that there would be severe consequences if they went to their constituencies for the long summer recess in such a black mood'. Another reason widely canvassed was that Mr Macmillan wanted to pursue a more expansionist economic policy (though without rejecting the principles of the incomes policy) and that Mr Lloyd was not the right man to do it. Also a change in July would give the new Ministers four months longer to establish themselves before a General Election. A final deciding factor may have been the last canvass returns before the by-election at North-East Leicester, due on Thursday, 12 July. These reached Central Office early the same week and forecast (correctly) that the Tory would come a bad third. Labour held the seat and the Tory share of the poll dropped by nearly a quarter. By now the Prime Minister had decided, it is said, to announce his changes the following Monday or Tuesday, 16 or 17 July. Only two or three colleagues — and none of those to be sacked — knew of them.

At this time of delicate poise the Press came elbowing in. Most of the morning papers on Thursday 12 July were concerned about Sir Winston Churchill's health, a Treasury opinion that the economy needed no stimulus yet, and the theft in Mayfair of paintings worth £400,000. Not so the *Daily Mail*. It had a banner headline, 'MAC'S MASTER PLAN', over a story by its Political Correspondent Walter Terry which began: 'A major Cabinet reshuffle by the Autumn, involving the departure of Mr R. A. Butler from the Home Office, will be part of the Tory master-plan for political recovery.' It went on to mention quite specific changes, some but not all of which were correct. Correctly Terry predicted that Mr Butler would become 'an even more active Deputy to the Premier', concentrating on Common Market and Central African problems; and that Mr Lloyd would be transferred from the Treasury. With less success he suggested that 'Mr Lloyd may find himself in the House of Lords as Lord Chancellor in place of Viscount Kilmuir', and that Mr Macleod might drop the Chairmanship of the Party. Lord Hill has recorded how this story looked to him:

'. . . this might well have been a "think" piece based more on influence and guesswork than fact. Yet — and by now I had had a good deal of experience in spotting the ways of the Press — it had read as if someone "in the know" had been talking out of school, and Terry's sensitive ear had heard his indiscretion.'[19]

Every sensitive ear in Westminster and Fleet Street strained for the overtones of the story. The *Daily Mail* in a retrospective piece proudly commented (16 July): 'Then it began. It was the talk of all the backbenchers. Senior Ministers button-holding backbenchers who were known to have social contacts with the Prime Minister, each other, and particularly political insiders among newspapers. Trying to find out. This is the way it goes in Cabinet reshuffles. The victims are always the last to know they are for the chop.' The rest of the Press had to catch up on the *Mail's* lead. With nothing hard to go on, Thursday's evening papers asked questions instead of answering them. The *Standard* took up Terry's phrase '*by* the Autumn' and suggested that changes might possibly come 'within the next three of four weeks. 'The Prime Minister has still to take a final decision on the timing, but he now, I understand, sees some advantages in getting them completed as soon as possible.'

By Friday morning, with the Leicester by-election out, the Press were taking for granted that the changes would come before the end of the month — in other words before the Parliamentary recess. But they were still speculating about the details without much confidence. 'The Prime Minister is actively planning a reconstruction of the government and has got down to names', *The Times* said. But like the rest it was much happier, when getting down to names itself, to talk of those likely not to be moved or dismissed. Several papers (among them *The Guardian* and the *Express*) predicted that Mr Lloyd would stay put. The stream of visitors to and from Admiralty House all day on Friday (Downing Street like the Cabinet was being reconstructed) removed all doubts about timing, and the official announcement of the changes was made at 7.00 p.m.

The speculation among politicians and the Press, started directly and wholly by the *Daily Mail* scoop, was the definite cause of the changes being brought forward from 16 or 17 July to the previous Friday and of the consequent embarrassments. Mr Macmillan acknowledged this quite openly (though perhaps disingenuously). His farewell letter to Lord Kilmuir began: 'The widespread speculation in the Press and the undesirability of a period of uncertainty made it necessary to complete the reconstruction of the government as rapidly as possible. This unhappily precluded me from being able to make immediately the kind of public tribute to you which I would have liked.' The *Mail,* of course, was delighted. 'MAC: I WAS PUSHED' was its headline when the resignation letters were published. 'To admit in one of them', it said, 'that the timing of the reshuffle had been forced by Fleet Street is amazing.' Lord Hill writes that the Prime Minister 'gave me to understand that he thought it would be very damaging — possibly even fatal — to the Government to postpone the announcement (of the changes). I later learnt from a well-informed source that someone had leaked to the Press what was coming and that the details of the changes would appear in the newspapers next morning whether by then they had been announced or not.'[20] The *Guardian* claimed also, plausibly enough, that Mr Macmillan thought publication before the weekend would avoid a field day of speculation in the Sunday papers.

The precise effects upon the manner of the changes through their being brought forward to Friday 13th were two. First and most irksome was that those dismissed had extremely short notice. The Cabinet Meeting on Thursday morning was absolutely normal without, Lord Hill says, 'any hint or suggestion that anything unusual was in the wind'. Hill himself was watching TV at home in Harpenden that evening when he was rung up by the Prime Minister's Personal Private Secretary and told that the Prime Minister would like to see him next day. His immediate reaction was to suspect a reshuffle. 'But I had no reason to complain', he writes, '. . . until I learnt that the changes were to be announced at seven o'clock that (Friday) evening. That seemed to me to be precipitately hasty as well as personally embarrassing to me, in that I had not yet told my constituency of my decision (to retire) of a year before . . .

Was it really necessary to give a departing minister but four hours' notice of his going, particularly when he had expressed a wish to go?'[21] Mr Selwyn Lloyd was asked for his resignation late on Thursday afternoon. Lord Kilmuir was given some inkling of the changes, though evidently not of the timing, on the Wednesday evening. Then, he records, 'as a meeting of the Cabinet was ending, Macmillan took me aside and said, "The Government is breaking up", and murmured something about "You don't mind going?" I was startled but merely replied, "You know my views".'[22] On Friday morning a message from the Prime Minister reached him in a Cabinet Committee and at 11.15 a.m. he saw the Prime Minister and was told of the resignations.

The second effect was to delay the usual exchange of letters. Some commentators suggested that Macmillan hoped to dispense with this formality. Mr Selwyn Lloyd evidently insisted on having the opportunity to make his position clear, for letters to each other from him and the Prime Minister were published at the same time as the details of the first resignations. Letters exchanged with the other six Cabinet Ministers were eventually released on the Sunday evening. Such a departure from precedent was bound to cause comment, all the more so because for one minister the normal practice was followed.

What, finally, were the full implications of the embarrassing way in which the government changes were made and for which the Press were so largely responsible? To some extent it is obviously difficult to separate these from the implications of the changes themselves. For example the Opposition could make capital out of such a big reconstruction regardless of the methods the Prime Minister used. The damage done more distinctly by the Press was within the Tory Party. The *Sunday Times,* for instance reported (22 July) that '. . . so many Tories consider that the manner of the purge will have a sharper and more unfavourable impact on public opinion which will outweigh the gains from the actual changes.' Lord Hill had a similar view. 'I find no pleasure', he remarked in his memoirs, 'in the reflection that, because of the way these changes were made, much of the advantage of bringing new blood into the Cabinet was thrown

away. . .'²³ There is no way of knowing what the exact
impact of the changes on public opinion was — or, indeed,
whether people did distinguish their opinions about the
manner of the changes from those about their substance. But
whether or not the manner did have a harmful effect on
public opinion does not matter at this point: the fact alone
that Tories feared it did was cause enough to damage Party
morale. The manner of the changes gave rise also to
explanations of the cause which could only do harm to Party
unity (if they had any effect at all). Thus the *Guardian*
suggested that Macmillan's haste was in reaction to an
'ultimatum' from Mr Butler, Mr Macleod and Mr Maudling,
who all threatened to resign unless an immediate drastic
reconstruction was made. This ultimatum was emphatically
denied by 'the highest sources'. But, of course, the rumour
spawned another. The ultimatum theory, it was suggested,
was possibly an attempt by anti-Butler and anti-Macleod
factions to involve them in the hostile reactions to Selwyn
Lloyd's dismissal. Round and round rumours went. They
would have gone round in some form anyway; some of them
probably even emerged from the *Mail* offices in an attempt to
thicken the smokescreen round Terry's sources. The manner
of the reconstruction gave them special impetus.

The major effect of the unfortunate manner of the changes
was the stimulation of substantial resentment within the
Tory party both at Westminster and no doubt in the
constituencies. This had two sides. One was an astonishing
wave of sympathy for the dismissed Ministers and particularly Selwyn Lloyd. His popularity was never greater than in
the manner of his going. On his first appearance in the House
of Commons after his dismissal he received warm cheers from
all parties. He had, the *Evening Standard* noted (17 July), 'a
remarkably affectionate welcome as he made what would
otherwise have been the lonely journey from the entrance of
the House to his more humble place (on the backbenches). It
was a sincere tribute to the victim of political misfortune.'
Some Tories felt that Mr Lloyd was being made the scapegoat
for an unpopular economic policy; and they felt at that rate
the slaughter might at least have been humane.

The other side was a reaction against the Prime Minister,

illustrated most sharply at the same sitting of the House. As Mr Macmillan entered for Question Time he was met by a thundering silence on the government benches. From the Opposition came mocking cries. 'That the manner in which he carried out his executions has done Mr Macmillan some personal harm', *The Times* Lobby man dryly remarked in his final analysis of the purge (23 July), 'nobody doubts high or low.' This harm took the shape of a short run reaction of hostility and challenge to his authority, and a more subtle long run loss of confidence. The hostility was greatest over the weekend after the resignations. Letters to soothe the feelings of the sacked Ministers were not yet published and the young new faces in the government were not yet unmasked. Several papers suggested that his dismissal had put Lloyd in a position of considerable potential strength as a rival for the leadership of the Party. During the following week, though, the Party regained its equilibrium. On Tuesday the Prime Minister was strongly criticised in a backbench Committee Meeting but at the 1922 Committee Meeting of all backbenchers on the Thursday he emerged, though apparently with some trouble, with his position intact.

Even the long run harm was probably caused less by the changes themselves than the maner of them, though one is inevitably speculating more here. The Conservative Party had been willing, as a result of the mood of the country illustrated in the by-election results, to accept major changes in the government. But if the process of change was such an awful experience, their point would be lost. The harm was analysed by James Margach in the *Sunday Times* of 22 July. He began his article:

The spell has been broken and things will never be quite the same again. The whips can lay on a massive demonstration of loyalty, the arithmetic of the division Lobby can show impressive numerical unity, but somehow nothing can make amends for or erase the memory of that sullen, studied, spontaneous silence in which the Prime Minister was received by his Party after his ruthless execution of so many Ministers. It was as unexpected as it was eloquent, and has effected a subtle change in the relationship between Mr Macmillan and his party. The chips are down.

In other words, Macmillan had reached the limit of his authority. Next time there was a reshuffle he would be the one to go. 'I once remarked', wrote Lord Kilmuir, '. . . that "loyalty was the Tories' secret weapon". I doubt if it has ever had to endure so severe a strain.'[2][3] *The Times* concluded in a characteristic phrase: 'If Mr Macmillan cannot bring about a change with so largely reconstructed a team, the question will not long be asked whether he could with any other.' In fact, of course, he remained in office another fifteen months. Even so, the night of the long knives was a turning point in his career as Prime Minister. Why he reacted to the Press in this apparently uncharacteristic way (scarcely consistent with his 'unflappable' image) is a fascinating but imponderable question. Certainly the results affected more Prime Ministers than just himself. Sir Alec Douglas-Home could never have contemplated such a drastic reconstruction with Macmillan's experience behind him; and Mr Wilson showed a preference for more frequent, small scale changes and every desire to avoid acquiring the reputation of a butcher by large scale hatchet jobs.

A case study like this needs to be hedged about. One may, for example, get it all wrong. Perhaps Mr Macmillan put the blame on the Press because he knew his purge would be a mucky business and he thought he might win sympathy this way. Indeed, perhaps he authorised the leak himself. If that were so, in fact, it would not show that the Press played no part in the circumstances and effects of the purge: only that it played a different part. But even if one's central judgements are sound, one's remarks may be a bit soft at the edges: the long run effects in this Macmillan case, as has just been said, are very much a matter of speculation. Most importantly, if one relies on such studies to build up a picture of the impact of the Press in Westminster and Whitehall, one is limited to whatever appropriate subject happens to crop up. The 1962 Cabinet changes may not be – indeed were probably not – the major political event affected in this way by the Press in the Macmillan years. But they were the unique example containing the special element of 'objective proof' which enables one to take the effect of the Press as given rather than infer it on the basis of one's own judgement in the first place. The whole range of impact by the Press on the political public is immeasurable; all one can hope to do with any reliability is pierce an occasional corner of the gloom when the chance arises.

Notes

1. Charles Hill, *Both Sides of The Hill* (London: Heinemann, 1964).
2. Paul Einzig, *In the Centre of Things* (London: Hutchinson, 1960).
3. Ibid.
4. *The Times*, 31 Jul 1967.
5. Jeremy Tunstall, *The Westminster Lobby Correspondents* (London: Routledge & Kegan Paul, 1970) p. 58.
6. Hill, *Both Sides of The Hill*, p. 182.
7. Cf. Jeremy Tunstall, *Journalists at Work* (London: Constable, 1972) p. 174; *The Westminster Lobby Correspondents*, pp. 44–5.
8. Francis Williams, 'The Office of Public Relations Advisor to the Prime Minister', *Parliamentary Affairs*, Vol. 9 (1956) pp. 260–67.
9. For an interesting and full account of the 'Apex' organisation of the Government Information Services in the twenty years after 1945, see Marjorie Ogilvy-Webb, *The Government Explains* (London: Allen & Unwin, for the Royal Institute of Public Administration, 1965) pp. 81–98.
10. Hill, *Both Sides of The Hill*, p. 186.
11. Ibid.
12. Williams, 'The Office of Public Relations Advisor', p. 266.
13. Ibid., pp. 204–6, 208.
14. See Marcia Williams, *Inside Number 10* (London: Weidenfeld & Nicolson, 1972) esp. Chapter 9 and pp. 53–4, 221–6.
15. Tunstall, *The Westminster Lobby Correspondents*, pp. 115–16.
16. See Macmillan's tribute to Evans, Harold Macmillan, *Riding The Storm* (London: Macmillan, 1971) p. 193.
17. Hill, *Both Sides of The Hill*, p. 247.
18. Ibid., p. 247.
19. Ibid., p. 246.
20. Ibid., p. 247.
21. Ibid., pp. 247–8.
22. Earl of Kilmuir, *Political Adventure* (London: Weidenfeld & Nicolson, 1964) p. 323.
23. Hill, *Both Sides of the Hill*, p. 248.
24. Kilmuir, *Political Adventure*, p. 324.

9 Two Styles of Government — Press Relations*

JEREMY TUNSTALL

One of the basic formal rules of the political structure within which the Lobby journalists operate is the rule of collective Cabinet responsibility. This rule includes strong mythical elements; quite apart from the question of how much 'responsibility' one Minister can really have for detailed policies emanating from a different Ministry, there is the political fact that within any British Cabinet some Ministers are political opponents on many issues and a few Ministers are direct rivals to the Prime Minister himself. One important aspect (among others) of this potential and actual rivalry within the Cabinet is the propensity of Ministers to pursue their rivalries by supplying information on a 'not for attribution' basis to Lobby and other political journalists. Of the many interrelated variables within this situation, the following are clearly only a selection:

(1) The political standing of the government including its House of Commons majority and its opinion poll rating.
(2) The political standing of the Prime Minister, including his personal opinion poll rating and the likelihood of his calling a General Election.
(3) The political standing of other leading Ministers.
(4) Rivalries between individual Ministers.
(5) Direct rivalry for the Prime Ministership or party leadership.
(6) The propensity of various Ministers to use press publicity as a weapon in political rivalry.
(7) The formal arrangements within the Cabinet and the government for relations with journalists.

*Reprinted from Jeremy Tunstall, *The Westminster Lobby Correspondents* (London: Routledge & Kegan Paul, 1970) pp. 102–7, with the permission of the author and publisher.

Each of the variables is probably influenced by, as well as itself influencing, the others. As an example one can take the last variable, the *formal arrangements* for government-press relations. During most of the period 1957—68 one of two types of formal arrangement existed. These can broadly be described as:

(a) The Macmillan or delegated arrangement.
(b) The Wilson or Prime Ministerial arrangement.

Under (a) The *Macmillan* or delegated arrangement, Government information in general became the full-time responsibility of a Cabinet Minister; day-to-day relations with journalists, including the twice daily Lobby briefings, were made the responsibility of a civil servant — Mr Harold Evans. On the whole the delegated arrangement worked fairly well for Macmillan. Charles Hill has described his role as co-ordinating Minister.[1] He appears to have seen the muting of rivalries between Cabinet Ministers in their press relations as one of his main functions; another function was the co-ordination of domestic and foreign publicity. Moreover, duting times of political crisis the strain of press relations was removed from the Prime Minister; another senior Minister was available to give quick and authoritative briefings to journalists — for instance after a 'crisis'-Cabinet meeting. The Macmillan system also worked fairly smoothly on a day-to-day basis; Mr Harold Evans, in the role of Public Relations Adviser to the Prime Minister, was popular with Lobby journalists, who welcomed his 'non-political' civil servant background.

The relative success of the Macmillan delegated system in muting the threats of press relations *rivalry* within the Cabinet, was probably bought at the expense of increasing the threat of *hierarchy* as a block to the upward flow of information. This at least appears to have been one interpretation which was placed upon the increasing failures in communication towards the end of Macmillan's administration by Mr Harold Wilson.

Under (b) The *Wilson* or Prime Ministerial arrangement of government information, co-ordination rested in the hands of the Prime Minister himself. Just as the Macmillan arrangements were partly a response to the press relations disasters of the 1956 Suez period, so the Wilson arrangements appear to have been partly a response to the Profumo and other scandals of the later Macmillan years. The press relations style of John F. Kennedy may have been another example; and clearly the special political circumstance of a minute Parliamentary majority in 1964 was a major factor. The main Cabinet responsibility for Government Information was carried personally by the Prime Minister. The day-to-day 10 Downing Street responsibilities — including the twice daily Lobby briefings — were taken on by Mr Wilson's 'Press Secretary'; the latter was Mr Trevor Lloyd-Hughes — not only a former Lobby correspondent but the former Lobby correspondent of the *Liverpool Daily Post*, a newspaper circulating in Mr Harold Wilson's own Parliamentary constituency. In contrast to this long-standing 'personal' tie, Mr Lloyd-Hughes was himself less experienced on the *national* political scene than had been Mr Clement Attlee's 'personal' appointment (Francis Williams, who was a former Editor of the *Daily Herald* and had other relevant national political experience — such as financial journalism, war-time service in a senior post in the Ministry of Information, and diplomatic press relations experience at the 1945 San Francisco Conference). Especially notable was Mr Lloyd-Hughes' lack of extensive civil service experience in Whitehall.

There were further 'personal' notes in the Wilson arrangements. By tradition each of the three political parties have been allowed one 'member' of the national Lobby correspondents; Mr Wilson's appointment, Mr Gerald Kaufman, was also installed at 10 Downing Street — and became in effect a personal 'political' press officer in addition to the personal, but 'non-political', Press Secretary. This personal or 'special assistant' role — with its flavour of Washington rather than Whitehall — was performed for some other senior Ministers after 1964; the most notable example was Mr John Harris, a former Labour Party Publicity Director. Such appointments appeared to stress not the communication of information to journalists but the communicating of information to the senior Ministers involved. One consequence of this and other related press relations practices was, however, the long-term encouragement of *rivalry* – between press officer and press officer, between Minister and Minister, and to some extent between Lobby correspondent and Lobby correspondent.

In the short-term the Wilson system under which the Prime Minister personally dominated government press relations appeared to work well; while perhaps justified by the special short-term political considerations of 1964–6, its continuation after the Labour government's success in the 1966 General Election was more dubious. The *rivalry* within the Cabinet which had been muted while the Election remained imminent, broke into public soon after.

Several press commentators at this period forecast disaster for the Wilson system. The *New Statesman's* political correspondent wrote two weeks after the 1966 Election:

> . . . the central weakness of the government's press relations. The trouble can be briefly stated – they hinge far too much on a Prime Minister who plays every situation by ear. Certainly, his affinity with working journalists has had no equal in recent times.[2]

Three months after the Election, when other Ministers were already speaking much more candidly to journalists, *The Economist* said:

> . . . Whenever there is a row about a press leak the people most deserving of suspicion are not the correspondents or (with some exceptions) the civil servants and the industrialists; in these matters ministers should be thought guilty until proved innocent.
>
> The peculiarity of this Government is that, while there has been some attempt to tighten up departmental security, at the centre it leaks like a sieve. This is how Mr Wilson likes to work and it is why he employs the personal staff that he does . . . But if this is to be the Wilson style for the next four years there is no need for anyone to get into a tizzy about it. Ministers who disagree with No. 10 on a policy issue have learned to look after themselves; some of them, too, were a little slow at first.[3]

The Editor of *The Economist* was Mr Alastair Burnet, a former Lobby correspondent.

Eighteen months later in early 1968, a number of Lobby correspondents commented that it was remarkable how Mr Wilson — who had seemed to understand journalists so well — had managed to make such a disastrous mess of his press relations. At this time, a few weeks after devaluation, I talked to most of the national Lobby correspondents — when the Prime Minister's popularity with both the public and the correspondents was at an extreme low point.

Subsequently some important changes were made in the formal arrangements for government press relations. And this is an example of the point that a Cabinet's internal relations and external press relations are interdependent. Another example would be the period after the March 1966 Election. The failure to change the Wilson personal type of press relations was one aspect of other failures to change — which led to devaluation of sterling in November 1967.

Perhaps I should re-emphasize the point of this discussion of formal government-press relations. The discussion is of only a brief and impressionistic nature; it is intended merely as illustration of the basic argument about a connection between Cabinet rivalry and Cabinet publicity. Some future adequately systematic study of the Macmillan and Wilson Cabinets will reveal other relevant variables which have been ignored here.

Undoubtedly the situation facing Harold Wilson when he became Prime Minister in October 1964 was quite different. Clearly also rivalry within a Conservative and a Labour government can be expected to take different forms. Perhaps the most important aspect of the inter-connection of Cabinet rivalry and Cabinet publicity is that the current press relations behaviour (including rival Ministerial leaks) is likely to affect the manner in which Cabinet decision-making is conducted. In the absence of any evidence, one can hypothesize that any Prime Minister who believes that certain types of decisions will be leaked by Ministers will be tempted not to discuss such issues at all in Cabinet meetings. Thus there may be a strong correlation between rival Ministerial press leaking behaviour and the propensity of the Prime Minister to take decisions personally, or through individual contacts with Ministers, or through Cabinet committees — rather than in full Cabinet meetings.

This discussion is of course even more speculative than the rest of the present chapter. The basic point I wish to make is that we cannot fully understand the workings of the Westminster Lobby system until we have an adequately systematic empirical study of behaviour within a recent Cabinet; and such an empirical study of Cabinet behaviour will in turn not be adequately comprehensive unless it takes into account the part which external relations with journalists play in the internal functioning of the Cabinet.

Rivalry: specialist journalists

Rivalry presents problems not only for Prime Ministers, but also for Editors of national newspapers. The mushrooming growth of semi-political specialization in journalism poses the threat that rivalries between different kinds of journalists will result in available information being lost to the employing news organisation.

Between 1964 and 1969 the number of 'feature and specialist writers' employed by national newspapers in Britain increased from 534 to 607; the number of reporters (some specializing a little, or standing-in for specialists on their days off) increased from 632 to 716. A highly complex and important story might appeal to correspondents from as many as seven different specialist fields within a single newspaper. The task of co-ordinating the reports of these different specialists rests largely with news executives and their assistants; the pressure of work upon these executives at the relevant times of the day is so great that any detailed weaving together of stories rarely occurs. Moreover, effective co-ordination would require the executive to play a part in *initiating* newsgathering activities.

The whole structure, ideology, and individual occupational experience involved in specialized journalism tends to operate against any such active co-operation. Specialist journalists treasure their autonomy and try to increase it; such autonomy centres especially on the choice of stories. Specialist journalists work on differing timetables — for instance, on a complex international political and financial story, the financial correspondents work on a timetable governed partly by the stock market, the Washington correspondent works on

US Eastern Standard Time, and the Lobby man works on the late evening timetables of Westminster. If in mid-evening the Lobby man did want to talk to the financial editor, the latter might be at a City banquet or on the way home by train; the Washington correspondent might be taking a late lunch.

Notes

1. C. Hill, *Both Sides of the Hill* (London: Heinemann, 1964).
2. M. Coady, 'The Premier and the Press', *New Statesman*, 15 Apr 1966.
3. *The Economist* (1966).

Part Three

THE CABINET AT WORK

10 Reflections on Cabinet Government*

LORD BUTLER interviewed by NORMAN HUNT

Norman Hunt: Lord Butler, you were a Cabinet Minister for over seventeen years; how far, looking back over those years, do you think it is true to say that the Cabinet is no longer the main forum for vital decision-taking that it used to be, say, at the turn of the century?

Lord Butler: It all depends on what issues go before the Cabinet. If they are purely technical issues that have been decided by a Cabinet committee, for example, then the Cabinet certainly has less power; or if they are issues where most of the work is done outside the Cabinet, the Cabinet also is disregarded. But I would say on the whole that for, say, a political decision by the government, the Cabinet still is the committee, which Walter Bagehot described as the buckle which ties together the legislative side of the government and the executive, and is still very important.

Hunt: But wouldn't it be true to say that more and more Cabinet committees are taking more and more decisions that in previous times would have come before the Cabinet?

Lord Butler: Most of my work when I was Minister of Education was done outside the Cabinet, and hardly referred to the Cabinet at all, and that was a major reform in our social affairs.

Hunt: Aren't Ministers more and more burdened with the detail of running their departments, and doesn't this also mean that the Cabinet as an effective forum for all policy decisions doesn't quite exist?

Lord Butler: I am certain from my experience that the majority of Cabinet Ministers come to the Cabinet over-burdened with briefs, and with life generally; it is not like the early days when Winston Churchill tells us he always had a memorandum for the Cabinet and treated it as a public

*Reprinted from the *Listener*, 16 Sept 1965, pp 407–11, with the permission of Lord Butler and Lord Crowther-Hunt.

meeting, and that the public meeting registered the results. It has rather changed, and I think it is important now for Ministers, when they come to the Cabinet, to realize that it is a place where great issues ought to be decided and discussed.

Hunt: Do you mean that they ought to be briefed on matters affecting other departments?

Lord Butler: They either ought to brief themselves or be armed to discuss these issues in the Cabinet, so as to make it the place where the decisions are taken.

Hunt: In your experience are they not so armed now?

Lord Butler: Not as well as they used to be. I think it's all part of the general rush of modern life, and the fact that the departments are so very big and busy. Take the issue of defence. A lot of the big defence issues will be decided by the Chiefs of Staff, and by the Defence Committee, and they would not themselves come to the Cabinet except for confirmation.

Hunt: So that when recommendations come before the Cabinet from the Defence Committee, the Cabinet is not in a very strong position to go against them?

Lord Butler: No, but it has the power to; and the point I want to make is that it is no good making generalizations about the British Constitution, saying this or that has happened, because it is always possible to retrace one's steps and still to use the Cabinet as the chief place in which these decisions can be made.

Hunt: But although it has the power to reverse a decision, or a recommendation of the Defence Committee, is it your experience, Lord Butler, that the Cabinet doesn't usually do this?

Lord Butler: No, it doesn't usually do so.

Hunt: The other fashionable idea that is put about these days about the Cabinet is that there has been a considerable increase in the power of the Prime Minister. Would you agree with this?

Lord Butler: I think that on the whole the Prime Minister has tended to stop being an equal among equals. There is a tendency not exactly to dictatorship, because I don't think the British Constitution would stand that in the end, but to be the leader who does control everything, and things are getting more and more into his own hands.

Hunt: Do you think that this increase in power is more an increase of power over personnel, over hiring and firing members of the Cabinet, than actually over the details of policy-formation of the government?

Lord Butler: So much depends on the extent to which the Prime Minister of the day intends to take the Cabinet into his confidence, and how much he intends to take decisions with the aid of a few Ministers outside the Cabinet. In my time there have been periods when the Prime Minister has got together two or three Ministers, taken a decision, and the Cabinet has then just become a rubber stamp. Strange to relate, I don't think this happened so much in the war under Churchill, who was extremely sensitive to popular opinion and to the views of other people in running the war, as it has tended to happen since.

Hunt: Have you noticed a progressive increase in power, as you have served under seven Prime Ministers over the years since the nineteen-thirties?

Lord Butler: Yes, I have. But if you look back at history, you see this going up and down in the course of history, as between a Prime Minister like Palmerston and a Prime Minister, who was perhaps more constitutional, like Peel. It depends really whether the Prime Minister is surrounded by a very powerful collection of Cabinet Ministers or whether he is not. And it tends — on the occasion when his colleagues are not so powerful — for the Prime Minister to assume a great deal of authority in his own hands.

Hunt: Of the Prime Ministers you have served under, Lord Butler, which one do you think wielded most power?

Lord Butler: I suppose the most powerful, although I thought he was one of the most constitutional, was Churchill. It would be difficult to find a man with more energy and ability. I should think the least dictatorial that I served under was Baldwin. Baldwin didn't attempt to enforce his way, although when he made his speeches to Parliament they were entirely his own, not inspired by his colleagues or written by them or written by his advisers. Baldwin was not primarily interested in foreign affairs, which for a Prime Minister is rare. I have been at the Foreign Office twice, both as an Under Secretary and as a Foreign Secretary, and I know that it is the habit of Prime Ministers to take a great interest in foreign affairs, as the present Prime Minister does.

Hunt: From what you are saying, Lord Butler, you seem to be suggesting that a Prime Minister may have a great deal of power over one particular aspect of policy, like foreign affairs, perhaps, or some other area of activity, but not in a sense have a great deal of power over the overall policy of the government?

Lord Butler: It really depends; because there is absolutely no doubt, in the British constitution as we see it operating today, that the Prime Minister has more power than he ever had before. I noticed an essay by Crossman on this subject in introducing the latest edition of Walter Bagehot's work. I would go a certain way with that essay, but I would still say that there were powers and forces in the British constitution which could still pull the Prime Minister down or pull him back. One of the forces which is most powerful is the private members in Parliament getting together and objecting to a dictatorial act on the part of a Prime Minister; similarly his colleagues getting together on finding that he is assuming too much power. I believe the British constitution always invents the power to counteract too much power, and that is important.

Hunt: In this general context could we look at one or two specific issues illustrating the role and power of the Prime Minister and the Cabinet — first your 1944 Education Act?

Lord Butler: It was rather exceptional, being war time, so the War Cabinet certainly would not have considered it. It used to go before a body called the Lord President's Committee, but I must tell you that the greater part of the negotiation and preparation for this huge measure, which is still unimplemented — this shows the size of it — today, was done outside the Cabinet, and outside the Lord President's Committee.

Hunt: Where did the basic ideas for this policy come from? Were they already existing within the department when you moved there, Lord Butler?

Lord Butler: Yes, they had been discussed when I moved there in 1941 by those interested in education; that is to say the local education authorities and the Board's officials; and therefore there was a plan which I could consider. What was not considered was the whole of what is called the religious settlement under the Act between the churches — that was the biggest bit of negotiation which I had to do myself; with the aid of my colleague, Mr Chuter Ede, who was then the Under Secretary. It was only at the later stages, when we wanted authority, that we went to a government committee to get authority for it.

Hunt: And was the Lord President's Committee able to alter your policy at all?

Lord Butler: No, I think they mostly endorsed what we had been doing; it was the result of a big piece of negotiation and therefore it would not have been sensible at that stage to alter it much.

Hunt: Would it be true to say that increasingly major measures are often the product of a department and the Minister in consultation with outside bodies, and that, once they have been agreed, it is then really very difficult for even a Cabinet committee, let alone the Cabinet, to alter them in any substantial way?

Lord Butler: Yes, and there I get back to what I said at the beginning, that it is when political issues arise that the Cabinet really comes in. The Cabinet does not alter the structure of the hard work done by a department in framing a measure, say a transport act or something of that sort. But if you are proposing to run down a lot of people, it is naturally politically unpopular, and that is the sort of thing which the Cabinet would come in to decide.

Hunt: Is it true to say that the Cabinet really, as such, has little control over the annual Budget?

Lord Butler: Yes, that is a convention which I must stress very strongly, having introduced five Budgets myself and having been Chancellor for the longest time, I think, recently — that is, four years. It is a fact that the Chancellor of the Exchequer does produce his own Budget, and the main reason for that is, first of all, that it requires a great deal of negotiation and thought with the interests concerned; and the second main reason is that it is desperately secret and if any of the secrets got out it would lead to great difficulty. What usually happens in the preparation of a Budget by the Chancellor is that he consults the Prime Minister, so as to have a friend at court in case of need and also a friend who can help him. He also quite likely consults the President of the Board of Trade or somebody deeply involved in the trade figures; but he does not consult the Cabinet as a whole until the very eve of the Budget. And I have only known one case in my five Budgets where the Cabinet tried to alter some regulation concerning Lancashire trade at the last minute, but not to alter the main lines of the Budget.

Hunt: You said that the reason this highly political question of a Budget — because it is both political and economic — did not come before the Cabinet and is not discussed by the Cabinet, is because of the need for secrecy. But are you really saying there that the Cabinet can be trusted with vital defence secrets but can't be trusted with vital economic secrets?

Lord Butler: I think there is a difference; because there is so much detail in the Budget. Supposing you are going to put some money on cigarettes or alcohol, it is essential that the Customs shall not let that be known; and if you consult a lot of people a long time before, it is undoubtedly the fact that it would get loose in their departments, and you simply couldn't keep a secret of what you were doing in the Budget. It is also awkward for the markets and, as the markets affect the pound, it is very important for the stability of the pound that the matter should not get out.

Hunt: In your early years as Chancellor, I think you had to work with the Treasury Advisory Committee — a small group of Ministers including Lord Woolton and Lord Swinton, I believe. Was this a useful innovation?

Lord Butler: I think it's quite useful, provided you can keep your own counsel about the Budget itself. I am personally a great believer in the Chancellor of the Exchequer having the right to introduce his own Budget. I would go further and say that I don't agree with having a separate Ministry for Economic Affairs. I think the whole thing ought to be centralized in the Treasury: it makes it much better for the Chancellor to take control of the situation.

Hunt: You don't think that the separate Ministry of Economic Affairs — a Department of Economic Affairs — is a useful spur to the Treasury civil servants and a useful spur to the Chancellor?

Lord Butler: No, I don't think so. The Treasury is so important a department, and the Chancellor so important a Minister, that he ought to be fundamentally in control of the economic life of the country.

Hunt: How far, when you were framing your Budgets, did you discuss policy detail with the Cabinet Economic Committee, for example?

Lord Butler: Not very much. But it is a striking feature of Cabinet government that the Budget and the economic situation are very much under the control of the Chancellor. Of course, the Cabinet does discuss the trade figures; it does discuss the trends in the economy. If the Chancellor wants to introduce some curtailing of hire purchase, for example, in order to cut down demand at home, he would discuss that with the Cabinet or a Cabinet committee, but he would not normally discuss his Budget.

Hunt: How far, in framing your Budgets, were you dependent upon the advice of Treasury civil servants?

Lord Butler: A great deal depends upon the Treasury civil servants. But also when you are at the Treasury you have the advantage of the Board of Inland Revenue and you have the advantage of the Customs to discuss things with. You also have the advantage of an economic section in the Treasury itself, which I think is a very good thing.

Hunt: Did you ever feel that you would like more political assistance in dealing with civil servants?

Lord Butler: I don't think so; one has one's own junior Ministers to discuss things with and that makes a big enough team. When I was appointed, Winston sent for me and said, 'I think you're far too young'. I was only forty-nine at the time, when I was Chancellor of the Exchequer, and he said, 'I'm going to appoint the cleverest economist who has ever lived — namely Lord Salter — who is a certain age, to look after you'. So I had the benefit of a senior man with me, appointed by Winston, as a friend of his.

Hunt: But you don't think as a regular matter it would be a good idea for the Chancellor of the Exchequer, when he comes into office, to bring his own little group of private advisers?

Lord Butler: Like a sort of French *cabinet?* No, I don't think so. I think that the relationship between the average civil servants and the politicians are extremely good.

Hunt: What is the role of the Bank of England in this? Do you have close discussions with the Bank in the pre-Budget period?

Lord Butler: I think the Governor of the Bank of England is the greatest friend of the Chancellor of the Exchequer, because he brings him the news of the City; and he is an independent man appointed by the government for a term of years and can be a person of absolutely capital importance in dealing with the matter. As you know, things are not always altogether easy between the Governor and the Chancellor, but the Governor sees the Chancellor at least once a week and tells him, of course, the position of sterling and the position of the pound in overseas markets, so the Governor is a man without whom the Chancellor of the Exchequer cannot easily get on.

Hunt: Would it be true to say that the Governor of the Bank of England knows more of what is in the Chancellor's mind in the pre-Budget framing period than some Ministers?

Lord Butler: I would certainly say that was true. It shows you one of the freaks of the workings in the British constitution.

Hunt: Would it follow from what you are saying about the role of the Chancellor of the Exchequer — and one gets this impression very much from the period when Mr Selwyn Lloyd was Chancellor of the Exchequer — that the Chancellor's policies were very much his personal ones or the Treasury ones and agreed directly between himself and the Prime Minister without the Cabinet really coming into this at all?

Lord Butler: No, I wouldn't say so; we used to spend hours discussing the incomes policy when Selwyn Lloyd was Chancellor of the Exchequer. But I think — as in my own case — he as Chancellor of the Exchequer had a great deal of individual authority.

Hunt: Where does Cabinet collective responsibility come

into this? When Selwyn Lloyd was dismissed, in a sense partly because his policies had not been as successful as they might have been, wasn't he then made the scapegoat for failures of Cabinet policy?

Lord Butler: That was much more an individual act by the Prime Minister of the day than a matter of collective Cabinet responsibility; and when you talked earlier about hiring and firing, you've got to realize that the Prime Minister is head of the government and has the right to terminate people's employment when he wants to, and to regulate the affairs within his own government.

Hunt: In your view does the sacking at that period of a third of the Cabinet illustrate the enormous power of a British Prime Minister? Because it really happened without a ripple.

Lord Butler: Yes, I think it does; and it illustrates what I said earlier, that the power of the Prime Minister has tended to grow.

Hunt: Did you see, coming out of that rather autocratic dismissal, the development of some of these countervailing powers, as it were, that you were talking about earlier?

Lord Butler: Of course, because all the people who go out have friends who mobilize round them.

Hunt: But if Mr Macmillan had not been ill and had not had to resign, no one would have been able to get rid of him as Prime Minister, would they, however strong the countervailing powers had been?

Lord Butler: No, it all depends on the extent to which the party and the House rally behind the Prime Minister, or the extent to which they become uneasy. What we are discussing here is not so much personalities as the stresses, counter-stresses, checks and counterbalances of the British constitution. All I say to you is that the tendency for the Prime Minister of today to have more power than he has had in English history before does create in the body politic of the Chamber of the House of Commons checks and counterbalances which can be called into effect if he goes too far.

Hunt: A Prime Minister would have to go a long way, wouldn't he, to be displaced by his Cabinet colleagues?

Lord Butler: There is power either in the Cabinet colleagues themselves, or in the individual members of the House, to achieve a change if that is necessary.

Hunt: Can we look at another occasion, Lord Butler, when some of these countervailing powers may have been building up as a result of what on the surface were very much personal and almost autocratic decisions by the Prime Minister? I am thinking of the time of the Suez crisis, when President Nasser took control of the Suez Canal in July 1956. I think at this time the Cabinet then formed a Cabinet committee to prepare counter-measures. How far was the whole Suez crisis handled by this Cabinet committee, without anything much really coming to the Cabinet at all?

Lord Butler: First of all you're wrong in saying that the Cabinet set up a Cabinet committee. It was the Prime Minister who set up a Cabinet committee, which is a different inflection constitutionally; the Cabinet would probably not have agreed to set up such a committee. The Prime Minister of the day thought these matters in the Suez were best handled by a Suez committee of the Cabinet, and that was a representative body, including the Defence Minister and Foreign Minister, which met regularly to discuss what is called the Suez crisis. The Cabinet came very little into the Suez crisis until towards the end.

Hunt: When this committee had been set up by the Prime Minister, would it be true to say that a lot of the important decisions taken during this period were nevertheless even taken outside that committee?

Lord Butler: There is no doubt that at that period of his career Sir Anthony Eden was very much in control of the affairs as he saw them and as he thought right. We must remember he was acting out of extreme conviction and honesty of purpose at the time. He was extremely anxious to keep these matters under his control and therefore at times he consulted only his nearest colleagues.

Hunt: When the ultimatum was finally given to Egypt and Israel, this was something that was reported to the Cabinet only four hours before the ultimatum was due to expire and certainly after it had been sent; so it wouldn't have been possible for the Cabinet to do anything about it at that stage?

Lord Butler: Oh, I think the Cabinet could have blown up

if it had wanted to, but the Cabinet had confidence in Eden at the time and what doubts there were were not expressed until, I think, a later stage.

Hunt: But wasn't this an occasion when these other countervailing forces that should have been developing never really came to the surface at all?

Lord Butler: You want to remember that the party in the House at the time of Suez was on the whole behind the Prime Minister and very indignant with Nasser; so there wasn't the seed-bed for opposition to the policy in the Conservative Party in the House that you would expect if the Prime Minister was acting contrary to the general line of what the back-benchers thought.

Hunt: A Prime Minister couldn't really wield dictatorial power if it were against the wishes and will of the back-benchers?

Lord Butler: No.

Hunt: But wasn't this an occasion when at any rate the Cabinet ought to have been kept more in touch with what was happening and there ought to have been more regular reports from the Suez Committee?

Lord Butler: The fact is that it was accepted by the Cabinet and by the party and the House that this should be the line of policy, and therefore there was no powerful reaction either in the Cabinet or in the House of Commons itself while the operation was taking place. Accordingly it is constitutionally true that the Prime Minister did have more power at that time than almost any Prime Minister has ever had.

Hunt:, But had the Cabinet gone as far as authorizing the idea of the use of British forces in an emergency without prior reference to the Cabinet?

Lord Butler: I would have said that it all came to the Cabinet in the end, and of course when Eden became ill and I took over the direction of the Cabinet to withdraw the forces and to deal with the problem of sterling in America, we did have regular support from the Ministers in the Prime Minister's absence.

Hunt: It then became much more of a Cabinet matter than it had been before?

Lord Butler: Yes. It just shows that in certain events in British history a Prime Minister of today, of modern times, has a great deal of power.

Hunt: During this period you were Lord Privy Seal and Leader of the House, with no departmental responsibility. Did you find when you were without departmental responsibility that you had a bigger voice and a bigger power in the Cabinet than at the time when you were head of a great department?

Lord Butler: I think a Minister with a big department behind him has a good deal more power in the Cabinet than a man like a Lord Privy Seal, who has no department with him. The real reason is that in putting a case for or against a particular action — it may be for or against a war-like action or not — one then has the whole force of one's department's advice behind one in putting it to the Cabinet. It is undoubtedly the case that if you were giving advice to a younger man, you would advise him in the Cabinet to have a big department behind him because his voice would be stronger.

Hunt: I can understand a man with a big department having a great deal of power and influence with the Cabinet over the matters affecting his own department, but how can he have power and influence over some of the other matters coming before the Cabinet, which do not affect his own department? How does a Minister of Health, for example, really have much power or influence over a Foreign Secretary?

Lord Butler: It depends entirely on the man, I think. When Nye Bevan was Minister of Health, he had a pretty good power in the Cabinet, because he was always talking and always powerful and always vociferous.

Hunt: Could we look at another matter which is very much a political question — the Common Market negotiations? This was both political and economic. Where were the vital decisions taken there about the question of Britain going into the Common Market?

Lord Butler: The negotiations were all so complicated that half the Cabinet didn't understand what it was all about.

After all, the Cabinet is an amateur body when they are discussing things outside their own departments. First of all it was left to the negotiators, Mr Heath and the late Sir Pierson Dixon, who were so clever at all these matters, and then it was left to a committee which was formed under my chairmanship called the Common Market Negotiating Committee. We used to take all the day-to-day decisions on the negotiations, upon agricultural matters, and all that sort of thing, and upon the trade matters which were very complicated. This is precisely the sort of thing in which the Cabinet is least apt to take a proper decision.

Hunt: But the Common Market Negotiating Committee was formed after the Cabinet had taken a decision in principle to try to get into the Common Market?

Lord Butler: Yes. There, the Cabinet took the political decision to try to go in, led by the Prime Minister of the day — Harold Macmillan.

Hunt: But this Cabinet decision must have been based on a great deal of previous study and previous information and perhaps previous Cabinet Committee reports. It wasn't just taken by the Cabinet?

Lord Butler: No. I can assure you that for the whole time of the Common Market negotiations we were deluged with pages of foolscap of a blue colour, which is what the government negotiations are written down on. And we all had a pretty good idea of what this all meant. But it was fundamentally a political decision about whether Britain was to be outside this wall of the Six, or whether she was to be inside and enjoy the advantage of an expanding Europe.

Hunt: Had a Cabinet Committee discussed the pros and cons of going in?

Lord Butler: Yes, at great length.

Hunt: And there was a recommendation from this Cabinet Committee . . .

Lord Butler: And a recommendation from the Prime Minister, which gave the political impetus to the decision to go in.

Hunt: So that even here, the Cabinet was faced by a very strong recommendation from the Cabinet Committee and the

Prime Minister that we should do this. Would it have been possible, apart from a technical possibility, for the Cabinet to have gone against that sort of recommendation at that stage.

Lord Butler: Oh yes, if there are enough people resolute enough to stand up to the lead given by the Prime Minister of the day, the Cabinet can kick over the traces, and there is an adjourned discussion. It's all rather painful. The Cabinet doesn't come to a decision, because it is clear that in the Cabinet there are enough people against it. The matter is then adjourned to another day, and the Cabinet can perfectly well react against that if it is strong enough. But the tendency of the day, with the rush of life which I mentioned earlier, is for the Cabinet Ministers not to give enough attention to the political issues when they arise.

Hunt: But even on a question like the Common Market, where you say the basic political decision was with the Cabinet, and it could have decided either way in spite of the fact that it had a recommendation to go one way, here was an issue that in a sense was suitable for Cabinet decision and yet the Cabinet decision was pre-empted.

Lord Butler: It was pre-empted to a certain degree, but remember that several of the Cabinet Ministers had to take serious decisions against their early youthful ideas upon imperial preference, for example, which has always been in the Conservative Party a great flagstone upon which people would base their careers. They had to take decisions about agriculture — whether British agriculture was going to be destroyed, and many of them had sat in agricultural seats for the whole of their lives. I should have thought the Cabinet took the decision to enter the negotiations with the Common Market with pretty good will.

Hunt: You have been drawing the distinction throughout, Lord Butler, between those matters which on the one hand the Cabinet can take real decisions about, and those matters which must be left to decisions elsewhere, and saying it's really the political questions that are the ones that the Cabinet can properly deal with.

Lord Butler: Yes. The Education Act, the Budget, and the Common Market are the three examples where practically all the work, and practically all the initial part of the decision was taken before it came into the Cabinet. On the other hand, the final jumping over the fence, as in the case of the Common Market, was a very big political decision for any government.

Hunt: But in a sense, as you were saying, on all these questions that we have been discussing the Cabinet was really faced with a pretty well unanimous recommendation to move in a certain direction. And so, even on political issues like these, the Cabinet really wasn't in a position freely to take a decision?

Lord Butler: I think if you take the Cabinet as covering the Cabinet committees and the committees of Ministers under it, you get a rather better conception of what the Cabinet is. If you just take the Cabinet meeting itself, you have to come to the conclusion that unless the people are very alive that day, and very political, much of the decision has already been taken before it reaches them. That is the conclusion I would come to.

Hunt: A lot of the decisions of government these days are concerned with allocation of scarce resources and really technical matters. Is the Cabinet at all suitable for dealing with these?

Lord Butler: The Cabinet in my day used to consider the allocation of resources, and it did particularly in the day when I was first Chancellor of the Exchequer in regard to materials, because all materials were short, and it did over investment in fields like health or local government and housing. While the whole of the work is done before it reaches the Cabinet, Ministers do like a say about whether, for instance, housing is to get more than roads. You do get a rivalry between those different investments, which the Cabinet is quite useful to resolve.

Hunt: But when it resolves a rivalry of that kind, doesn't it tend to resolve it on the basis of a bit for each Member of the Cabinet?

Lord Butler: That's the trouble, yes.

Hunt: Isn't this the thing that makes it really not a very good forum for resolving problems of that kind?

Lord Butler: But I fail to see a better place for the final decision to come.

Hunt: The only other possibility, presumably, would be a very small Cabinet of people without departmental responsibility making the vital decisions about these matters?

Lord Butler: That I think is what is gradually developing in the modern age.

Hunt: Would you like to see this develop?

Lord Butler: If you were asking me how Whitehall was going to develop in the modern age, I would say that you would tend to see a smaller Cabinet which had the time to consider the final political judgements on issues worked out elsewhere. I will give you an example. I should have thought that not only has the Ministry of Defence been amalgamated under one Defence Minister, but I think you will see an External Affairs Minister who will take charge of Foreign Affairs, Commonwealth Affairs, and Colonial Affairs, and he will be a member of the Cabinet. Similarly, you will see only one Minister, I hope, at the Treasury, in charge of the economic situation. And similarly, I think you will see, as time goes by, the social services much more amalgamated under one Ministry, although they will have under them people dealing with old age, with the young, and so forth. That will mean that there are a series of Ministers who have greater power over fields, and the Cabinet can therefore be smaller.

Hunt: But won't this mean that the individual Ministers will be even more burdened with departmental responsibility — the External Affairs Minister, for example, having taken on Commonwealth problems as well as foreign policy, will he therefore be able to have a worthwhile view on, say, the social affairs side?

Lord Butler: I would like to take you up on that, because I think one of the troubles about the Foreign Secretary at the moment is that in dealing with at least three parts of the world — Malaysia and Aden, for example, quite apart from Cyprus, which makes a third — he has to work all the time with a Commonwealth Secretary or a Colonial Secretary, and much of his time is taken up in arguing and eventually getting some line which they can jointly put to Cabinet. I think it would be better if there were an External Affairs Minister who could take that decision. He would have with him a

Secretary of State, or two Secretaries of State, who would do much of the work. But the ultimate decision would be his.

Hunt: But this wouldn't really enable the External Affairs Minister to be particularly effective in his contributions to Cabinet discussions on home policies.

Lord Butler: There again it depends entirely on the man, as to whether he has the ability to expand or not. I can imagine Ernie Bevin when he was Foreign Secretary, for example, having some pretty hot ideas on the trade unions.

Hunt: This smaller Cabinet with Ministers having a wider area of responsibility — what will this in your view then mean for the doctrine of collective responsibility, in so far as we really do have a doctrine of collective responsibility now?

Lord Butler: Oh, I think it would make it easier, because there would be fewer people brought together in the knot of the Cabinet. I think it would have the effect of giving the Prime Minister a much more efficient committee or Cabinet from which to deal, and I think it would tend to reduce the power of the Prime Minister.

Hunt: So your reflection on this, Lord Butler, is that we are not going to move in the foreseeable future, in your view, towards what sometimes has been called presidential government; that the power of the Prime Minister is not going to go on increasing, that it will now start diminishing?

Lord Butler: Yes, I should hope myself that the checks and balances inherent in the democratic system in a House of Commons, which at present is very lively, would counteract the tendency to go towards a presidential system. I also think that the responsibility of Ministers to the House is much better than the separation of the powers in the American continent, and we cannot in our position have a government which has not a majority in the House of Commons. That I think is a very important feature of our constitution.

11 On Being a Minister*

ROY JENKINS

There are only three Departments of State which are strong both in tradition and in power. There are others which have acquired power recently, and others again which once had power but have lost it in the evolution to modern Whitehall. But only the Treasury, the Home Office and the Foreign Office occupy roughly the same relative positions in 1970 as they did a hundred years ago when Mr Gladstone was Prime Minister for the first time, Prussian troops were invading Paris, and Papal Infallibility had just been proclaimed.

Of the Foreign Office I have little direct knowledge. Over the other two Departments I presided for a combined period of four-and-a-half years. Lord Butler and Mr Callaghan have each held both offices for a longer period, but they moved in the opposite direction from me and their comparative judgements might be influenced by this as well as by other considerations. I have the doubtful distinction of being the only man to move direct from the Home Office to the Treasury since Sir John Simon.

Simon's Home Office was no doubt different from the one I first knew, but I have the strong impression that there has been more change in the past five years than in the preceding 25. A flexible and forward looking Permanent Under-Secretary has assisted this recent evolution. It has made some of my recollections out of date, but not inaccurate.

In 1965 the Home Office was surprisingly detached from the rest of Whitehall. To some extent, this was a result of the nature of its work. Very large sections of this can be and are done without any inter-departmental or inter-ministerial consultation. This meant that senior officials met their opposite numbers elsewhere somewhat less than was the case in most other departments. And the effect of this was considerably fortified by a deliberate policy of exclusivity.

*Reprinted from the *Sunday Times*, 17 Jan 1971, with the permission of the author.

210

There was very little cross fertilisation. Home Office men had a strong tendency to end where they began, with perhaps a very brief period outside in the middle. Both the Deputy Secretaries had begun as Home Office Assistant Principals, the one entering in 1937, the other in 1938. The Permanent Secretary was not a Home Office man in this sense. But he came from its sister department across the border, having been Secretary of the Scottish Home and Health Department for nine years before becoming official head of the Home Office in 1957. He had been the head of a department for 17 years. He was firmly in the tradition of strong, long-lasting Home Office Permanent Secretaries.

This tradition dated back at least to Sir John Anderson and probably well before that. It was epitomised by a story relating to Anderson in his heyday. A paper originating with an Assistant Principal bearing the initials (let us say) of HMT worked its way up to the Secretary of State. The Minute from HMT recommended Course A. This was not merely opposed but excoriated by everyone else on the way up. The general tenor of the subsequent minutes was that any man in his right mind must clearly accept Course B. But not the Secretary of State. He was not one of the more distinguished occupants of this post. But on this occasion he allowed an element of daring to creep through his habitual timidity. 'I think I rather agree with HMT,' he somewhat tentatively wrote. The next minute was less tentative: 'I have spoken with the S. of S. He no longer agrees with HMT. JA.' Anderson had intervened. The file was closed.

This tradition produced a somewhat rigid and hierarchial atmosphere. Christian names were rarely used. I never heard anyone, including myself, call the Permanent Secretary anything but Sir Charles. It also produced a highly-centralised system of submitting advice, which indeed had grown much more so since Anderson's day. All advice to the Secretary of State was submitted in the form of a single co-ordinated minute under the initials of the Permanent Secretary. Even the HMT incident would have been impossible under this system. I admired the speed of comprehension and decisiveness of expression on the part of the Permanent Secretary which made the system possible, but feared that the system effectively removed the point of decision from the Home Secretary. It also produced a certain reluctance, on the part of officials, to disagree with each other at meetings within the department. Co-ordinated views on paper tended to produce co-ordinated silence around the table.

The old Home Office system, although exclusive, did not appear to me to produce a totally self-confident outlook. The Department, although not anxious to change, was uncertain about its place in the world. There was slighly defensive expectation that whenever the Home Office attracted public attention it would also attract public blame. I remember seeing a sympathetic and semi-jocular minute written by one of my predecessors. 'Poor old Home Office,' it ran, 'we are occasionally right, but we always get the blame.' That struck me as depressing.

The Treasury, as I knew it, was more self-confident, less centralised, more relaxed. It operated upon the basis of an easy informality. Christian names were always used. All my private secretaries automatically called the Permanent Secretary by his. There was never the slightest difficulty in provoking argument and disagreement at meetings. Most people had plenty to say, and didn't mind to whom they said it, or whether the recipient of their views agreed with them or not.

At the same time, a great number of things were decided and done at a comparatively low level. Draft answers to Parliamentary Questions, for example, rarely went above Assistant Secretary level before being submitted to Ministers. In the Home Office they nearly all went to the Permanent Secretary. Much the same applied to briefing for Cabinet meetings and Committees. Senior officials were interested in advising on major policy, not in preventing Ministers making fools of themselves. If they couldn't avoid this with the help of an Assistant Secretary, either the Minister or the Assistant Secretary, or both, oughtn't to be in the Treasury at all.

A hostile critic would argue that all this easy informality and confident delegation of authority was based on the assumption of an aristocracy of talent and an essential community of outlook and view. It was open and democratic only in the sense that Whig society in 1780 was so. There is something in this, but not very much. Very few Treasury officials look or sound at all like Lord Holland or Lord Rockingham: or, what is perhaps more to the point, like each other. They are highly disparate, in background, appearance, manner.

They are also far from holding the same views. You could, I think, find nearly as wide a spectrum of economic outlook in Great George Street as amongst any collection of financial journalists or academic economists. If there is greater caution in the Treasury than in Fleet Street it is not so much through lack of intellectual adventurousness as because the official, if his advice is taken, has to sit and administer its consequences. The journalist (or the academic) can move easily on to giving the next set of advice.

This does not mean that certain rather set official Treasury positions cannot sometimes develop and be generally accepted, at least for a time, throughout most of the hierarchy. But this is different from the view that the official Treasury over the past 20 years or more has been steadily responsible for a consistent body of mostly wrong advice, with the received wisdom handed down, in a sort of apostolic succession, from generation to generation of senior officials.

I never detected, among those officials, a sufficient degree of reverence for their predecessors to make this system possible. And, indeed, on the principal occasion when I thought I saw signs of an obsessively rigid view developing among Treasury officials it was not in defence of a traditional position, but as an over-violent reaction against what they regarded as the mistakes of themselves or their predecessors a few years before. The Treasury has had its fair share of being wrong, but not in nearly as consistent a direction as is frequently supposed.

Nor is it so foolish as to believe in its own omniscience. What it probably does believe is that its members are at least as likely to be right as anybody else. It does not expect to be popular, and does not desperately care whether it is or not. But it is in no way sorry for itself. I would be amazed if anyone has ever minuted 'Poor old Treasury.'

In addition, the Treasury compared with the Home Office is much more of melting-pot. It is not at all inward looking.

It has not only exported people all over Whitehall and sometimes taken them back again (which might merely be regarded as a means of increasing its own influence), but it also absorbs into the highest ranks a great number of people who were not original Treasury entrants. Of the top three officials today not one entered the Civil Service as a Treasury Assistant Principal, and of the next eight officials only three had this provenance. There was throughout most of my time only one administrative grade Treasury official who was there before 1939.

In part this policy of the far wider open door is a result of Treasury work, paradoxically in view of the allegedly arcane mysteries of finance, being in some ways rather easier to pick up than Home Office work. The Treasury does not require the same meticulous standards of detailed administration. It deals little with the public. A lot of the work turns more on giving opinions, often somewhat by-and-large opinions, than on making or recommending decisions. And opinions can rarely be absolutely right or wrong, or at any rate cannot be proved to be so. Judgement and originality are often more important than accuracy and knowledge.

This does not apply to the Home Office. When I became Home Secretary it was only one year free of the death penalty. This sombre institution had to some extent pervaded the whole atmosphere. The Secretary of State's room was hardly made gayer by the presence, even if the discreetly concealed presence, of a board adjusted from day to day and recording the imminence of all pending executions. The responsibility for making recommendations as to what should be done in these cases weighed heavily upon all the officials concerned.

Such a duty could only be discharged by sensitive men if attempted with a clinically strict regard for precedent and consistency. This affected the approach to other cases dealt with in the Criminal Department, and persisted after the death penalty itself had disappeared. It is indeed necessary in cases involving the decisive exercise of executive power over individuals even if the dreadful finality of an execution is absent. The use of the prerogative of mercy in relation to prison sentences or decisions about deportation must have a defensible pattern of consistency. Otherwise there would be an intolerable sense of arbitrariness.

But consistency, while it may not be the 'hobgoblin of little minds,' is certainly the enemy of the broad sweep and the adventurous thought. A mistake in the Home Office may often be less damaging than one in the Treasury, but it is much more likely to be found out. The one may keep a man in prison who ought to be let out, or *vice versa.* The other may cost the country a massive loss of resources. But the former is much more precisely identifiable and will also have a much more direct impact upon a particular individual, who will quite rightly make as much noise as he can. Meticulous and precise administration is therefore an essential part of the Home Office tradition, and with it, as the reverse side of the same coin, tends to go a certain rigidity of outlook.

It was, I think, precisely in order to try to temper this that Home Office officials, for 20 years or more past, attached considerable importance to the slightly anomalous retention of the Children's Department. They thought it might have a humanising influence over the rest of the office. I doubt if it was powerful enough to exercise this influence, or if the nature of its work was quite right from this point of view. The acquisition of much wider and more positive responsibility for race relations in 1966 (hitherto the main responsibility had been the purely negative one of restricting immigration) probably did much more good in this direction. It was general work, involving a broad sweep of policy, and a great deal of contact with other Departments and outside bodies.

Even so, the Home Office, compared with the Treasury, necessarily and inevitably remains a department with a great deal of individual casework and much of its policy building gradually out of a multiplicity of minor decisions rather than coming down as part of a grand design.

This contrast affects not only official outlooks but also the pattern of work which is required from the Ministerial heads of the two Departments. The climate of the two offices is quite different. That of the Home Office is one of tropical storms that blow up with speed and violence out of a blue sky, dominate the political landscape for a short time, and then disappear as suddenly as they arrived. When they are on it is difficult to think of much else. When they are over it is difficult to recall what the fuss was all about.

A typical example was the escape of Frank Mitchell, the so-called 'mad axeman', from Dartmoor in December, 1966. It happened on the afternoon of the Second Reading of the Criminal Justice Bill, a fairly major measure by any standards, which introduced the parole scheme, suspended sentences, and majority verdicts by juries, abolished corporal punishment in prisons, simplified committal proceedings, changed the law relating to bail, and introduced much stricter control over shotguns.

I was told about the escape when I came out of the House of Commons chamber, after making my own speech and listening to Mr Hogg's reply. It was obvious at once that Mitchell's escape was going to kill all immediate public discussion of these long-term issues. Mitchell dominated the Press and television bulletins for three or four days. There was great apprehension that he would attack someone with his axe. In fact the reverse happened. He was carved up by those who helped him to escape. His name can now barely be recalled. The same is true of the psychiatrically disturbed boy whom the visiting magistrates at Maidstone Prison ordered to be birched, but whose decision I set aside. The violence of that storm is matched by the anonymity in which he is now happily shrouded.

The climate of the Treasury, on the other hand, during most of my time there was that of a long dark arctic winter, only slowly melting into a tentative spring. Changes, whether pleasant or unpleasant, could usually be foreseen at least a few weeks ahead, and were part of a general ebb and flow of events rather than some sudden unexpected occurrence. Occasionally, however, some minor freak storm did arise, as when Sir Gerald Nabarro startled the country with some particularly ludicrous allegations about Vehicle Excise Duties. But the untypical nature of such incidents for the Treasury is underlined by the fact that when they arose one's natural reaction was to say: 'It's just like the old days at the Home Office. It's the sort of incident we had with the mad axeman or the boy who was ordered to be birched.'

It follows from this that the rhythm of work at the Home Office was more agitated than at the Treasury. Weekends and holidays were more liable to be interrupted. The telephone call late at night or on a Sunday was more likely to mean unexpected bad news. The steady pressure of responsibility was less, but anxiety could flare up more quickly. And the ministerial job of administering the Home Office was heavier than that of administering the Treasury. There were far more individual decisions to be made. There was also more Parliamentary work.

The special burdensomeness of the Chancellor's job, which is proverbial but also true, arises out of three special factors: the endemic nature of Treasury crisis; the size of the stakes if things go wrong; and the amount of time which has to be devoted to dealing with one's colleagues. Abstract these factors, in other words postulate a calm situation with the economy going well and the rest of the government on holiday, and the Chancellor's job would be peculiarly light, unless it were the period of run-up to the Budget. It would be difficult to find more than a couple of hours' work a day. The Home Secretary, even without Northern Ireland on the boil, which it was not in my day, would always have more to do than this.

But of course these conditions could never prevail for long in the Treasury. Even if no other crisis intervened, other Ministers would return from holiday. And Cabinets have only to be resumed and the schemes of other Departments to be propounded for the Chancellor to be fully engaged. He has to attend all major ministerial meetings, and nearly always be either protagonist or antagonist. He can rarely sit through such a meeting, as a Home Secretary can often do, allowing the discussion to lap gently around him, intervening if he wishes, thinking his own thoughts if he does not. Only a few meetings would need to be passed in such a state of happy reverie for him quickly to discover that he was committed to expenditure involving major Budget changes.

Another facet of the same point is that for a Chancellor, unlike a Home Secretary, relations with other Ministers are crucial. A man could, I believe, be a tolerable and even a good Home Secretary while not on speaking terms with most of his principal colleagues. It might not be a happy state of affairs, but it would be a possible one. Many of a Home Secretary's most important decisions are exclusively reserved for his individual judgment. They need not be taken to Cabinet and they ought not to be so taken. And even among the rest, there are few which provoke great collective discussion. Home Office issues often excite more popular than strictly political interest. Very few of the storms of my period as Home Secretary led to collective ministerial discussion. I did not invite it; others did not demand it.

But no Chancellor can hold his position unless he can hold his colleagues, explain his policies to them and win their agreement, extracted either by loyalty or fear, for disciplines which are in themselves generally unwelcome. A substantial part of his time and energy is consumed in achieving this result.

Another substantial part is of course consumed in discussion and argument within the Department. But this is also true of the Home Secretary. This does not mean, except in unusual circumstances, that a Minister has to batter his head against a brick wall of determined departmental opposition. If he knows what he wants to do he will not in general have much difficulty in getting his policy carried out. Most civil servants, including the most able, prefer it this way. If a Minister is putty in their hands they have a nasty suspicion that he will be putty in the hands of everybody else too, and that policy will not be so much made by the civil servants as never properly made at all.

At the same time, it is of course the duty of civil servants to point out to a Minister the likely consequences of his actions. As 'likely consequences' frequently involves judgment and not merely objective fact prejudices can obviously enter the picture. But it is for the Minister to make up his own mind about this. If he has any will of his own he will do some things against advice, but after considering the argument more carefully than if he were going with the tide. Equally, unless he is incredibly rash and pig-headed, he is bound to be deflected by the weight of argument from certain courses to which he was originally attracted. Were this otherwise there would be no point in having advisers. And he will occasionally regret, amongst decisions which could have gone one way or the other, both those made with advice and those made against it.

If I were to attempt a distinction between the Home Office and the Treasury in this respect it would be this: in the Home Office it is more difficult for a Minister to make small changes, but perhaps easier for him to affect the general climate. Because of the great importance attributed to consistency he will find more resistance to granting a free pardon in a motoring case where the conviction looks to him odd, if the Department does not agree, than he will to the initiation of a new policy on race relations or the law relating to homosexuality.

In the Treasury he will not have much difficulty with small issues. If he wants to be liberal towards some piece of expenditure, then, provided the departmental Minister does not object — and they rarely object to generosity — it will go through. But on wider issues of policy he may have to face harder arguments mainly because the general world economic climate is less within his control, or that of his officials, than is the case with Home Office social policy.

A Chancellor's work is central to the Government, although, except perhaps at Budget time, rather remote from individuals and from the public as a whole. The Home Secretary is constantly dealing with personal cases and his principal duty is to hold a balance between the State and the individual. Either can greatly affect the reputation of a government, although in different ways. A Chancellor has relatively few decisions to make but the importance of each, and it is mostly considerable, is usually fairly obvious in advance. A Home Secretary has to take a multiplicity of small decisions, necessarily at considerable speed, if the work is to be got through.

Most of them are relatively easy, but lurking among the easy ones, like an inverted version of an occasional pearl in an oyster, is the rare exception, the case that can suddenly explode in face of himself and the Government. He must hope that a mixture of luck and instinct will enable him to spot them. Deportation cases, as Lord Brooke's experience showed, need particularly careful watching.

In some ways the Chancellor's job is the grander. He is usually, although by no means always, the higher in Cabinet precedence. He has No. 11 Downing Street, the annual set-piece occasion of the Budget, the prestige often regarded (by cartoonists, at least) as the second man in the government. But the Home Secretary, while less at the centre of affairs, has a more independent command, and the office is far more steeped in historical ceremonial. He has more appointments at his disposal. He signs more impressive looking documents. Although no longer present at Royal births, he still sees much more of the Sovereign. He is the senior Secretary of State.

The Chancellor by contrast is by tradition a clerk. He is even referred to in some documents as 'the Under Treasurer,' for he is not the nominal head of the Treasury. The First Lord is that, which is why so few appointments fall to be made by the Chancellor on his own authority. But there are some compensations in this work-a-day role. A Home Secretary is frequently expected to be in formal dress — to swear in a bishop, to call out the names of new knights, to attend the arrival of a foreign Head of State at Victoria Station. While these ceremonies continue a Chancellor often has to sit at the bedside of an ailing economy, but at least he is spared having to do so in a morning coat.

12 Two Imaginary Cabinet Meetings*

LORD GORDON-WALKER

I. An imaginary Cabinet Meeting of Foreign Affairs

[Note: This account is based in part on the three debates in Mr Harold Wilson's Cabinet in May 1967 (particularly the first one on May 23rd) concerning proposals to attempt to forestall the threatened outbreak of war between Israel and Egypt after the latter had closed the straits of Tiran:[1] and in part (particularly on pp. 231–4) on the debates in Attlee's Cabinet in 1951 on the Abadan crisis.[2] I myself used the argument in p. 233 attributed to the 'Minister of Libraries'. The remarks attributed to Ministers with proper official titles are in part — though not wholly — imaginary.]

Prime Minister: I have called this meeting at very short notice. You all know what it's about — the seizure of our uranium deposits and works by the government of Lorentia. I'm afraid there's been no time to prepare papers — things have just been happening too fast. I'll ask the Foreign Secretary to put the Cabinet in the picture.

Foreign Secretary: Prime Minister, we are faced with a grave and difficult situation. I have thought a great deal and very anxiously about the advice I should give my colleagues. But before coming to that — let me bring the Cabinet up to date about the latest situation. I was up to a very late hour last night reading the telegrams as they came in: I was woken up once by the Office in the middle of the night: I saw the latest telegrams this morning. So, Prime Minister, if my account isn't in the best logical order, I hope my colleagues will forgive me.

The latest situation is that the strike in Ariadne, where our works are, is still going on. I now have firm information,

---

*Reprinted from *The Cabinet* (London; Jonathan Cape, 1970), pp. 139–57 with the permission of the author and publisher.

from sources I don't want to mention, that this strike was fomented and organized by the new government of Lorentia—

Minister of Libraries: When did the strike start?

Foreign Secretary: About a week ago. Two days ago the government started riots among the strikers. Yesterday government officials came to the offices of British Uranium and told the managing director that the company had been sequestered by the government of Lorentia and that he must leave the office at once. He protested, but left when the officials threatened to bring in soldiers to arrest him. He went to our Consul who has been in constant touch with us ever since. He has kept his head and is doing a good job. We have found out through him that there are about eighty British subjects in the uranium field, including about fifteen women and the same number of children. In the town of Ariadne there are several hundred more. I have told the Consul to advise the women and children to make at once for Ariadne. The men, according to the Consul, don't want to leave and I haven't yet told him to give them any advice, pending this meeting of the Cabinet.

Minister of Investment: I'm sorry to interrupt, Prime Minister, but could the Foreign Secretary tell us if our people are safe in Ariadne itself?

Foreign Secretary: Yes, I should have mentioned that. I'm obliged. The answer is that they appear so far to be in no immediate danger. All British staff except the managing director are still in the works: but owing to the strike there's nothing they can do except do their best to keep safety precautions going. Quite a large number live together in the compound and these could hold out for a time if attacked. Others live scattered about the town. Nothing has happened to them yet. Is that what you wanted to know, Minister of Investment?

Beside the very great British interests directly involved, there are wider aspects of this crisis, Prime Minister, that cause me very great concern. Lorentia's neighbour, Alcidan, has always laid claim to the area to the west of Ariadne. The present instability of the government of Lorentia may tempt Alcidan to move into this area. Alcidan has recently been scared of an attack by Lorentia upon the small islands which command the straits of Ariadne. This would amount to a blockade of Alcidan. Our latest information is that, just because of its present nationalist fervour, Lorentia may be about to launch such a military operation. Alcidan may well strike first to forestall such an operation. The danger of hostilities is great. Both sides have made warlike noises and moved troops forward. That's the situation. It's a threatening one and if hostilities broke out, our interests would be further hit. Our trade with both these countries and with the whole area is very considerable.

My greatest fear is that the war would spread. Russia is pouring in arms. The war might reach a stage at which we couldn't keep out.

What should we do? We can't dodge a decision one way or the other. If we do nothing, that too is a decision: and it could lead to a spread of the war with the possible consequences I have described. If we act, we will protect British interests and keep the peace.

I've given long and anxious thought to this, Prime Minister, and I spoke to you about it this morning. I have come to the conclusion that we ought to send naval units to the Ariadne estuary. The Defence Secretary will be able to tell us about the logistics. I want as many marines on board as possible. We would be able to rescue British subjects at need: and we would be in a position to seize back our works. But most important of all, we would have ships between Lorentia and the islands. The only thing that can, in my judgement, prevent war is to give Alcidan a visible British guarantee against attack. The presence of British ships would be such a guarantee.

At the same time we should take steps at the UN to prevent an outbreak of hostilities between Alcidan and Lorentia. I would like my colleagues' authority to try and get a resolution through the Security Council and the General Assembly calling on both countries to keep the peace and sending an observer team to the area. If hostilities break out, we should get a resolution calling for a cease-fire. I should tell the Cabinet that I have alerted our Ambassadors and High Commissioners in countries represented in the United

Nations to go into action and urge the need for speedy and effective action in New York.

I am sorry to spring these vigorous proposals upon the Cabinet without preparation. I had to do so because we must quickly decide one way or the other. There are risks in my policy. I know that. You needn't tell me. But there are risks whatever we do. I beg any of my colleagues who may be reluctant to accept my suggestions to think what might happen if we do nothing. The habit of seizing British property might spread: British lives may be lost. If fighting starts between Alcidan and Lorentia, the war may spread in a very dangerous way that might draw us in. We would suffer heavy economic loss — much worse than the seizure of our works in Ariadne. I for one am not prepared to run *those* risks.

Prime Minister: Secretary of State for Defence, could you tell us about the military aspect of the Foreign Secretary's proposals?

Defence Secretary: Yes, Prime Minister. I consulted the Chiefs of Staff immediately after our talk with the Foreign Secretary this morning. We have sufficient naval forces in or near the area. We could get some ships there in twenty-four hours. We have not enough marines within reach: but we could embark a couple of infantry battalions at Port Pontino. That is why it would take us three days to get effective forces to Ariadne. That's what you might call the pure logistics — but I'm afraid there's more in it than that. We couldn't send large ships close inshore: they would be sitting ducks in these narrow waters to shore batteries, torpedoes and aircraft. We could send in small ships: but what would happen if they were fired on? They could probably look after themselves: but we couldn't reinforce them. All they could do would be to return fire and withdraw. A shipborne military operation in well-guarded narrow waters is a nonsense. I can see the logic of the Foreign Secretary's policy but there's no way of giving naval teeth to it.

Foreign Secretary: But, Secretary of State for Defence, why have you so suddenly changed your mind? I didn't think *you* were a wobbler. Only this morning you agreed with me and the Prime Minister — if anything you rather pushed me along.

Defence Secretary: Prime Minister, I would like to support the Foreign Secretary. I want the same things as he does. But after our meeting I consulted my expert advisers and have come to the conclusion that what seemed politically attractive this morning is in fact militarily unattainable. That's all there is to it.

Prime Minister: Chancellor of the Exchequer, what about the financial and economic aspects?

Chancellor of the Exchequer: Well, Prime Minister, this has come rather suddenly upon me. I don't know as much as the Foreign Secretary and the Secretary of State for Defence seem to. But I am pretty clear in my own mind about the economic issues involved. It is true that the outbreak of fighting in the area, and even more its spread, would have an adverse effect on our balance of trade — though it would check imports as well as exports. Much the worst consequence would be the need to pay hard currency for the uranium that we wouldn't be getting from Lorentia. That is one thing we must look into right away — how far we can economize and where we can get alternative supplies from. On the other hand the course you and the Foreign Secretary propose, Prime Minister, would cost us a great deal of money and lead to higher taxation: but—

Minister of Investment: I am sick and tired of the Chancellor's constant veto on everything we should do. I think we must stand by—

Chancellor of the Exchequer: Prime Minister, I had not finished. In a matter of this gravity each of us ought to be allowed to speak without interruption.

Prime Minister: Go on, Chancellor. There will be time for everyone to speak.

Chancellor of the Exchequer: I was actually in the middle of a sentence. I was about to say that far graver than the budgetary cost would be the effect upon the pound. A disturbance of this kind in which we ourselves got involved could lead to a run on the pound. The outbreak of fighting would itself be bad enough: but if you add to this the upset of the international market, increased overseas expenditure and our need to raise taxes — well, the Foreign Secretary's proposals would involve us in an immediate economic crisis that would be worse than the effects of losing the uranium for a time.

Prime Minister: Minister of Investment.

Minister of Investment: I apologize to the Chancellor for interrupting him and getting a bit heated. But, Prime Minister, I feel very strongly on this issue. At the bottom of all the complications is a very simple principle. We can talk till we're blue in the face about dubious and doubtful economic consequences, but there are times when principles must come first. The fact is that Alcidan is a progressive, democratic state. It has many friends in this country, especially in the Churches. We ought to stand by it and make clear to Lorentia that we won't stand any nonsense. I am not sure about all the objectives of the Foreign Secretary's proposals: some of them seem problematical to me. But on the main point I'm with him. We ought to send the Navy in and prevent Lorentia from attacking Alcidan.

Minister with Portfolio: }
Minister for the Isles: } (together) — Prime Minister.

Prime Minister: I want next to call the Minister of Nuclear Energy. What will be the effect of cutting off our supplies of uranium?

Minister of Nuclear Energy: Prime Minister, I have begun to go into this question with my Office. I'm afraid we haven't got far yet, as the whole thing is rather complex. We don't yet know how much uranium is en route: nor how much is already processed at Ariadne, which we might still get out. It is not uranium as such that matters in the short run. It's the plutonium that counts. It may be that we can economize here and eke out our supplies for quite a while. If the crisis goes on, we'll certainly have to pay dollars to keep up necessary supplies: but we may be able to scrape up a certain amount from other sources. That's all I have been able to find out in the short time at my disposal. I have set up a high-powered working party to go into the whole thing. I agree with the Chancellor that we must find out as quickly as possible where we stand. One thing that we ought to do at

once is approach all governments concerned to see that they
don't buy uranium that belongs to us.

Prime Minister: Minister with Portfolio.

Minister with Portfolio: Prime Minister, I don't see how
we can follow the simple line suggested by the Minister of
Investment. We have been told that either of these countries
may attack the other, we don't know which. They're on a
par. A progressive state can be an aggressive state. The
principle that matters is that aggression must be condemned
whether or not it is committed by a state that we — or some
of our people and some members of the Cabinet — happen to
like. We should not take sides. But I go further than that,
Prime Minister. Fighting may indeed break out in this area,
but why should we get involved? We have no duties or
obligations here — all these countries are now independent.
Why should we take enormous economic risks for something
that doesn't concern us more than anyone else? We might
well be involved in military risks, too. Once marines or
troops are landed, we may have to send in more forces to
extricate them. We may be in up to the neck before we are
finished.

Foreign Secretary: Could I come in again, Prime Minister,
just for a moment? The Minister with Portfolio thinks we
should keep out. I frankly don't like his rather weak and
neutralist line. But the real question is — can we keep out? If
we intervene to protect British interests and lives and to
prevent the spread of war we would certainly be involved in
the way the Minister with Portfolio objects to. But say we
follow his policy and do nothing, fold our hands, keep
safe — and then fighting breaks out and spreads, we are also
involved in another way. A spread of the war might bring in
the Super Powers at least indirectly and it would be difficult
for us to keep out. We have allies and friends amongst these
independent states and we could not simply let them down.
Moreover, Chancellor, a war that was extended in time and
space would have far more costly effects for us than the
preventive action I propose.

Prime Minister: Minister for the Isles.

Minister for the Isles: I think there is a lot of force in
what the Foreign Secretary says. My sympathies are with

Alcidan. It is in danger of being attacked. If it were provoked into forestalling action, that would not be aggression, but self-defence. We should do all we can to nip aggression by Lorentia in the bud. As the Foreign Secretary has convincingly argued, this would also be in our national interest.

Prime Minister: The Cabinet is clearly very evenly divided. I would like to tell my colleagues my own views. I support the Foreign Secretary. I appreciate what the Secretary of State for Defence has said and we must take his warnings into account. But I believe we could bring our influence to bear on Lorentia without undue risk. They are a shaky government, unsure of themselves. They would hesitate to fire on our ships and bring even more trouble upon themselves. Over and above that we will run great political risks if we do not do all we can to protect and rescue British subjects. Another factor weighs heavily with me that has not yet been mentioned. We may be facing a spread of war that would enable Russia to enter this area. America is reluctant to get directly involved — but it would strongly back action by us along the lines suggested by the Foreign Secretary. That is the view of our Ambassador and my own conclusion. We have not had very good relations with America lately. Here we could at one and the same time serve our own interests, get on good terms with the United States and help to keep world peace. I would not consider the American angle if there were not also direct British interests: but is is an extra factor of considerable importance.

I must confess that I am worried about reactions amongst our own people if we do nothing. We have to take some risks for the sake of the great issues at stake. Britain must sometimes stand up. This is a time for stout hearts. I strongly support the Foreign Secretary.

Defence Secretary: Prime Minister, to go back to what you said about Lorentia not opening fire on our ships — I did what I was asked to. I examined a particular proposal for action. In my considered view, the military risks are too great to run. I repeat, the Foreign Secretary's proposals would make no military sense. We might assemble a naval force some way off, to bring pressure to bear: but to go into narrow waters in the hope that a wild and inexperienced government, which has already seized our works, would not open fire — this would expose us to risks against which we could not retaliate.

Prime Minister: Yes, I understood your point. I said we must fully take it into account. Chancellor of the Exchequer.

Chancellor of the Exchequer: I don't want to add anything to what I said about the economic and financial aspects. Nothing that has been said has shaken me in my views. On the more general issue I must protest against the tone of some of the remarks made about those of us who do not agree with you and the Foreign Secretary. The Foreign Secretary described us as neutralists. And you, Prime Minister, said that we need stout hearts — implying that those who take a different view are cowards.

Prime Minister: I certainly implied no such thing, Chancellor.

Chancellor of the Exchequer: I'm glad to hear that, Prime Minister. I cast no doubts on the sincerity of anyone who takes a different view from me. I hope my sincerity will be equally acknowledged.

The Foreign Secretary said that there might be a spread of the war and that this might well involve us in still heavier economic cost. Well, Foreign Secretary, like you I have to balance risks. I prefer to be cautious in the beginning — as far as I can see with clarity. I know what the immediate costs of the proposed operation would be. I don't believe the risks of a spread of the war are considerable. Who would want to spread the war? It might spread amongst some of the neighbours of Lorentia and Alcidan — though I don't for the life of me see why. But even if the war spread that far, it wouldn't be a general war. America and Russia might give arms and other aid: but they are not going to risk a direct confrontation.

I have listened very carefully to what you and the Foreign Secretary said — but I think you are both overlooking stubborn facts. We simply have not the resources for that sort of thing. Our first duty is to consider our own national interests. I can't see what national interest compels us to intervene militarily. It certainly wouldn't get us any uranium. Even if you seize and hold the works you can't compel the

Lorentians to work. Even if you put in pioneers and kept the works going, you couldn't get uranium from the field: you can't dig uranium with bayonets. Of course the loss of uranium is going to be awkward: but sooner or later Lorentia will have to sell us the uranium again. It's valueless to them without a market: they can't eat uranium. As the Minister of Nuclear Energy said, we must take immediate steps to stop foreign governments or companies buying our uranium. We must then threaten to bring action in the International Court to protect our interests. If America is so keen for us to help them, Prime Minister, we should ask them to join us in keeping other purchasers out, themselves included.

Prime Minister: Minister of Libraries.

Minister of Libraries: Prime Minister, this is perhaps the most serious issue this Cabinet has yet had to face. I agree with the Chancellor of the Exchequer. I think it would be madness to proceed as suggested by the Foreign Secretary. We simply are not concerned. We can no longer take on ourselves an obligation to keep peace everywhere in the world — even in areas where we once had authority. The Foreign Secretary and those who agree with him greatly exaggerate our effectiveness. The Foreign Secretary said that Alcidan wants a guarantee against attack, but it is not *our* guarantee that would satisfy her, only an American guarantee. We must—

Prime Minister: But America won't act and wants us to.

Minister of Libraries: That may well be so, Prime Minister. But that doesn't mean that a guarantee by us would be effective. If America won't or can't act, that clearly means that no military action of any kind is possible and we must think of other means — such as those proposed by the Chancellor. Oh, there was a point I was about to make when you interrupted me, Prime Minister. We must not overlook that if we took military action we would in many countries and almost certainly in the UN be branded as an agressor. We might possibly take the military initiative but would be on the political defensive. The arguments of the Chancellor and the Defence Secretary are very powerful. I think the Foreign Secretary should give his mind to the diplomatic possibilities open to us. I wholeheartedly welcome his proposals about activating the UN.

Prime Minister: Commonwealth Secretary.

Commonwealth Secretary: I agree on the whole with the Minister of Libraries: indeed his main argument seems to me unanswerable. But I'm not sure about the proposal that we should by ourselves try to activate the United Nations. We are, or appear to be, an interested country. We are always liable to attack for neo-colonialism. We should try to get other nations to take the initiative: we might join in as one of a number of sponsors. We must, too, be careful in which countries we set our Ambassadors to work. Over-eagerness can blow back on us. The final vote could be pretty close. We want every vote that can possibly be got.

Prime Minister: Minister for the Isles.

Minister for the Isles: Prime Minister, I am totally opposed to what the Minister of Libraries said. This is no time for pacifist talk. You can always find reasons for not doing something. We still have some power and influence in the world. Power and influence are there to be used on proper occasions. This is a proper occasion if there ever was one. That other nations want to keep out is all the more reason why we should not. The logical conclusion of the argument of the Minister of Libraries is that we shouldn't keep any forces at all: that's what follows from his argument that we can't effectively use even a show of force in a relatively minor operation. If you can't use your forces, get rid of them — that's what the Minister of Libraries *should* say.

Foreign Secretary: Can I come in here again, Prime Minister? I am glad the Minister for the Isles has spoken as he has. It needed saying. The Minister of Libraries has taken a simply defeatist line. Some of my colleagues don't seem able to get it into their heads that it is peace not war that I want. If we don't damp down the fires, there may be a spread of war that would involve us in much worse and — Chancellor — more expensive dangers. I will try and not interrupt too much, Prime Minister — but I feel strongly about this. Some of the things that have been said I deeply resent. They totally misrepresent my policy.

Prime Minister: Don't apologize, Foreign Secretary. I haven't liked all I have heard this morning. Secretary of State for Defence.

Defence Secretary: I haven't yet spoken on the merits or rather the demerits of the Foreign Secretary's proposals. Let me say in a word that I agree with the Minister of Libraries that, since we cannot bring effective force to bear, we should not try to.

(Four or five Ministers speak briefly. All but one — who says,

'We can't leave Alcidan in the lurch' — are against military action.)

Prime Minister: Before we come to a conclusion we must consider more closely the safety of our people in Lorentia. One of the main objects of the Foreign Secretary was to put us in a position to rescue our people if necessary. Who would like to speak on this point? Minister of Investment.

Minister of Investment: I'm glad you've brought us back to this point, Prime Minister. To my mind it is one of the most important of all. If we stand by and do nothing and then British people are killed there will be a public outcry against us and quite right too. If it is found that we can't do anything even after their danger becomes clear, I wouldn't give much for our chances for survival.

Prime Minister: Minister with Portfolio.

Minister with Portfolio: We've got to keep a sense of proportion. What is military nonsense for one purpose is still military nonsense for another: it's not the objective, but the nature of the operation that matters. If we can't move, we can't move. We would be just as much exposed to political attacks on us for aggression. It would be said that little countries can't rescue their people when in danger in another country: only big countries can do this against little countries.

Chancellor of the Exchequer: I have spoken strongly against the Foreign Secretary's proposals. But if the issue is limited to the rescue of British subjects, that's a different matter. There's a strong tradition in this country that if it is at all possible to rescue British subjects we should do so. In spite of what the Minister with Portfolio said, an operation limited to this purpose would, I believe, be understood in the world. Indeed, if we did nothing, we would be condemned.

Defence Secretary: I think, Prime Minister, the best thing we could do would be to keep some ships some way off but near enough and in sufficient strength to show that we could act if we were forced to. It would still be dangerous to send ships close inshore. But if one or two ships went in alone with the sole object of getting our people out, I think we could probably get away with it. That would be something openly and palpably different from a military operation. We could allow it to be known that our ships were in the vicinity for this purpose and none other.

Minister with Portfolio: We must be careful, Prime Minister. We might provoke the very thing we are trying to avoid. Lorentia might be provoked by a show of force into attacking our people.

Prime Minister: Minister of Libraries.

Minister of Libraries: Prime Minister, I too spoke very strongly against the Foreign Secretary's proposals as a whole. I feel equally strongly that the part of the Foreign Secretary's policy that relates to the rescue of our people is right. I don't think there is as much risk as the Minister with Portfolio says: even if there is, we must run it. The risk may not be that the government of Lorentia will be provoked into attacking British subjects but that it won't be capable of protecting them against public riots and looting. If we make it clear that we are sending ships in and landing men solely to rescue British subjects in imminent danger and are going to withdraw at once — then, as the Chancellor said, our action will be understood. But we must make it clear that our action is limited in this way. I suggest there are two particular steps that we should take. First, make strong and public representations to the government of Lorentia about the safety of our people and say that we will hold it responsible for anything that happens. Secondly, we should concentrate all British subjects in the compound so that we can reach and rescue them quickly.

(Several Ministers say briefly that they agree.)

Prime Minister: Well, there is a clear preponderance of view in the Cabinet against a military operation. But we are agreed that we must rescue British subjects if they are in danger. This would involve, if necessary, landing men from ships to get our people out and on board. I want the Cabinet to be quite clear about this, as we might have to act at a moment's notice before the Cabinet can be recalled. We will not openly initiate action in the UN: but will associate ourselves with any resolution about keeping the peace or accepting a cease-fire. We will, with discretion, approach some friendly governments.

We must urgently approach all countries that have uranium companies to get them to agree not to buy Lorentian uranium so long as our property has been taken without compensation. Lord Chancellor, would you look into the legal position in international law with the Law Officers and the Minister of Nuclear Energy?

Lord Chancellor: Certainly, Prime Minister.

Foreign Secretary: Have you finished, Prime Minister? Well, I'd like to say this — I agree about the proposals for action in regard to the United Nations. They're too cautious, but it doesn't much matter which way we proceed.

But, Prime Minister, I totally disagree with what you said about no military operation. I am frankly disgusted by the way this discussion has gone. I've never seen such a lack of guts.

Prime Minister: You know I have a good deal of sympathy with your general proposals, Foreign Secretary. But the preponderant view of the Cabinet is clear. We won't get any further by going on any longer.

Chancellor of the Exchequer: Could I suggest, Prime Minister, that you set up a working party to go into the effects of the seizure of our works upon our balance of payments. To do this we need to know how much uranium we can still get out, how long Lorentia can hold out and so forth. I think you should send out an emissary to see things on the spot and report back. To the Foreign Secretary let me say that it needs just as much guts in a situation like this to say No as to say Yes.

Prime Minister: I think those are good proposals, Chancellor of the Exchequer. Is the Cabinet agreed with my summing up and the additional points made by the Chancellor?

(Silence, with a few muttered 'Agreeds'.)

Very well. Could you have a word with me, Foreign Secretary, about whom we might send out?

II An Imaginary Cabinet Meeting on Home Affairs

Prime Minister: The next item concerns proposals arising out of the Stockington Report. Welfare Minister and Minister of Communications to come in.

(The Assistant Secretary of the Cabinet opens the door. Both Ministers come in, red boxes in hand. The Welfare Minister finds a vacant seat by the Deputy Secretary to the Cabinet: the Minister of Communications sits on a chair against the wall, which he half draws up to the table.)

Prime Minister: Sorry to have kept you both waiting rather long. We have before us a report of the committee I set up under the chairmanship of the President-General. I will ask you to open, President-General, and the Minister of Welfare to follow.

President-General: Prime Minister, I don't know that I can add much to the paper I have circulated. The proposals of the Welfare Minister consist of three main points. First, that there should be a tax on sweets: secondly, that the advertising of sweets on TV should be forbidden and should be restricted in other media: and, thirdly, that free toothbrushes should be issued to children under eleven in the schools — one free brush a year.

As I say in my report, opinion on the committee was very evenly divided. I'm afraid I wasn't able, Prime Minister, to get any acceptable compromise. You've got to accept or reject at any rate proposals one and three — they hold together. You could leave out the proposal on advertising without wrecking the scheme — but it has strong advocates. In the annexe to my report I set out in some detail the technical problems that would be involved by the adoption of the three proposals: none of these would be insoluble. My own view, Prime Minister, tends to favour the proposal. It is a neat one. The revenue from a tax on sweets could be so adjusted that it exactly paid for the cost of the free toothbrushes. This proposal would in a sense cost nothing. The Welfare Minister will speak about the effect on children's health. There is of course also a political angle — I'm inclined to think the proposals would be popular. Certainly the Opposition wouldn't be able to attack them except in detail — because they like this sort of thing. Some of our own fellows will object — most of them, probably, would be opposed in their hearts — but we're getting near enough to an election — whatever date, Prime Minister, you choose — to make attractive any proposal likely to be popular in the country. So, on balance, I support the proposals.

Prime Minister: Minister of Welfare.

Welfare Minister: Prime Minister, I urge these proposals as strongly as I can on my colleagues. I am grateful to the President-General for the way in which he has introduced the papers — but one thing he said I disagree with. The prohibition of TV advertising and the restriction on other forms of advertising is essential. After all we are not really concerned with elections, but with the health of our children. This whole thing started with the Stockington Report which showed conclusively the deleterious effect of an excessive sugar-intake on children's teeth and on their health. Those with good teeth grow better, suffer less from illness and even seem to be more intelligent. My three proposals are interlocking and self-balancing. As the President-General has pointed out, the Treasury won't have to pay a penny. If we don't restrict the advertisement of sweets, we might as well drop the whole thing. The sweet manufacturers would simply be undoing the whole point of free toothbrushes. Clearly we can't stop children eating sweets — indeed the Stockington Report shows that, up to a point, this does no harm. It's a sugar-intake over a certain level that causes all the damage. Manufacturers want to get children to eat sugar over the danger level — that's what they're in business for, whatever they may be saying. We want to keep children's teeth safe. Where a private interest is in conflict with a clear public interest it must give way.

Regarding the free toothbrushes, Prime Minister, I know the argument that the Education Secretary is going to use — but there's no alternative to a distribution through teachers in schools. Any arrangement for mothers to get free toothbrushes for their children would be excessively complicated and expensive and, over and above that, full of loopholes for abuse. If it can't be done through the schools, it can't be done at all: and that would be a disaster. The

Stockington Report has been very well received in all informed quarters and I have for some time been under pressure in the House to carry it into effect. I don't think I can stall much longer.

I beg my colleagues to agree to a policy that will cost nothing and which will do real good. The policy can be properly administered, as is made clear in the annexe to the paper before us, which was prepared by officials of all the departments concerned.

Prime Minister: Secretary of State for Education, you are much concerned in this.

Secretary of State for Education: Yes, Prime Minister, I am. The simple fact is that we cannot put any more chores on the teachers. They are already overloaded. They object to being treated as free labour, doing one service after another for the State, which it ought to pay for itself. The teachers are discontented about their salaries. If we put this extra task upon them we can expect them to press for an earlier increase than the one we must in the normal course expect towards the beginning of next year. Probably they would simply refuse to co-operate. I cannot agree, Prime Minister, to bringing the teachers into this. If the Welfare Minister wants his scheme, he must find another way of carrying it out.

Prime Minister: Chancellor, what have you to say about the fiscal aspect of these proposals?

Chancellor of the Exchequer: Well, Prime Minister, let me first deal with the Welfare Minister's point that his proposals would cost nothing. It is true that the proposed tax on sweets could be made to equal the cost of the free toothbrushes. But the free toothbrushes will cost just the same amount, however financed. From the taxpayers' point of view they will be paid for out of extra taxation.

Moreover, Prime Minister, I could never agree to the ear-marking of a tax for a specific expenditure. That is against all our traditions and would be a most dangerous precedent.

Finally, we have before us a proposal to levy a tax. I cannot, as Chancellor of the Exchequer, agree to consider tax proposals apart from my budget. When the time comes I will have to consider my proposals, if any, for tax changes in the light of the general economic situation and of public expenditure as a whole. I can't deal with this proposal in isolation and at this time of the year. I must oppose the proposal.

Minister with Portfolio: But, Chancellor, this is not a tax in the ordinary sense. Its purpose is to deter an activity that undermines the health of our children.

Chancellor of the Exchequer: Prime Minister, whatever its purpose, it is a tax and therefore falls within my prerogatives as Chancellor.

Minister with Portfolio: Can I go on, Prime Minister?

(Prime Minister nods.)

The Minister of Welfare's proposal is one of very great social importance. There can be no doubt about the good effect it would have on the health of our children: indeed of a whole generation as the children grow up. If we do nothing, we are making ourselves a party to keeping our children less healthy than they could be. I hope the Chancellor will in these special circumstances reconsider his rather doctrinaire stand. What he says about taxes and budgets may have been all right in Gladstone's time: but we live in different circumstances today.

Prime Minister: Minister for the Isle of Wight.

Minister for the Isle of Wight: I oppose on principle the Chancellor's line. It's time that the Cabinet had the right to discuss, at any rate in broad outline, taxes that the Chancellor might impose or alter. The present method by which the Chancellor tells us of his proposals all together a day or two before the budget deprives the Cabinet of its proper rights: it just sets it aside.

Prime Minister: That's taking us rather far afield. We could perhaps discuss that on another occasion. Let's keep to the issues before us, which are big enough.

Minister for the Isle of Wight: Well, Prime Minister, on the issue immediately before us, I would like to say this. This government badly needs some measure of social progress. It's this kind of thing that really interests people. And very many people would be interested — not only doctors and nutrition experts but mothers—

(The Education Secretary throws a folded note across the table to the Minister of Investment. 'Dear Bill, Please come in and say a word against this barmy proposal — Christopher.' The Minister of Investment reads the note and nods his head.)

and fathers. Even if teachers don't want to take part, they want healthier children to teach. By the way, although I must defer to the Education Secretary in his own field, don't forget that there was an eminent teacher on the Stockington Commission and I have read letters in the papers from teachers backing the Stockington Report.

Secretary of State for Education: I can assure you the teachers as a body won't stand for it.

Prime Minister: Minister of Communications.

Minister of Communications: Prime Minister, I am sure we'll be in terrible trouble with the television companies if we put a discriminatory restriction upon them. And I must say I think they would be right. Why should we pick on them?

Welfare Minister: That's not true. One of the proposals is to restrict advertising on other media.

Minister of Communications: First of all, there's a distinction between *banning* advertisements on TV and *restricting* them on other media. Secondly, there will be no restriction on other media because we don't want the whole press against us; besides, it would probably push some papers out of circulation. No: in effect the proposal is to pick on television and I think that is wrong.

Prime Minister: Minister of Investment.

Minister of Investment: I'd like to make two brief points, Prime Minister. First, what does the Minister of Welfare mean when he says he's under parliamentary pressure? It's just a bunch of cranks and interested members who ask questions, quite a lot of them from the other side of the House. We are all under this sort of pressure and we stand up to it. That's one of the things we, including the Welfare Minister, are paid for. The second point is this; we must be careful about pushing people about. I agree there with the Minister of Communications. Who are we to stop people seeing certain sorts of advertisements on TV or on the hoardings? If we restrict newpaper advertising we will put some papers into still greater danger. And if people want to eat sweets or want their children to, why on earth should we stop them? We don't want to be a government of kill-joys. And one other thing — I just don't believe you can stop children eating sweets. To try to is against nature.

Chancellor of the Exchequer: Can I come in again, Prime Minister, with just one word. I agree with what has just been said. We must not unnecessarily interfere with people's lives. Let me briefly repeat that I cannot agree to a tax being decided upon in isolation.

Prime Minister: We are getting near one o'clock. I have to see the Ambassador of Neutria then. Can we come to a conclusion?

I think the view of the Cabinet is quite clear. The proposal to stop TV advertising is an issue separate from the other two. The general view is that we should drop this proposal.

I agree with the Chancellor that we cannot decide upon a tax before he has considered his budget as a whole: though the discussion we have had has done no harm. We can look at this again when the Chancellor brings his budget proposals before us. If he finds it right to impose a tax on sweets, we can consider the whole matter again. The scheme could, if we wished, be introduced in the next Session. Meanwhile, Minister of Welfare, you will have to resist pressure in the House.

Clearly we cannot impose this extra burden on the teachers. So if the scheme for free toothbrushes is to work, a new way of administering it must be found.

What I propose is that the matter goes back to the committee. Officials can try and work out an alternative method of administration to be considered by the committee. But the whole thing must depend upon the Chancellor's proposals.

It is vitally important that strict confidence is kept over all this. It would do great harm if it got out that we had been considering such far-reaching proposals. It would make it harder for us to agree on anything if there were leaks. And it would be extremely embarrassing if we decided in the end to do nothing.

Any comments?

Well, then, that finishes the agenda.

Notes

1. Lord George-Brown, *In May Way* (London: Gollancz, 1971) pp. 136–7, 223; Harold Wilson, *The Labour Government, 1964–70* (London: Weidenfeld & Nicolson and Michael Joseph, 1971) pp. 396–7, 401.
2. Herbert Morrison, *An Autobiography* (London: Odhams, 1960) pp. 271–2.

13 Cabinet Reform Since 1914: Major Trends*

HANS DAALDER

Since 1914, the place of the Cabinet in the British political system has not fundamentally changed. The Cabinet is now, as it was then, a committee of leading parliamentarians who, with the general support of the majority party in the House of Commons, in permanent debate with the Opposition, responsible to King and Parliament, and constantly in the public eye, take or approve the main political decisions – in the process reacting to impulses from the civil service and from social forces outside the immediate government institutions.

But changes in the scope of government have resulted in definite shifts within these terms. Sometimes these shifts implied only slight changes in atmosphere; at other times they brought considerable modification in structure and operation. Even a hasty perusal of the preceding chapters makes one conclusion inescapable: these changes cannot be regarded as an unequivocal adjustment of the organization of British central government to changed administrative duties. New tasks did require special administrative arrangements. But personal factors and existing departmental divisions and loyalties threw up serious obstacles;[1] new administrative organs, or sections, often encountered suspicion; and political considerations demanded their toll. In many cases only the emergencies of war could break down irrational opposition.[2] But wartime, in turn, introduced numerous administrative improvisations. The administrative machinery was complicated with new departments, which mortgaged corporate loyalties just as heavily as did older departments.

It is nevertheless possible a posteriori to distinguish certain

*Reprinted from Hans Daalder, *Cabinet Reform in Britain, 1914–63* (Stanford, California: Stanford University Press, 1964) pp. 241–65, with the permission of the author and publisher

trends in the development of British central government over the last fifty years. These may be conveniently grouped into six categories: the effects of the increase of government tasks on the existing interdepartmental structure; attempts to improve coordination between departments; further differentiation in the ministerial hierarchy; changes in the relation between ministers and civil servants; the increasing involvement of experts and scientific advisers in central government; and changes in relation between ministers and Parliament.

The effects of the heavier burden of government on the existing interdepartmental structure

Since 1914, the burdens on the central government machinery have vastly increased. This is evident even from the sheer quantitative angle. The number of civil servants employed in the service of the central government — excluding the personnel of the armed forces and the nationalized industries — increased fourfold, from a little more than a quarter million in 1914, to about a million forty years later.[3] At same time public expenditure rose considerably. Supply expenditure, which was only 6 per cent of the gross national product in 1910 and 12 per cent in 1930, had risen to 22 per cent by 1960; total public expenditure of all kinds, including that of local authorities, national insurance funds, and the capital expenditure of the nationalized industries, now represents about 42 per cent of the gross national product.[4] The size of the higher civil service increased even more: the administrative class grew from less than 500 in 1914 to about 3,500 in 1955. The number of Treasury personnel grew almost ten times, from about 140 in 1914 to about 1,300 in 1955, while over the same period the size of the Foreign Office increased thirty times, from 190 in 1914, to 5,710 in 1955.[5]

But changes cannot be measured in quantative terms alone. Since 1914, goverment business has become more complicated and interrelated. The borderline between the public sphere of government and the private one of the individual and society has increasingly disappeared as government policies and popular demands in close interaction have resulted in increasing State intervention. The civil sevice has moved out of the restricted environment of Whitehall, as service functions have come to be added to regulatory ones. International factors too have complicated even national decision-making processes.[6]

The ensuing change in the tasks of government had various consequences for the interdepartmental structure.

Individual ministers and existing departments were burdened more heavily. This was more true for some ministers than for others. While some departments saw their powers increase rapidly, others grew only slowly. Not every new government task brought an equal addition to the task of the minister and his highest administrative advisers. Some departments managed to absorb new functions more easily than others.[7] But the accumulation of tasks became in certain instances so heavy that some duties had to be relinquished at all costs.

New departments were instituted. The reason for their establishment might vary. Sometimes a new department became necessary because of a sudden expansion of government authority over a new field. But more usually, new departments had their basis in government functions that already existed. If so, the *raison d'être* for a departmental split-up might be the political interest that a specific field of government suddenly acquired in the constant tussle between the Government and the Opposition. Or a new department might be the result of a desire of a heavily burdened ministry or department to surrender some of its powers to others. Or a particular range of tasks that had hitherto been dispersed over various departments might be concentrated into one department, for efficiency's sake. Whatever the specific cause, the number of government departments increased considerably. This had immediate consequences for the size of the Cabinet.

There was constant pressure to enlarge the Cabinet. This force was at work even before 1914. Ministers at the head of new departments have never gladly suffered exclusion from the Cabinet. The Cabinet increased from 12 to 14 members around 1875 to 23 in 1915. It changed again from 16 members in 1922 to 23 in 1939, and from 16 in 1946 to 21 in 1962. Many politicians have judged this inflation of the Cabinet to be detrimental to the value of Cabinet discussion. 'Six are fully as many as can usefully converse on any subject,' an experienced Lord Chancellor sighed more than a hundred years ago.[8] A council of some twenty members tends to degenerate into a public meeting. Factions may form, and considerations of prestige may block agreement. Parkinson has thought it possible to fix 'the coefficient of inefficiency' between 19 and 22.[9] So, apparently, thought the designers of the Cabinet room, in 10, Downing Street, which can hardly hold more than 22. Prime Ministers have usually found it desirable but difficult to keep the number of Cabinet members below that limit. This, in turn, had two further consequences:

The principle that every minister at the head of an important administrative department has a claim on Cabinet membership was perforce abandoned. Even in the nineteenth-century Cabinets this principle had not always been respected. Before 1914, however, those who were not admitted to the Cabinet usually occupied offices that were not really comparable to a large department of government. Ever since the War Cabinet of Lloyd George, however, heads of important departments have been excluded from the Cabinet. Conversely, the removal of the direct link between the Cabinet and individual departments has removed a brake on the further increase in autonomous departmental units. Non-Cabinet ministers have usually had all the formal trappings of their more fortunate Cabinet colleagues. They have 'Cabinet rank.'[10] They receive the same salary. They are made Privy Councillors. They are sent the most important Cabinet papers and are invited to attend parts of Cabinet sessions. But they have remained outside the Cabinet as such. Whatever the arguments in favour of this situation, few have found it really satifactory in practice. Hence:

It was also consciously attempted to decrease again the number of independent departments. This number rose particularly rapidly during the two world wars, when the government assumed many new tasks and when the insitution of the War Cabinet had removed the normal link between the

Cabinet and the departments. The re-establishment of the traditional Cabinet was generally accompanied, on the other hand, by the deliberate dissolution of various new departmental units. Since 1951, attempts have also been made to decrease the number of departments in charge of ordinary civilian tasks by amalgamating them with other departments. Some of the traditional ties between the Cabinet and the departments have thus been restored.

Attempts to improve coordination between departments

As government tasks became more interdependent, new instruments of coordination became vital.

The increased pressure of business made it necessary to hold more formal Cabinet meetings. The number of Cabinet sessions per year rose from about forty before 1914, to about sixty after 1918, to an average of eighty-nine between 1946 and 1957.[11] There is, however, an absolute limit to the time and thought that ministers can give to Cabinet business. It was therefore necessary to resort to other expedients if business was not to become clogged at Cabinet level.

Cabinet procedure was further formalized.[12] This was true of both the preparation and the execution of Cabinet decisions. The Cabinet Secretariat was charged with keeping off the Cabinet agenda all business that was not absolutely essential. The agenda itself acquired greater importance. New rules were adopted for the composition and the timely circulation of Cabinet memoranda to all departments concerned, before certain problems could be raised in the Cabinet. Officials were instructed to solve interdepartmental controversies on the lowest possible hierarchical level. Issues were to be brought to the Cabinet only when all other means of settling them had been exhausted, and when the points of contention had been so well defined that the alternatives were clear. Cabinet minutes came to stay. The Cabinet Secretariat introduced a detailed register of business that was still under consideration, as well as an index of decisions taken. It was charged to notify all departments concerned of Cabinet decisions, and, if necessary, to draw attention to omissions in execution. 'Much Cabinet business is now almost formal,' two British authors wrote recently.[13]

At the same time it was tried to lighten the Cabinet's burden by introducing an extensive system of Cabinet committees. Cabinet committees were known in the eighteenth and nineteenth centuries, but at that time they were usually nothing but an expedient for settling specific problems. Only the CID introduced a *system* of permanent committees, which like the parent committee, were initially not technically Cabinet committees. When Lloyd George severed the Cabinet from the departments, the Government attempted to bridge the threatening gap by holding special Cabinet sessions, establishing the Cabinet Secretariat, and introducing Cabinet committees. Lloyd George's rather chaotic methods did little to rationalize the system. Nor did his successors do much in this direction. Between 1919 and 1939 there existed many committees, but hardly a committee system. Only the War Cabinet of the Second World War and the Labour Government consciously built a pyramid of committees that were to facilitate decision-making below Cabinet level. Depending on the temperament of successive Prime Ministers, such a committee system has since been more or less formal, and more or less extensive. But under all of them the number of committees has been considerable. An inquiry in the early 1950s revealed the existence of at least 700 interdepartmental committees, of which more than 100 were technically Cabinet committees.[14]

The complexity of the committee system has created a new coordination problem. When numerous conflicts of confidence flared up in 1950, during a period of active rearmament and great economic stress, a special Coordinating Section was instituted within the Cabinet Secretariat. It was charged

to follow the work of the many committees dealing with defense and economic questions and to ensure that there is no duplication; in cases of doubt to suggest which particular committee should consider a particular question; and generally to see that the new problems emerging are dealt with smoothly and efficiently.[15]

This formal Coordinating Section has since disappeared. But even now it is the task of the Cabinet Secretariat not only to service but also (if at all possible) to kill committees — provided the Prime Minister and ministers concerned consent.

The existence of Cabinet committees has made it possible to reduce the time normally spent on Cabinet sessions to two sessions of two hours each per week. But for some ministers, notably the Chancellor of the Exchequer, the great number of Cabinet committees has posed an extra burden. This is one reason why an attempt has been made to reduce their number by charging individual ministers rather than committees with special coordinating tasks.

Special coordinating ministers were appointed. These ministers were charged with relieving the Prime Minister and the Cabinet as much as possible of the responsibility for coordinating groups of departments in certain specific fields of policy. Sometimes, as in the case of the Minister of Defence, the coordinating minister was given a department of his own. Occasionally, the duties of a coordinating minister were publicly announced, as in the case of the Minister of Production. At other times, only a vague indication of his tasks was given in Parliament, as in the case of the Overlords and ministers like Morrison, Richard Stokes, and Charles Hill, who in 1945, 1951 and 1957, respectively, were charged with the general coordination of govermnent information services. But more often, coordination duties have been kept secret. Normally, a coordinating minister exercises his duties as chairman of a cabinet committee, the composition of which is also not disclosed. Whether he occupies a sinecure office or heads one of the more important departmental posts in the ministerial hierarchy will depend on personal and political factors rather than on formal ones.

Less official agents also play a considerable role in improving interdepartmental coordination. Prime Ministers have often relied on informal meetings to resolve interdepartmental disputes. Occasionally, they have asked ministerial colleagues to act for them on incidental matters without attributing any formal authority to them. An important part is played by unofficial means of communication: telephone converations, casual notes passed by one minister to another on the Treasury Bench or during a Cabinet session, informal talks over luncheon and dinner tables, short chats in the lobbies of Parliament, etc. In addition, the network of private secretaries serves to smooth out many less important problems and to ensure ready communication.[16] In the Prime Minister's immediate environment there have always been a few high-placed civil servants — technically residing in the Cabinet Office, the Treasury, the Foreign Office, or in a somewhat more formalized Prime Minister's Secretariat — who by long experience have become 'masters of . . institutional understanding . . . able to prod and stroke, caress and jab, the relevant parts of the English organism, so that somehow or other, in a way that [makes] organizational diagrams look very primitive,' certain vital matters are seen through.[17]

Finally, some formal agencies play a coordinating role. Certain agencies have been deliberately placed in a central position because they represent some high-level *expertise* useful to the entire government or because they supply common services. Economic advice, statistical coordination, certain defense matters, and central information and intelligence services have thus at various times been concentrated in a non-departmental central coordinating agency. In addition, certain departments have always provided special services for other parts of the government machinery in such matters as office buildings and office requirements; legal, actuarial, and audit services; etc.[18]

Further differentation in the ministerial hierarchy

Since 1914, the ministerial hierarchy has become further differentiated in various ways.[19]

The position of the Prime Minister has been reinforced. Various factors have contributed to this. The increased importance of foreign affairs and defence matters (both nationally and internationally) has led to a more constant intervention of the Prime Minister in these sectors. The growing complexity and interdependence of government has enhanced his role of supreme coordinator. The House of Commons and the public have become more prone to appraise government acts not as measures of individual ministers or departments but as parts of government policy as a whole. This has tended to raise the Prime Minister's stature over that of both his party and his colleagues. The Government, in other words, is judged as much by its Prime Minister as the Prime Minister is by his government. Since the days of Lloyd George, the right to advise the King to dissolve Parliament has become in practice the Prime Minister's alone rather than the Cabinet's. Elections have tended to be a competition between alternative Prime Ministers as well as between rival parties or programs. The increased length of the ministerial hierarchy has augmented the Prime Minister's powers of patronage and heightened a sense of dependence on the part of his appointees. Those at the bottom of the ladder know that they can move up only by the grace of the Prime Minister. Those on the highest step must often ponder the fact that below them are many who would be only too happy to shed crocodile tears over their possible dismissal, but who are yet ready to take their place immediately at the Prime Minister's bidding. Some observers have also stressed the enduring importance of the Prime Minister's having his own staff in the Cabinet Office. This might conceivably (but in practice not too frequently) brief him against proposals of his departmental colleagues, and enhances his powers over the Cabinet agenda and the circulation of Cabinet papers and Cabinet minutes.

It is somewhat farfetched, however, to conclude from this that the British system of government is, in fact, tending towards a presidential system.[20] Nor should one accept without question the statement that 'Britain is not governed by the Cabinet but by the Prime Minister, his senior colleagues, junior ministers, and the leading civil servants, with the Cabinet acting as a coordinating body and clearing house for business.'[21] This sentence is either a truism or an underestimation of the Cabinet's role as a political as well as an administrative agency. No Prime Minister is fully independent of the Cabinet or its most influential members. Each Prime Minister governs at the mercy of party; and not withstanding superficial affirmations to the contrary, a British political party is more than a group of the Prime Minister's friends and idolaters. The tradition of collective responsibility and the corporate strength of vested departments is too strong to allow easy control by one central minister, let alone by his non-departmental private secretariat. Even the sheer burden of office prevents any Prime Minister from intervening at all closely except in the most urgent matters. If he can make his will prevail in any matter he chooses, he can only do so by leaving most things alone.

In recent times, a Deputy Prime Minister has become a more regular feature of British Cabinets. The first person to bear this unofficial title was Attlee, who was termed Deputy Prime Minister in 1942. Morrison was recognized as Deputy Prime Minister from 1945 to 1951. In the autumn of 1951, Churchill nominated Eden 'Foreign Secretary and Deputy Prime Minister.' The King refused to agree to the latter title, however, because it might interfere with his free choice of Churchill's eventual successor.[22] But whatever the nomenclature, many Cabinets have had one minister who was expected to take the chair at Cabinet meetings in the Prime Minister's absence. The minister was sometimes, but not necessarily, the Prime Minister's logical successor. In a real coalition government, for instance, the two are not likely to coincide. No one expected that Attlee might be appointed Prime Minister of the National government after 1942 if Churchill should die. On the contrary, in June 1942, Churchill formally recommended that the King entrust the formation of a new government to Eden, in case he himself should die on a journey to the United States.[23] Again, in 1944, Churchill formally advised the King to send for Anderson if both he and Eden should be killed on their journey to Yalta.[24] Bevin, Dalton, and Cripps were not likely to conclude from Morrison's unofficial title of Deputy Prime Minister (Morrison presumably was so designated because he was the officially elected Deputy Leader of the Labour Party) that he was the only possible choice as Prime Minister of the Labour Cabinet after 1945, in case something happened to Attlee. Between 1951 and 1955 Eden was both the unofficial crown prince and the actual Vice-Prime Minister of the Cabinet.[25] Under Eden himself, Butler acted as Deputy Prime Minister, but it did not prevent the appointment of Macmillan over his head in 1957. Butler has remained in the number two position since then. In October

1961, when he relinquished his Leadership of the House of Commons but remained Home Secretary, it was officially announced that he was 'to give special assistance to the Prime Minister over a wide field of public duties, and, in particular, to head the ministerial group charged with the oversight of the Common Market negotiations.' In March 1962, Macmillan still refused to nominate a Deputy Prime Minister holding that the office did not technically exist under the constitution.[26] But after the ministerial upheaval of July 1962, Butler gave up the Home Office to accept the new post of First Secretary of State. It was intimated that he would act as Deputy Prime Minister, even though again that title was not formally conferred by the Queen. According to *The Times* of 18 July 1962, the new title lent 'an appropriate dignity to Mr Butler's position, the title Deputy Prime Minister having an insufficiently archaic ring about it by British standards.' But even as First Secretary, Butler could be far from certain that he would, after all, become Prime Minister.

Other leading ministers, too, have seen their positions strengthened. For a long time past in British history, a connection had been noted between the growth of the Cabinet and the disposition of leading ministers to prepare and at times to take important decisions in informal meetings outside the Cabinet. If Peel 'had started upon a more limited scale, he would have had no difficulty in keeping out its deformities.' Lord Ripon stated over a century ago. 'He must now only take care that they have no power or influence.'[27] The appointment of coordinating ministers who at the same time preside over the more important Cabinet committees has perhaps led to a certain institutionalization of an Inner Group. However important personal factors continue to be, it is now practically unthinkable that such officeholders as the Chancellor of the Exchequer, the Foreign Secretary, to a lesser extent the Minister of Defence, and (if they are important committee chairmen) the Lord President and the Lord Privy Seal, can be kept outside the privileged circle of actual Cabinet leaders for long.

The development of the committee system has also had an impact on the position of the sinecure offices. Instead of being honorific advisers or ministers incidentally charged with specific tasks, the most important sinecure holders have often become essential links in the complex policy-making mechanism. Many factors have caused this process. The existing sinecures regained some of their earlier political influence when Lloyd George utilized them to form a non-departmental War Cabinet above the departments, thus establishing a precedent that was also followed for a time during the Second World War. The occurrence of coalition government in 1915, 1931, and 1940 enhanced the position of a second man in the Cabinet, who owed his rank not to an important ministerial portfolio or a strong political position within the Prime Minister's party but to his place as Leader of a party that represented an independent force within the coalition. Such politicians have often preferred a sinecure office to a large department.[28] Bonar Law, for instance, abandoned the Treasury for the Privy Seal in 1919, and Austen Chamberlain followed this example in 1921. Baldwin similarly preferred the Lord Presidency to the Treasury in 1931. Attlee became Lord Privy Seal in 1940, Deputy Prime Minister and Secretary of State for the Dominions in 1942, but again Lord President of the Council in 1943. In addition, the evolution of the Cabinet-committee system has done much to raise the status of sinecure-holders acting as chairmen of important standing committees. A sinecure post has also often served as an office for the Leader of the House. At times, however, various ministers who have resembled the traditional 'elder statesmen' rather than directors of the central government machinery have still been appointed to the Lord Presidency or the Privy Seal. The fact that Butler thought it necessary to assume the Home Secretaryship in addition to the Privy Seal in 1957 has often been regarded as proof that even a powerful coordinating minister cannot wield sufficient political strength from a sinecure office against the main departments of government.[29]

Recent developments have also served to increase the actual burden on the holders of sinecure offices. Two of them (the Lord Privy Seal and the Paymaster-General) have in fact become second Cabinet ministers in the Foreign Office and in the Treasury, respectively. The office of the

Duchy has been assigned to the Leader of the House of Commons, who is also party chairman. And the Lord President of the Council, Halisham, has collected such an assortment of duties that his post can hardly be described as a 'sinecure.' A confirmation of this development may be seen in the reappearance of ministers without portfolio in the Cabinet.

The separation between Cabinet ministers and ministers of Cabinet rank outside the Cabinet has led to further differentiation within the ministerial hierarchy. Membership in the Cabinet, by itself, has never implied equality of status. The remark of a former Socialist minister that 'the youngest and most junior member can sometimes get his colleagues to change their minds' conveys more of a sense of hierarchy among Cabinet members than of a prevailing egalitarianism.[30] But even so, the cleavage between the least important minister within the Cabinet and the most important one outside it has become deep, whatever the personal influence of ministers concerned.[31]

The appointment of Ministers of State has added a new category of ministers between heads of departments and parliamentary secretaries. The first Minister of State was Beaverbrook, who was appointed to this newly created office in 1941. He was a member of the War Cabinet, as were Lyttelton and Richard Casey, who were successively appointed Minister of State Resident in the Middle East. Since then the office of Minister of State has declined in rank. In 1943 a son of Bonar Law, Richard Law, was appointed Minister of State at the Foreign Office. As such, he was subordinate to the Foreign Secretary. Ministers of State have been appointed when a minister's burden threatened to become unduly heavy but to divide his duties among seperate departmental ministers seemed impossible or undesirable.[32] In the Foreign Office for instance, a second Minister of State has been appointed since 1953.[33] In the Treasury an Economic Secretary was joined to the Financial Secretary in 1947. For a time in 1950 and again in 1951, this minister carried the personal title of Minister of State, and since 1957 both the Financial Secretary and the Economic Secretary have been paid the same as the Minister of State (but they are less often Privy Councillors and are included under the heading 'junior ministers' in the official list).[34]

When the Board of Trade absorbed the Department of Overseas Trade in 1946, it was still found necessary for a special Minister of State to occupy himself full-time with problems of overseas commerce under the general direction of the President of the Board of Trade.[35] In 1948, when the emancipating of colonies began to gain momentum, a separate Minister of State was appointed to the Colonial Office. The development of various areas toward self-government greatly increased the tasks of the Secretary of State for the Colonies until each colony gained independence.[36] Eventually, however, the work of the Colonial Office began to shrink, while that of the Commonwealth Relations Office increased *pari passu*. A separate Minister of State for Commonwealth Relations was added. Finally, in July 1962, Macmillan appointed Sandys Secretary of State at both offices thus leaving the Minister of State and the Undersecretary of State at the Colonial Office as the sole full-timers in that department. The Secretary for Technical Cooperation, appointed in 1961, also ranks as Minister of State, although he is not statutorily responsible to any other minister.[37] A Minister of State has also been appointed in the Scottish Office, which is responsible for a range of government tasks that in England are the responsibility of various departments. In December 1957, finally, a Minister of State for Welsh Affairs was appointed, largely as a concession to nationalist sensitivities; he is under the Minister of Housing and Local Government, who is technically also Minister for Welsh Affairs, and works mainly in Wales, as his Scottish counterpart does in Scotland. Both Ministers of State are peers.[38]

It is difficult to generalize about the extent to which Ministers of State have been able to relieve the burden on more senior ministers. In practice, much depends on the personalities concerned, and on the willingness of Parliament to transact business with the Minister of State rather than the senior minister in charge, which depends largely on political circumstance. The Ministers of State have not become substitute ministers; as we saw in the two vitally important

cases of the Foreign Office and the Treasury, Cabinet
ministers rather than ministers below the line have recently
been added to help shoulder the impossible tasks of the
ministers in charge. Thus, increasingly, a system of having
two senior ministers in a department has been found
necessary, rather than a further strengthening of subordinate
staff. This has posed new problems of dividing responsibility
at the highest level of government, as well as further
differentiation within the Cabinet.

*At the same time, the number of parliamentary secretaries
has increased.* In 1914, there were only 14 undersecretaries
and parliamentary secretaries. In 1919 this number had
increased to 27. In 1939 the number had declined to 23, but
it now stands at 32. This increase partly reflects the increase
in the number of departments that were given their own
parliamentary secretary. But in addition, more than one
parliamentary secretary has sometimes been appointed to a
single department; statutory limitations on the number of
parliamentary secretaries who could serve in any particular
department were removed in the Ministers of the Crown
(Parliamentary Secretaries) Act of 1960. From 1939 to 1958,
the number of Joint Undersecretaries in the Scottish Office
increased from one to three, and since 1961 there have been
three parliamentary secretaries at the Ministry of Transport.
There are now two Joint Parliamentary Secretaries in five
other departments: Home Affairs, Foreign Affairs, Commonwealth Relations, Agriculture, and Pensions and National
Insurance. In such ministries as the Foreign Office and the
Treasury, the grading of ministers at lower levels has become
quite complicated: in addition to the First Lord and the
Chancellor of the Exchequer, the Treasury now houses a
Chief Secretary (who is in the Cabinet), an Economic
Secretary and a Financial Secretary (who practically rank as
Ministers of State), and the Parliamentary Secretary and the
junior Lords (who serve as whips and as such do not deal
with Treasury business). Similarly, the Foreign Office has its
Foreign Secretary (who is in the House of Lords, and for
whom both the Prime Minister and the Lord Privy Seal
answer in the House of Commons), the Lord Privy Seal (who
is a Cabinet member especially concerned with European

problems), two Ministers of State, and two Joint Under-secretaries.[39]

Considerable pressure has been exerted on the House of Commons to be satisfied with junior ministers as spokesmen on various matters of departmental policy. On less controversial issues, this seems to have had some effect. Civil servants too, have learned to regard the desk of the senior minister as a potential bottleneck and hence have been more ready to clear business with lower-ranking ministers (always providing that personalities, politics, and the parliamentary responsibility of the senior minister permit this). Junior ministers would thus seem to have gained some prestige on the administrative and parliamentary level. But at the same time, the ministerial ladder has become steeper and the intermediate steps more important. To hold office as a junior minister is more necessary for further promotion than ever before. But remuneration is low, and at times concern has been expressed about whether persons of sufficient quality are readily coming forward to undergo this testing.

A more subtle but no less real differentiation grew between the older departments and the newer ones. As we saw, this distinction was not unknown before 1914. Earlier, attention was drawn to the strong resistance encountered by such departments as the Ministries of Labour, Health, Transport, and Air, which were established after 1916. Similar obstacles confronted various departments that originated during World War II, including the Ministries of Supply, Town and County Planning, Fuel and Power, Civil Aviation, and National Insurance. The more powerful politicians generally continued to prefer the long-established departments. New departments were therefore often given to politicians who could not expect or demand higher office: older politicians who had reached the top of their pole, or younger ones who considered such posts as no more than a steppingstone. Thus these newer departments often became part of a vicious circle. They were not important enough to attract politicians of the first rank. And because they were not led by first-rate ministers, they often did not become really influential in the ministerial hierarchy.

Symptomatic of the lesser prestige of the newer departments were the more frequent reorganizations they had to undergo. There were various drastic shifts, for instance between the Ministries of Health, Works, and Town and Country Planning. The Ministry of Supply was tossed about, and finally disbanded in 1959. Such departments as Pensions and National Insurance, Transport and Civil Aviation, and Food and Agriculture were joined together without much ado. Others simply disappeared. Such occurrences were hardly likely among the older departments (the Service departments forming a notable exception): their traditional prestige, their corporate pride, and the political power of their ministerial heads made them to a large extent inviolate.

But all these status differences were in their turn affected by other factors, such as personality, or the political or administrative importance that a department might assume at a particular period. Powerful politicians — Morrison or Hore-Belisha at the Ministry of Transport, Bevin at the Ministry of Labour, Bevan at the Ministry of Health, Dalton at Town and Country Planning, Macmillan at Housing and Local Government, Sandys at Aviation— were able to enhance the repute of their departments. The political importance of the ministries of Labour and Agriculture increased in conjunction with the rising political importance of their clienteles. Technical factors for a time enhanced the prestige of the Cinderella of the Service departments, the Air Ministry. In a crisis, the political importance of a particular ministerial post might even soar overnight.

In other words, traditional differences in prestige, considerations of status, personal influences, political circumstances, and the relative significance of particular government tasks at any given time make the ministerial structure into a complicated hierarchy, the pattern of which may differ considerably from one moment to the next.

The relation between ministers and civil servants

The relation between ministers and officials, too, underwent substantial changes as a result of the development of modern government.

The entire administrative apparatus grew considerably in size and complexity.[40] It therefore became more and more difficult to direct it. This increased both the burden of ministerial work and the strain of nervous tension. As a former Labour minister wrote, 'The real strain arises not from what ministers do but from what they feel they ought to be doing.' Or in the words of Sir Ivor Jennings, 'It is not work, but worry.'[41]

Ministerial control over the civil service therefore became more problematical. This is as true of ministers individually as of the Cabinet as a whole. Thousands of decisions about which ministers do not and could not know are taken daily in their name. The measure of leadership that ministers give cannot but differ from person to person. But in practice, ministers can do little more than initiate certain proposals, decide controversies that proved impossible to settle at lower levels of the civil service hierarchy, and intervene in issues that touch a political nerve or happen to have their special interest. 'Ministers,' Franks has written, 'criticize, they reject, they alter, they judge and decide.'[42] They are far from being the only springs of policy.

The position of the higher civil servants has acquired correspondingly greater importance. Even more than before the highest officials have become 'permanent politicians,' serving as alter egos of their ministers.[43] The institution of the *Cabinet du Ministre* as France knows it did not develop in Great Britain. Nor is there any inclination to adopt the American practice of changing the highest officials when a new party arrives in office. On the contrary, even now the parliamentary secretary sometimes enjoys less contact with his minister than do the main permanent officials; and the career private secretary is nore frequently found in his minister's company than is his parliamentary private secretary.

The higher civil servants seem to be becoming less anonymous than they were in 1914. No longer can it be said of civil servants that 'like the Fountains in Trafalgar Square, they play from ten to five, with an interval for lunch.' The urgency of coordination and the fact that ministers can be challenged in Parliament on every issue within their general competence compel senior officials to occupy themselves personally with a large variety of government business. Work in evenings and on weekends is the rule rather than the exception. One can ask, with Wilfred Harrison, 'Why do they do it?' and reply, with him, in the simple statement, 'Because the work would not get done if they did not.' Harrison formulates the dilemma in one sentence: 'As government activities increase and work multiplies, the load that converges on them increases; and the process is cumulative because with the constant pressure and absence of relief the working tempo becomes reduced.'[44]

It is a moot point whether ministers or senior civil servants are the harder pressed by the burdens of modern government. A minister has many responsibilities outside his departmental duties. To quote Chester:

> The work is likely to be more strange to him and therefore more difficult. He has the ultimate responsibility for all decisions and must face any public criticisms. He has also many other claims on his time — attending the House of Commons, speaking on public occasions of all kinds. And he is constantly in the public eye with the possibility that any public utterance of his may get widespread publicity.[45]

But ministers have the *ultimum remedium* of leaving much real work to the civil servants. The latter are permanent, and can never take their leave, even at the hands of an ungrateful electorate or Prime Minister.

The increasing role of experts in the making of policy

The growing complexity of goverment tasks has made it more necessary than formerly to include experts in the policy-making process. This has come about on various levels:

The number of experts within the departments has increased considerably. The scientific civil service now is about four times as large as the administrative class of the civil service; the professional, scientific, and technical classes *in toto* include about one and a half times the number of persons of the administrative and executive classes jointly.[46]

Special advisers and advisory organs have been added to the machinery of government. Apart from the desire of ministers and departments to obtain the expert advice of government scientists, the Cabinet itself has sometimes wanted to have special advisers at its disposal so departmental proposals could be tested from angles not influenced by specific departmental loyalties. To this end, various persons and agencies have been established in staff positions at the top levels of central government. Such central advisory agencies often found their origin in the modest staff of the CID, which served as model for the Cabinet Secretariat and for the many joint bodies under the Chiefs of Staff Committee. These agencies, in turn, stimulated the demand for similar organizations elsewhere in the government. Personal factors sometimes led to the appointment of experts to such specially created posts as Economic Adviser to H.M. Government and Chief Industrial Adviser. During World War 2, the Economic Section and the Statistical Office were established in the Cabinet Office. After 1945, a number of these specialist posts and agencies were drawn into more departmental orbits. The Treasury absorbed the economists of the Cabinet Office. The military members of the Cabinet Secretariat formed the nucleus for the Ministry of Defence in 1946. All this had little effect, however, on the formation of policy at the highest levels. High-level economic experts, the top of the Treasury, the leading professional and scientific staff in the Service Departments and the Ministry of Defence, and the members of the Cabinet Office remain in immediate contact with one another and with the Prime Minister and leading Cabinet ministers. They form a small, closely knit group that exercises an immediate influence on policy in a measure determined as much by personality as by the position each member may formally occupy in the hierarchy.[47]

At the same time advice was also increasingly drawn from circles outside the immediate apparatus. The complexity of modern government is such that the state cannot hope to appoint its own expert staff in all fields into which the government enters. Particularly when government begins moving in unexplored terrain, it tends to be highly dependent on available outside knowledge. Close consultation with interested parties, to obtain advice and consent, is indicated. Various means have evolved to ensure the service of non-governmental experts for government purposes. Special regulations have made it easier for academic experts to serve in the government for a short period (and, conversely, for a few civil sevants to spend a period of study and reflection in the universities). Advisory committees are playing an increasingly important role.[48] They may range from formally instituted Royal Commissions to casually arranged discussion groups. Some are only temporary, others permanent. According to a recent study, there were some two hundred standing committees attached to the central government in 1939. This number had increased to almost five hundred in 1958, of which no less than 60 to 70 per cent were expert committees rather than consultative or administrative ones.[49] Undoubtedly, many such advisory bodies have served more than one purpose; they have been instruments for the government to get its case across to interest groups and interested experts. But, in turn, these groups have also obtained a more ready influence on government policies.

The Government has also become increasingly aware of the importance of both pure and applied research for the military strength, economic prosperity, and social welfare of the British people. Since the First World War support for research has been increasing. It ranges from block grants to the universities to highly specialized subventions or government research contracts. As long as such sponsorship did not clearly reside under any one department, such activities were promoted under the aegis of a number of agencies under the Privy Council. Among them were the Department of Scientific and Industrial Research (established in 1916), the Medical Research Council, the Agriculture Research Council, and the Nature Conservancy, which nominally reported to the Lord President of the Council.[50] In 1959, however, the importance of research had become so much of a political issue that the Conservative Party included the appointment of a special Minister of Science in its election program. The new minister was duly appointed in October 1961. But not much changed in practice.

But the increasing role of science has also affected the extent of ministerial control. The ideal image of the ever-wise, triumphantly commonsensical amateur has come in for increasingly sceptical comment. More and more concern is being expressed about whether modern science and democratic control are even compatible. Various expedients have been tried to preserve political supervision. Parliamentarians have formed their own specialized scientific committees. Ministers have more readily concentrated on certain fields. But through advisory committees and through the appointment of rival experts in government service, the government has tried to lower political dependence on any one scientist. But no final solution has been found, or seems possible. Especially in certain fields where national security seems to dictate 'closed politics,' the prestige of function and personality allows a few experts a preponderant influence. 'Court politics' has sometimes led to the elevation of advisers to ministerial status, as in the cases of Cherwell and Mills.[51]

Ministers and Parliament

Considerable change has come about in the relation of ministers to Parliament. The pressure and complexity of administration has forced successive governments to ask for increased power. Apart from the issue of delegated legislation, this has also led to certain problems for the ministerial hierarchy.[52]

It has strengthened the element of individual ministerial responsibility, both in a legal and in a political sense. Numerous government powers are legally no longer vested in the Crown but in individual ministers.[53] The heavy burden of modern government makes it imperative that ministers accept sole responsibility over a wide field, without burdening their colleagues. The extension of government powers has increased the number of issues on which ministers can be technically challenged in Parliament. This burden has not hit all ministers equally. The introduction of the rota system in question time, for instance, has had the effect of lessening ministerial answerability for a considerable number of ministers.[54] Oral questions have become increasingly a political game, which may require debating skill as much as a thorough grounding in a particular issue. Nevertheless, parliamentary questions pose a considerable burden on some ministers and their senior official advisers. Also, the MP's increased practice of asking written questions and using private correspondence to seek information or redress about particular official decisions has considerably augmented the burden of ministerial office.[55]

This has strengthened the tendency to seek to lessen ministerial responsibility for a number of tasks. Devolution of powers to autonomous organs of government — e.g., public corporations, administrative committees, and administrative tribunals — has absolved ministers from certain responsibilities in specific fields or at least has narrowed the scope of their answerability to general direction, rather than to day-to-day administration.[56] The existence of such bodies as well as of advisory committees has given ministers the opportunity to disclaim responsibility or at least to defer it until such time as these bodies may decide or issue a report.

At the same time, the element of collective responsibility toward Parliament has increased as well. In many cases it became impossible to divide goverment tasks neatly among separate departments; in the making of policy various interests merged. 'The Government' became for both parties and for the electorate a collective body, which must accept responsibility for the welfare of the entire nation and for each individual citizen.

The increase of State tasks demanded more efficient legislative procedures.[57] No longer could the quiet tempo of legislation be preserved. Parliamentary business has become more complicated and time-consuming. More and more mornings are given over to committee meetings. The government has had to resort to stricter procedures such as the closure and the guillotine to expedite legislation. Stricter rules have been adopted about the parliamentary agenda, and question time has been further rationed. Private Members' Time has sometimes been taken over for government Business. The task of piloting bills through Parliament has come to require more concentrated attention, the more so because each bill that has not been adopted before the end of the session automatically lapses.

No longer is the Prime Minister able to combine his increased duties with the Leadership of the House of Commons. During the two world wars, Lloyd George and

Winston Churchill had set the precedent of delegating this function to other ministers. In 1942, Churchill appointed Cripps Leader of the House, as Lord Privy Seal. Since then Eden has acted as Leader from 1942 to 1945 as Foreign Secretary, Morrison from 1945 to 1951 as Lord President of the Council, Chuter Ede in 1951 as Home Secretary, Crookshank as Minister of Health and Lord Privy Seal until 1955, Butler as Lord Privy Seal and Home Secretary till 1961, and since then Macleod as Chancellor of the Duchy of Lancaster. Personalities, not portfolios, determined these choices. But at all times, one leading minister has had to concentrate on parliamentary business. Morrison has deemed it necessary that this minister should at the same time, preside over the Legislation Committee of the Cabinet.[58]

With the government's growth in size, the percentage of parliamentarians of the majority party directly tied to the government has increased as well. This increase has taken place on the level of ministers, Ministers of State, parliamentary secretaries, and parliamentary private secretaries. In 1947, only 49 members of the House of Commons enjoyed a paid office under the Crown. This number had risen to 68 in 1962.[59] Including the parliamentary private secretaries, just over a hundred members of the governing party in the Commons now hold some kind of office.

From time to time, traditional concern about 'placemen' was resuscitated. A Select Committee on Offices or Places of Profit under the Crown, appointed during the session of 1941—42, recommended that the number of ministers who could sit and vote in the House of Commons be limited to sixty; that the proportion between ministers and parliamentary secretaries as specified in the Ministers of the Crown Act in 1937 be maintained strictly; and that the convention of having only one parliamentary private secretary per department be adopted.[60] At the time, few of these recommendations were effected. But in 1957, a House of Commons Disqualification Bill was passed. It limited the number of senior ministers in the House of Commons to twenty-seven and the number of all ministers to seventy. Pressure on these limitations continues, however. Somewhat pessimistically, Ross has proposed to increase the number of parliamentarians, rather than seek to restrain the number of officeholders.[61]

As the position of the most senior ministers was enhanced, the psychological distance between them and the backbenchers in Parliament became wider. Becoming more occupied with departmental duties, ministers have found less opportunity to maintain informal contacts with backbenchers. They have come to Parliament to speak rather than to spend part of their day listening to the debates or talking politics in the lobbies or the smoking room. Even more so than formerly, they appear on the scene as prima donnas rather than as colleagues in a club. Backbenchers have felt frustrated by this and have found inadequate compensation in the increased committee work of the House. More and more, they have come to feel themselves ill-paid and little-esteemed numbers in a parliament where others dispose of their votes and their political future. Their frustrations have sometimes broken out in two psychologically closely connected attitudes: rebellious eruptions against the party leadership and attempts to somehow gain a place on the ministerial ladder. To maintain constant and cordial relations between party leaders and party followers has thus become more vital and more difficult. The importance of the whips has increased, and so has their number. In each party, small liaison committees between leaders and backbenchers have been established — department by department or between backbenchers and frontbenchers generally — to supplement the more formal proceedings of the meetings of the Parliamentary Party as a whole.[62] But no arrangement has been able to close the gap.

Complaints about the functioning of British central government

These varied adjustments notwithstanding, complaints continue to be heard about the malfunctioning of the central government apparatus. This phenomenon is not new. Ever since Balfour argued that 'democracy threatens to kill its servants by the work it requires of them,'[63] ministers and high officials have constantly warned, irrespective of political persuasion, that the machinery threatened to break down. Haldane spoke of Asquith's Cabinet as 'a congested body of about twenty in which the powerful orator secured too much attention,' a system in which the Prime Minister 'knew too little of the details of what had to be got through to be able to apportion the time required for discussion' and whereby 'business was not always properly discussed and the general point of view that vitally required decision almost never.'[64] Lloyd George's experiments ended in chaos rather than a new system. The Cabinets of Bonar Law and Baldwin restored some peace and order in the higher ranges of government but suffered from indecisiveness. MacDonald declared in 1924 that his duties were so heavy 'that if you stopped to go much beyond the surface of things, you got caught up in doubts that were like nightmares and that the only thing to do was to plunge boldly in the knowledge that the next man would have to do the same.'[65]

Lord Robert Cecil, who served under Asquith, Lloyd George, and Baldwin, was equally pessimistic in 1932. The pressure of government business, he argued, affected the health of leading ministers, resulting in breakdowns and early deaths, insomnia, exhaustion, indecisiveness, and an inclination to postpone or not to shoulder responsibilities. Cecil spoke of 'the Prime Minister's disease . . . an instinctive refusal to decide anything if decision could by any means be avoided.'[66] Jones, who was Deputy Secretary of the Cabinet until 1931 and a close companion of Baldwin and many other leading politicians in the 1930's, gave in his diary many examples that substantiate Cecil's general picture. He reported that Baldwin and Neville Chamberlain refused in 1932 to heed a summons for the Cabinet in vacation time because of the fatigue they had suffered at the Ottawa Conference of that year. He gave extensive information about the poor health of MacDonald and Baldwin between 1931 and 1937. He suggested that Hoare suffered from fainting fits because of overwork when he was Foreign Secretary.[67]

During this period the Cabinet Office under Hankey was accused of being partly responsible for overburdening ministers with an excess of activities. But Hankey himself was to write thirteen years after he resigned as Cabinet Secretary:

'An imperative necessity is to reduce the paralyzing strain of overwork on ministers, Parliament, and public servants, which threatens the country's constitution of all its strength.' In the light of the 'proliferation of Coordinating Commissions, Boards, Councils, Committees, Subcommittees, Working Parties, Panels, and the like,' he deemed 'a drastic and immediate overhaul' urgently necessary.[68]

Churchill had little sympathy for committees. However, in 1942, Cripps complained that Churchill tolerated such inefficient ways of administration as a needless proliferation of the committee system, inadequate delegation of authority, and old-fashioned ways of communication.[69] After 1947, Cripps himself became the classic example of a minister who practically met with death through insufficient delegation of duties to others. In 1947, Bevan proposed to postpone the discussion about nationalizing iron and steel because ministers 'were all too tired to size up all the points.'[70] The fate of Bevin and Cripps, the exhaustion of Butler as Chancellor of the Exchequer, of Eden as Foreign Secretary, and of other ministers made one member of Parliament, Martin Lindsay, brand in 1954 the system one of 'Government by Endurance.'[71] The Lord Chancellor, Kilmuir, declared in April 1956 in a Rectoral Address at St Andrew's University that it was doubtful 'whether a minister ever has sufficient time to consider the most profound problems of his country's future.'[72] In that same month an article appeared by a former Socialist minister, Patrick Gordon Walker, who argued that 'the rush of affairs is so tumultuous that the fine machinery of Cabinet is in constant danger of getting clogged up with a surfeit of business.'[73] Only six months later came the Suez crisis and Eden's resignation. Again the problem of the physical strain of ministers was painfully brought home. Desmond Donnelly, Labour member of the House of Commons, requested Macmillan to appoint a Select Committee to investigate the entire problem of the heavy burden that rested on ministers. For the time being, Macmillan refused the suggestion. But he asked Attlee and some other Privy Councillors to hold an informal inquiry. Their report apparently brought little solace.[74]

Whatever the reforms in the organization of central government, therefore, the complaint is still being made that ministers are seriously overworked, with the inevitable result that insufficient attention is given to matters of long-term policy, that business is not transacted efficiently, and that hurried compromises often take the place of well-thought-out decisions.

Proposals for general reform of the Cabinet structure

Criticism has generally been accompanied by proposals for further reform. These proposals have evoked discussions that are interesting for a number of reasons. They throw light on some basic problems of central government and give some indication of the direction in which public administration thought has been developing over the last decades in Britain. And they offer an opportunity for a critical appraisal of the politics and the political theory that would seem to form the basis of public administration doctrines that are common in this field. One caveat seems in place here. These various reform proposals are not fully representative of British thought and experience in this matter. Proposals for changes from inside the government are either reflected in the actual changes that have taken place or have not been disclosed so far. This study therefore restricts itself in the following chapters to the thoughts of some British writers who have played a prominent role in actual politics or have strongly influenced contemporary academic thought about central government.

Reform proposals have been made by different persons in a wide variety of settings. They show many nuances. Nevertheless, three themes recur with great frequency in the debate: (a) there should be a fundamental redistribution of tasks among departments; (b) a small, non-departmental Cabinet chiefly concerned with policy-making should be established; and (c) Cabinet membership should be restricted to the most important ministers, while an extensive system of Cabinet committees should be utilized.

In reviewing these proposals, one should remain constantly aware of the tasks the Cabinet should perform in the British political system. These can be summarized as follows:

1. The Cabinet should be able to decide the most important policy questions encountered by the central government both in day-to-day practice and in long-term perspective. This implies that ministers should have the time to concentrate on such questions; that they should have at their disposal the best expert advice available from departmental and non-departmental advisers; and that they must remain aware of the more important ideas and social movements found in the country at large.

2. The Cabinet should supervise the machinery and processes of administration and make sure that the bureaucracy functions effectively and in unison. To do this, the Cabinet must have adequate insight into actual administrative procedures. It must be able to intervene in specific issues and to ensure coordination where necessary. But it must not be burdened to such an extent that the normal flow of administration becomes hampered and insufficient attention is given to long-term policy considerations. Decisions must be effectively prepared, and once taken they must be fit for execution *and* be recognized as such by the departmental and other official organs that will have to implement them.

3. The Cabinet should be able to make valid its claim to represent the political desires of at least the majority of politically articulate groups in the population. This requires that the relations between the Cabinet and the Parliamentary Party and its constituent groups be so close that steady support is secured; that enough voters continue to view the Government as effectively promoting their articulate or inarticulate interests; that the nation as a whole (not withstanding group and party differences) be willing to abide by the leadership of the Cabinet; and that the internal relations within the government allow a softening of political and personal conflicts to such an extent that external homogeneity can be preserved and a constant clearance of political, policy, and administrative decisions can be affected.

4. In all its functions — as decider of policy, administrative coordinator, and focus of political desires — the Cabinet should be able to proceed without impairing the legal and political responsibility of individual ministers and of the Government as a whole toward Parliament. This requires that

Parliament remain able to hold individual ministers responsible for the efficient discharge of their duties; that collective responsibility remain intact; and that, in addition, Parliament be able to judge the more general question of whether the process of decision-making is that of an efficient and responsible government.

Notes

1. Of these, formal ones were the less important. The Prime Minister has long ago acquired a substantial say attributing different tasks to his ministerial colleagues; his political ascendancy over Parliament assured the necessary legislative and budgetary approval for most changes he thought desirable. The availabilty of the sinecure offices and the theoretical indivisibility of the office of Secretary of State offered him further flexibility for introducing changes. In the Ministers of the Crown (Transfer of Functions) Act of 1946, provision was formally made for allowing the transfer of statutory powers from one minister to another by Order in Council.

2. Cf. W. A. Robson, 'The Machinery of Government, 1939–1947', *Political Quarterly*, Vol. 19 (1948) pp. 1–7.

3. See Moses Abramovitz and Vera F. Eliasberg, *The Growth of Public Employment in Great Britain* (Princeton, N. J.: Princeton UP, 1957) Table 1, p. 25.

4. Cmnd. 1432 (1961), para. 10.

5. Cf. D. N. Chester, 'Recent Trends in British Central Government', *Administration* (Dublin), Vol. 4 (1956) pp. 13–16. See also Political and Economic Planning (PEP), 'The Growth of Government', *Planning*, Vol. 23 (1957) pp. 232–5, 247–8.

6. M. Beloff, *New Dimensions in Foreign Policy: A Study in British Administrative Experience, 1947–1959* (London: Allen & Unwin, 1961).

7. D. N. Chester (ed.), and F. M. G. Willson, *The Organisation of British Central Government 1914–56: A Survey of a Study Group of the Royal Institute of Public Administration* (London: Allen & Unwin, 1957) pp. 343–5.

8. A. Aspinall, 'The Cabinet Council, 1783–1835', *Proceedings of the British Academy* (London: UP, 1952).

9. *The Economist*, 3 Nov 1956; reprinted in C. N. Parkinson, *Parkinson's Law and other Studies in Administration* (Boston: Houghton Mifflin, 1957) pp. 33–44.

10. The title 'Minister of Cabinet Rank' has officially lapsed (W. J. M. Mackenzie and J. W. Grove, *Central Administration in Britain* (London: Longmans, 1957) p. 339).

11. Data provided by the Treasury Library; cf. I. Jennings, *Cabinet Government*, 3rd ed. (Cambridge: UP, 1959) p. 249.

12. Ibid., pp. 242–64; I. Jennings, *The British Constitution*, 3rd ed. (Cambridge: UP, 1950) pp. 179 ff; D. N. Chester, 'Development of the Cabinet 1914–18, in G. Campion et al., *British Government since 1918* (London: Allen & Unwin, 1950) pp. 37–41; R. J. P. Hewison, 'The Organisation of the Cabinet Secretariat', *O & M Bulletin* (The Treasury), Vol. 6, No. 6 (1951) pp. 36–41; Mackenzie and Grove, *Central Administration in Britain* pp. 338–42; Beloff, *New Dimensions in Foreign Policy*, pp. 165–6. F. A. Johnson, *Defence by Committee: The British Committee of Imperial Defence*, 1885–1959 (London: UP, 1960), pp. 239–42.

13. Mackenzie and Grove, *Central Administration in Britain*, p. 339.

14. Bosworth Monck, *How the Civil Service Works* (London: Phoenix House, 1952) p. 100. Whether an interdepartmental committee is a Cabinet committee is 'not defined by membership but whether or not it is served by the Cabinet Office' (Beloff, *New Dimensions in Foreign Policy*, p. 27).

15. Hewison, 'The Organisation of the Cabinet Secretariat', pp. 38–9; for a similar duty of Hankey, even in 1914, see his *The Supreme Command 1914–18*, 2 Vols. (London: Allen & Unwin, 1961), pp. 226–7.

16. T. Jones, *A Diary with Letters 1931–1950* (London: Oxford U.P., 1954) pp. xix–xxi; Mackenzie and Grove, *Central Administration in Britain*, pp. 191–4.

17. C. P. Snow, *Science and Government* (Cambridge, Mass.: Harvard U.P., 1961) p. 61.

18. Chester and Willson, *The Organisation of British Central Goverment*, pp. 274–80.

19. The following discussion refers, of course, to a ranking according to *political* criteria. Since 1914, ministers have tended *formally* to become more equal. This is apparent, for example, in the use of the title 'Minister' for many offices that formerly had more archaic designations. Salaries, too, have been equalized to a great extent. This process began during the First World War, when it was temporarily decided that all ministers would pay their salaries into a common fund, and draw equal amounts from it. The Ministers of the Crown Act (1937) provided for a salary of £5,000 for all ministers who headed a government except the Postmaster-General and the First Commissioner of Works, who were to get £3,000, and the Minister of Pensions, who was thought worth only £2,000.

20. See the correspondence in the *Daily Telegraph*, touched off by a provocative letter on 2 August 1960 from Professor Max Beloff; cf. *The Economist*, 13 Aug 1960.

21. This statement appeared on the jacket of J. P. Mackintosh, *The British Cabinet* (London: Stevens, 1962). For a good critical review, see D. N. Chester, 'Who Governs Britain?', *Parliamentary Affairs*, Vol. 15 (1962) pp. 519–27.

22. J. W. Wheeler–Bennett, *King George VI: His Life and Reign* (London Macmillan, 1958) p. 797.

23. Cf. Lord Avon, *The Eden Memoirs: Full Circle* (London: Cassell, 1960) p. 266.
24. Wheeler-Bennett, *King George VI*, pp. 544—5; J. W. Wheeler-Bennett, *John Anderson, Viscount Waverly* (London: Macmillan, 1962) pp. 315—18.
25. When both Churchill and Eden were ill in 1953, Salisbury directed foreign policy, and Butler 'assumed authority for Home Affairs': Lord Avon, *Full Circle*, p. 52.
26. 655, House of Commons Debates (13 Mar 1962), Col. 1117; D. J. Heasman, 'The Prime Minister and the Cabinet', *Parliamentary Affairs*, Vol. 15 (1962) pp. 467—8.
27. Aspinall, 'The Cabinet Council', p. 163.
28. Another indication that the ministerial status of the sinecure offices has risen is that since 1916 various holders of these offices have been able to claim the house at 11 Downing Street, which is normally the home of the Chancellor of the Exchequer; in other cases they have at least shared these quarters with the Chancellor. In 1919, for instance, Bonar Law continued to occupy the house when he exchanged the Exchequer for the Privy Seal. When Clynes was Lord Privy Seal and Deputy Leader of the Labour Party, he worked at No. 11 in 1924. As Lord President of the Council, Baldwin lived there from 1931 to 1935: Neville Chamberlain did the same in 1940. Attlee and Cripps shared the house with Chancellor of the Exchequer Sir Kingsley Wood when they held the office of Privy Seal in 1941 and 1942, respectively. Morrison worked there between 1945 and 1951 as Lord President, and in 1951 Cherwell moved in as Paymaster-General. (Data provided by the Treasury Library.)
29. Cf. *The Economist*, 27 Apr 1957, and M. Dogan and P. Campbell, 'Le Personnel Ministériel en France et en Grande Bretagne (1945—1957)., *Revue Française de Science Politique*, Vol. 7 (1957) pp. 313—45, 793—824.
30. P. Gordon Walker, 'On Being a Cabinet Minister', *Encounter*, Vol. 3 Apr 1956, p. 20).
31. A recent, somewhat perfectionist study (D. J. Heasman, 'The Ministerial Hierarchy', *Parliamentary Affairs*, Vol. 15 (1962) pp. 327—8) has even attempted a rather fanciful division of non-Cabinet ministers into five categories:

> First, heads of autonomous departments that are concerned with the formulation of important policies who might, therefore, in other circumstances, be in the Cabinet (for example, the Minister of Pensions and National Insurance and the Minister of Health); secondly, heads of essentially administrative departments whose responsibilities do not warrant their presence in the Cabinet (specifically, the Minister of Works and the Postmaster-General); thirdly, holders of minor sinecures and ministers without portfolio whose assignments are of an auxiliary nature; fourthly, the three Service

ministers, the importance and expenditures of whose departments exceed, by far, those of (say) the Minister of Works
(since 1946 the list of 'ministers not in the Cabinet' has been
headed almost invariably by the three Service ministers), yet
who are clearly subordinate, as the Minister of Works is not, to
a member of the Cabinet; and finally, Ministers of State.

32. The half-way position of Minister of State between senior ministers
and junior ministers was, as it were, arithmetically fixed in 1957,
when they were awarded a salary of £3,750. A minister normally
receives £5,000, a parliamentary secretary £2,500.

33. After Eden returned to the Foreign Office in 1951, he told
Morrison that he found his duties twice as heavy as they had been
in 1945 (H. Morrison, *An Autobiography by Lord Morrison of
Lambeth* (London: Odhams, 1960) pp. 297–8; and H. Morrison,
Government and Parliament: A Survey From the Inside (London:
Oxford U.P., 1954) p.63; for graphic descriptions of the very heavy
burden on the Foreign Secretary, see Lord Grey of Fallodon,
Twenty-five years 1892–1916 (London: Hodder & Stoughton,
1925) Vol. 2, p. 251 ff. and Lord Strang, *Home and Abroad*
(London: Deutsch, 1956) pp. 298–300. Eden himself thought that
in normal times, the Foreign Secretary and the Chancellor of the
Exchequer bore heavier burdens than the Prime Minister, Lord
Avon, *Full Circle*, p. 317.

34. Heasman, 'The Ministerial Hierarchy', p. 328.

35. According to the Ministers of the Crown Act (1937), the Secretary
for Overseas Trade, the Secretary of Mines, and the Financial
Secretary to the Treasury enjoyed a salary of £2,000 – i.e., £500
more than the other junior ministers.

36. Cf. Sir Charles Jeffries, *The Colonial Office* (London: Allen &
Unwin, 1956) p. 118. Parkinson's Law is partly based on the
'experiences' of the Colonial Office; see *Parkinson's Law and Other
Studies in Administration*, pp. 10–11.

37. F. M. G. Willson, 'The Organisation of Pritish Central Government
1955–61', *Public Administration*, Vol. 50 (1962) pp. 159–200.

38. The Home Secretary acted as 'Minister for Welsh Affairs' from
1951 to 1957; since that time, the position has been filled by the
Minister of Housing and Local Government.

39. Cf. Peter Bromhead, The British Constitution in 1961', *Parliamentary Affairs*, Vol. 15 (1962) pp. 148–9.

40. Cf. PEP, 'The Growth of Government', pp. 232–5, 247–8;
Chester, 'Recent Trends in British Central Government', p. 14.

41. 'On being out of office', by a Fallen Cabinet Minister, *Sunday
Times*, 11 Nov 1951; Jennings, *The British Constitution*, p. 156.

42. O. Franks, *Central Planning and Control in War and Peace*
(London: Longmans, 1947) p. 52; R. S. Milne, 'Britain's Economic
Planning Machinery', *American Political Science Review*, Vol. 66
(1952) p. 410; cf. I. Jennings, *Queen's Government* (Harmonds-

worth: Penguin, 1954) P. 114: 'The civil service governs, the Ministers control the process of government.'

43. The term 'permanent politicians' is taken from J. D. Kingsley, *Representative Bureaucracy* (Yellow Springs, Ohio: Antioch Press, 1944) p. 269.

44. W. Harrison, *The Government of Britain*, 2nd rev. ed. (London: Hutchinson, 1952) p. 149.

45. Chester, 'Recent Trends in British Central Government', p. 19.

46. See annual data in *Britain: An Official Handbook* (HMSO); see also H. J. Laski, *Reflections on the Constitution: the House of Commons, The Cabinet, the Civil Service* (Manchester: Manchester UP, 1951) pp. 204—12; F. Brundrett, 'Government and Science', *Public Administration*, Vol. 34 (1956) pp. 245—56;

47. Snow, *Science and Government*, pp. 54—7.

48. Cf. R. V. Vernon and N. Mansergh (eds.), *Advisory Bodies; A Study of their uses in relation to Central Government* (London: Allen & Unwin, 1940) *passim*; PEP, *Advisory Committees in British Government, 1960* (London: Allen & Unwin, 1960) *passim*; S. E. Finer, *Anonymous Empire: A Study of the Lobby in Great Britain* (London: Pall Mall Press, 1958).

49. PEP, *Advisory Committees in British Government, 1960*, pp. xi, 10—11.

50. Cf. Chester and Willson, *The Organisation of British Central Government*, pp. 249—73.

51. Snow, *Science and Government, passim;* PEP, *Advisory Committees in British Government 1960*, pp. 94—5.

52. See, for example, Sir Cecil Carr, *Delegated Legislation* (Cambridge: UP, 1921); Lord Hewart of Bury, *The New Despotism* (London: Ernest Benn 1929); Sir C. K. Allen, *Law and Orders* (London: Sweet & Maxwell, 1956); *Report from Committee on Ministers' Powers*, Cmnd 4060 (1932); *Report from the Select Committee on Delegated Legislation*, House of Commons, 310—I (1953); W. A. Robson, *Justice and Administrative Law* 3rd ed. (London: Stevens, 1951).

53. Jennings, *Queen's Government*, pp. 95—6. But cf. S. E. Finer, 'The Individual Responsibility of Ministers', *Public Administration*, Vol. 34 (1956) pp. 377—96.

54. D. N. Chester and N. Bowring, *Questions in Parliament* (London: OUP, 1962) pp. 145 ff.

55. Ibid., pp. 96—108.

56. Ibid., pp. 92—6.

57. For details, see Lord Campion, *An Introduction to the Procedure of the House of Commons* (London: Macmillan 1947); G. Campion, 'Developments in the Parliamentary System since 1918', in G. Campion, et al., *British Government since 1918*, pp. 28—9; Morrison, *Government and Parliament*, pp. 221 ff.

58. Morrison, *Government and Parliament*, p. 117.

59. Cf. the table in P. G. Richards, *Honourable Members: A Study of*

the British Backbencher (London: Faber, 1959) p. 214; the number of parliamentary private secretaries in the House of Commons has risen from 16 in 1910 to 36 in 1960. There are also a number of unpaid Assistant Whips.

60. House of Commons 120 (1941); cf. House of Commons 349 (1956).

61. J. F. S. Ross, *Electors and Elections: Studies in Democratic Representation* (London: Eyre & Spottiswoode, 1955) p. 123.

62. Morrison, *Government and Parliament*, pp. 121–33; cf. Richards, *Honourable Members*, pp. 93–107, 143–56.

63. L. Broad, *Winston Churchill 1874–1945* rev. ed., (London: Hutchinson, 1946) p. 78.

64. R. B. Haldane, *An Autobiography* (London: Hodder & Stoughton, 1929) pp. 216–18.

65. M. de Wolfe Howe (ed.), *The Correspondence of Mr. Justice Holmes and Harold J. Laski, 1916–1935* (Cambridge, Mass.: Harvard UP, 1953) p. 628.

66. Viscount Cecil of Chelwood, *The Machinery of Government*, Barnett House Papers, No. 16 (Oxford, 1932) pp. 11–13, 19.

67. Jones, *A Diary with Letters*, pp. 56, 158; see also H. J. C. L'Etang, 'The Health of Statesmen and Affairs of Nations', in *The Practitioner* (1958) pp. 113–18.

68. Lord Hankey, *The Science and Art of Government* (Oxford: Clarendon Press, 1951) p. 23.

69. C. Cooke, *The Life of Richard Stafford Cripps* (London: Hodder & Stoughton, 1957) pp. 313–14.

70. M. Dalton, *High Tide and After: Memoirs 1945–1960* (London: Frederick Muller, 1962) p. 250, cf. p. 264.

71. *Sunday Times*, 18 Jul 1954.

72. *The Times*, 21 Apr 1956.

73, Gordon Walker, 'On Being a Cabinet Minister', p. 21.

74. 568 House of Commons Debates (11 Apr 1957), Cols. 1296–8; cf. the letter from Desmond Donnelly, MP, in *The Times*, 14 Dec 1956.

14 The Brains Behind The Throne*

JAMES FOX

Someone in Whitehall was describing how Lord Balogh — the head of Harold Wilson's Economic Unit in the Cabinet Office — had been 'viciously neutralised' by the Civil Service machine during the early days of Labour's slim majority. My informant is a relative newcomer to Whitehall but, for professional reasons, he made it his business to find out what had happened. He discovered that Balogh simply stopped getting information: the flow of Cabinet papers dried up; he was either not told of crucial committee meetings or was asked to attend three at the same time. Decisions were being made elsewhere while everyone, in the meantime, was being unspeakably nice to him. After 1966 Balogh had frequent access to the PM and to his papers, so his influence grew. But he was never accepted into the machine as an equal.

Lord Rothschild, however, has been accepted on both fronts, thus straddling the ground where politicians and civil servants dispute the balance of power. It is a delicate operation.

Rothschild's success so far — his survival — is the result of two things: firstly, his intellectual powers and his 'degree of natural authority', which, it is said, have won him respect and tentative acceptance by the machine; secondly, his direct access to Heath. That was something not spelled out in the White Paper that set up the Central Policy Review Staff, but Rothschild saw from the outset that it was crucial to his effectiveness. And while any interpretations of the shifts and balances of power at the centre are necessarily subjective, this access has also seemed crucial to Heath's own concentration of power around the Prime Minister's office. Since he came to power, Heath, partly by reforming and using the machine

*Reprinted from the *Sunday Times*, 25 Mar 1973, with the permission of the publisher.

in a particular way, has extended his control over Whitehall
to a degree that had been achieved by no other Prime
Minister since Attlee. Rothschild's access to Heath in this
context can be seen as mutually reinforcing. Only a handful
of senior officials have direct access.

The think tank, with its 15 versatile brains, was conceived
as a monitoring unit with antennae all over Whitehall. It was
designed to act for the Cabinet as a whole, to produce
analyses to help Ministers make independent policy decisions
and to keep a close watch on government strategy, all of
which it does. (Members of the CPRS insist on a formal
distinction between Tory strategy and post-manifesto government strategy.) But, by allowing Rothschild access, Heath has
brought the unit directly into his orbit. To a large extent it is
now he who approves their work programme — most recently
by allocating them specific research projects for Phase Three.
Unmistakably it is a shift of power towards the Prime
Minister, a subtle alteration that has made the think tank, in
the view of many Whitehall observers, a Prime Minister's
Department in all but name.

If this sounds alarming, it should be remembered that the
Prime Minister has traditionally received worse advice than
any other Western head of government, largely because he
has never had his own direct source of information. Whitehall
and Rothschild point to the constitution and the formal rules
to disprove shifts in the balance of power. Others — Whitehall
reporters, for instance — look at the personalities and alliances that make central government tick. It is a contentious
area. Much of the strengthening of the Prime Minister's
power base and his use of the think tank, for example, is
the direct result of Heath's own dominant personality, his
quasi-autocratic style of government in Cabinet and his
ascendency over his colleagues — partly a legacy of his
personal election victory. Indeed Mr Heath, to quote one of
the Tory inventors of the think tank, has had to use
'tremendous skill' and prudence to prevent the think tank
being seen, in effect, as a Prime Minister's Department. But
Ministers are already said to be showing signs of uneasiness.
They would be the first to suffer a loss of power. 'Ministers
are suspicious of the think tank,' said one Whitehall watcher,

'because they can see that sooner or later this will actually turn into a Prime Minister's Department. It increases the power of the Prime Minister and they don't want him poking around in their departments.'

Lord Rothschild denies these trends, and there is a school of thought which seeks to reduce alarm by saying that, in the cause of efficiency, the balance must shift towards No. 10, where the Prime Minister needs it badly. He, they say, is the only one who can take a grip on the machine, which is threatening to seize up with elephantiasis. Rothschild himself says that any moves towards presidential government would be incompatible with the British Cabinet system. But Heath's concentration of power obviously gives the idea (and it *is* certainly the wish of some influential Tory planners) that presidential power is slowly creeping up on No. 10 with what a *Financial Times* reporter called 'Grandmother's Footsteps'. 'Whenever anybody turns round to challenge him, the Prime Minister is always standing virtuously still.'

These days Rothschild can not only see the Prime Minister and brief him orally, bypassing Permanent Secretaries and Ministers alike, but he can also, at a pinch, report to the Prime Minister without first consulting Sir Burke Trend, Secretary to the Cabinet and the supreme Whitehall mandarin. What there was of a Prime Minister's brief used to be the responsibility of Sir Burke alone, but now Mr Heath gets briefs from Rothschild as well. Along with Sir Douglas Allen at the Treasury, Sir William Armstrong at the Civil Service Department and Trend himself, Rothschild has become one of the four top bureaucrats in Whitehall with access to Heath. For an outsider this is an extraordinary achievement. In addition, for reasons set out later, Rothschild and his staff have become the Treasury's direct rivals for the central policy position.

These are problems that concern the very nerve centre of parliamentary government, and in Whitehall it is almost a forbidden subject.

For two years officials have been saying quite bluntly that the CPRS is not attached directly to the Prime Minister but to the Cabinet as a whole. Answering my questions in his office in the Kent Treasury building in Whitehall, Lord

Rothschild was especially cautious about the question of his access to the Prime Minister. 'We are not the Prime Minister's men. We are the Cabinet's men,' he said, 'but you tend to have more discussion with the chairman of a committee than you do with its individual members. So although I would be very sad if I did not have access to the Prime Minister — when he's not too busy — it is rather on that relationship than on a personal advisory basis.' On Robin Day's *Talk-In* some months ago on BBC TV he said he saw Heath about once every five to seven weeks. In fact, it seems, there is scarcely a week in which the two men do not meet.

For Whitehall, the nerve centre has been invaded by what they call Lord Rothschild's 'idiosyncratic' behaviour. It may be partly Rothschild's ability to ask 'peculiarly direct questions — the kind that would embarrass seasoned civil servants'; or it could be to do with the framed headline in his office which proclaims: 'Lord Rothschild stars in Nude Pantomime'. The mandarins' reaction has been described by one informed observer as 'a suppressed howl of rage and indignation'. They are heard to complain that, while Whitehall respects personality and intellect, Lord Rothschild's method of work has left the original prospectus for the CPRS rather a long way behind. They mean, perhaps, that he has got too big for his boots.

It is all the more remarkable because of the unanimous predictions at the outset that the think tank would quickly be either absorbed or rejected by the Civil Service departments. The machine, in fact, has done neither, but has simply, to quote a source in Whitehall, 'put up with it'.

Much of the think tank's survival has undoubtedly been due to Rothschild's intellectual brilliance and the speed with which he has mastered the Whitehall game. But he was not the natural first choice as leader for the CPRS. Whitehall tried to find an insider — in fact they would have liked the whole thing kept internal, with additions made to the Cabinet Office which nobody would have found particularly remarkable. It was an idea which would have well suited Sir Burke Trend, who considers it unseemly for the Cabinet Office to be exposed to view. But it was denied him by the Tory manifesto, which made the plan public.

One possible candidate was definitely approached before Rothschild: Professor Hugh Ford, head of Mechanical Engineering at Imperial College and, like Lord Rothschild, a Fellow of the Royal Society, was offered the job and turned it down within 24 hours. Ford was definitely on the list of the 'great and the good' for some time. Among other things he was a member of the Science Research Council, and a Thomas Hawksley Gold Medallist for his research work on iron and steel. A technocrat *par excellence*, he was acceptable to the machine and to the planning group around David Howell, the smooth young Tory Junior Minister who had written the pamphlets for 'managerial revolution'. Another possibility was Dick Ross, now Rothschild's second-in-command at the tank, an economist who had worked at the OECD for seven years. He was put up, it is said, by Sir Burke Trend. The theory was that Ross, the academic, would work quietly away at blueprints for the future, out of the political limelight. However, he was never directly approached.

Finally, through the good offices of, it is thought, both Lord Jellicoe and Sir William Armstrong, Rothschild got the job.

Ross included, the 15 members of the think tank were chosen with great care from a very specialised pool, which turns out to have a fairly narrow social base of Oxbridge, stars from the Civil Service, and Rothschild's own acquaintances. Many are young, hence the slightly unfair epithet 'the teenage Old Etonians'. They dine at the Mirabelle with Rothschild (he pays). They go to Chequers with their strategy charts. With their considerable potential to question the entrenched views of the great departments and throw grit into the machine, they are seen either as brash outsiders or stimulating new arrivals, depending on whether or not they support what you are doing. 'We are just a few friends between the enormous Leviathan,' said one member wistfully.

The outsiders in the tank were said to be impressed by Whitehall and the brain-power they encountered, but were amazed that they had to lock their soap and towels in their desks so they would not be filched from the Cabinet Office conveniences.

The think tank is vulnerable to suggestions that the future of society is being mapped out by a group of elitist intellectuals. Still, with the help of selected outsiders, they are *finding out* about job alienation and about how irreversible the shake-out of labour in British industry really is. They are helping to plan Phase Three, for which they are, for example, trying to discover whether the wage demand spiral is due to grievances against the basic unfairness of society. Do the Tory backbenchers know that? Is the think tank getting out on a limb politically?

In fact the secrecy of the think tank's operations angers some MPs. They would like Rothschild's unit to be investigated regularly by a Select Committee. Rothschild argues that the Cabinet Office never reveals its secrets. But the MPs have a point, since this is the first time the Cabinet Office has been involved in policy-making like this. If it is working on blueprints for the future of society, MPs want a say.

Rothschild's (published) report on the scientific research councils sent shudders through Whitehall with its suggestions that money for the councils' research should be allocated on a contractor-consumer basis and that control should move towards different executive departments of government. It put up a great many backs, which was the last thing Whitehall's barons wanted.

One failure was thought to be the think tank's suggestion that Heath should impose a pay and prices freeze long before it was finally adopted. Rothschild denies he suggested it, but the story had currency to show how he lacked at the beginning the subtlety needed to master Whitehall politics.

There was also hostile feedback from the departments and criticism in the House of Commons about the unit's proposals for regional policy. As a short term project it also looked at Concorde, a study which some Whitehall-watchers saw as a tactical mistake — everyone in Whitehall believes the project is hopeless but nobody can get it killed.

On the future of the British computer industry, it reversed the recommendations of the Select Committee, which proposed a £60 million investment, and said the industry would have to wait until its corporate structure was stronger — i.e. backed by European or US money. On energy, it played a key part in the decision to resuscitate the coal industry, or at least to halt its decline. There it seems to have imposed its view on Whitehall, which, said Lord Robens, 'had been mesmerised by nuclear power'.

The think tank has commissioned a study from outside on how the government should relate to the City. It is studying the crucial question of population, which industries will decline in the next 10 years, what to do about roads and transport. More immediately, it was largely the think tank which persuaded Heath to open the tri-partite talks with the TUC and the CBI and has since been closely involved with Heath's counter-inflation policies in general.

Every Monday morning the think tank assembles in Rothschild's office for its weekly meeting. 'What? Get them all together?' he said when I asked for a photograph. 'Impossible. You don't seem to realise. This is a bunch of 15 anarchists.' The atmosphere, clouded by Rothschild's extraordinary consumption of cigarettes, is democratic — except, that is, for Rothschild himself, who can be fearsome and autocratic with all his wit and charm.

I had 45 minutes of his time straight after one of these sessions. 'We had rather a good Monday morning meeting this morning,' he said. 'Most of us were there, and Adam didn't pretend to go to sleep, which he usually does just to get a rise out of me. William says, "I know what you're going to say next." Rather putting off. Adam usually lies on that sofa. Very unruly lot.'

Adam is Adam Ridley, an Old Etonian economist who came from the Department of Economic Affairs, was at Oxford with Emma, one of Victor Rothschild's three daughters, and married an Asquith. He is in his early thirties. William is William Waldegrave, who is much talked about as a bright and ambitious young Tory. His engagement to Victoria, youngest of Lord Rothschild's daughters, was the subject of congratulations in the House of Lords — much to their embarrassment. (His father is the 12th Earl Waldegrave.) Waldegrave is 26 years old and has the reputation of having known the control panel of the Tory Party from an early age — in fact he is used by Rothschild as the link-man with the Party, as a policy-acceptability tester. He is a good friend of

Peter Walker, and is said to be in his element at Chequers. He has all the attributes of excellence of a classically Bright Young Man: from Eton he got a scholarship to Oxford, where he obtained a Classics First. Since then he has become a Fellow of All Souls. At a loose end, in a manner of speaking, he wrote to Lord Jellicoe, now Lord Privy Seal, to ask what a bright young man should do now. Lunch with Rothschild secured him the job. They found themselves thinking along similar lines.

In the interview Rothschild had been saying that nobody knew the political views of civil servants. 'But I know what you are, William,' he said turning to Waldegrave. 'You're a radical.' 'Thank you,' said Waldegrave, who in fact is thought to stand politically in the centre of the Tory Party.

Among the first members of the tank, hired at the end of 1971, were two former personal assistants of Heath, William Plowden and Peter Carey (ex-Ministry of Technology, who has since gone to the DTI). There was Robin Butler, who has gone to No. 10. Later on, in 1972, Brian Reading, Heath's closest economic adviser in Opposition, architect of the 'At-a-Stroke Programme', joined the think tank. William Waldegrave, climbing the Tory ladder, joined early on. The first, if unofficial, member, even before Rothschild, was John Mayne. Formerly Healey's Private Secretary in the Ministry of Defence, he had worked closely with Trend on the CPRS's *modus operandi,* and on the White Paper that created it. It was Mayne who knew how it should work. (He is still linked with Trend's office and is teased by Rothschild for being Trend's 'spy'.) From the Foreign Office, where he was a star, came Robert Wade-Gery, Wykehamist and All Souls Fellow. He is a key figure in Rothschild's diplomatic front with Whitehall.

Among the early arrivals were Chris Sandars, from the Ministry of Defence — originally appointed as Rothschild's personal assistant; Adam Ridley and Hector Hawkins. Ross also put up Richard Crum, economist, who he had known from East Anglia University. There was Madeleine Aston and, from Shell, Tony Fish, who has since left. Later additions picked by Lord Rothschild include Kate Mortimer, daughter of the Bishop of Exeter, and Peter Bowcock, ex-Tory Central Office, both of whom came from the World Bank. There was

Jean Rosenfeld, also from Shell, who has also left; John Burgh, originally at the Board of Trade, then on the Community Relations Commission; John Guinness, of the Guinness family, formerly at the Foreign and Commonwealth Office. New additions are John Crawley, from the Inland Revenue, and Ian Read, from Shell.

'We looked around,' said Rothschild. 'I sometimes go to the Barbados, and since Dick Ross told me he knew a very good man on one of these sugar boards called Hector Hawkins, I made it may business to have a rum punch with him — perhaps two — and I thought Hector was very nice and very good so I asked if he would make a sacrifice and join me in the Cabinet Office. [Hawkins had been in the Department of Overseas Development under Barbara Castle.] Well, then Peter Bowcock was recommended to me by Lord Jellicoe. Kate Mortimer I knew because she was a contemporary of my daughter Emma's at Oxford, so I knew her quite well.

'Madeleine [Aston] I think Peter Carey recommended.' A scientist and an economist, Madeleine Aston was at first the only woman in the think tank, and when Lord Rothschild took all of them to the Mirabelle, London's very posh restaurant, for an annual celebration, Madeleine was chivalrously placed on his right. But not for long. The seating, master-minded by William Waldegrave, changed no fewer than three times during the meal.

'Adam we all knew was a very clever fellow,' says Rothschild of Ridley. 'I think I got hold of William [Plowden] because his father's rather a friend of mine and I asked his father if he might like it. I knew quite a lot about William because I knew him from his Cambridge days.

'I'm afraid,' says Rothschild, 'that the selection in some people's eyes might be considered rather random.' Or rather personal? 'Personal, perhaps, except some of them were very strongly recommended by departments.'

There is a Whitehall version of Rothschild's own appointment which says that the cardinals of the bureaucracy (to use Lord Rothschild's phrase) were taken by surprise when he was paraded as a Socialist, and Waldegrave, it is said, owes part of his job to the need to 'get some Tories'. Rothschild is not a Socialist in any way that is discernible. He has not taken the Labour Whip for 11 years, is known to spit with rage at the mention of Harold Wilson, and moves most easily in Tory aristocratic circles. He is ill at ease outside this circle and embarrassed in the company of middle-class Socialists. 'Victor,' said a friend, 'is an aristocrat. He is a Socialist because he thinks Socialists are nicer people. For a Jew of his generation, remember, Tories were notable for their lack of opposition to Fascism and will say that Mussolini's trains ran on time and so on.'

Rothschild and Heath get along well, despite Rothschild's description of their first meeting. 'The PM is a man of few words. He said: "I don't think we've met before?" After my reply that, no, we had not, there was a long, rather wintry pause. I then said are you sure you don't want an economist in this position, to which he replied with a rather characteristic, monosyllabic, "No".'

'Another wintry pause and the interview came to an end.' (It was, in fact, not the only interview. They met several times in the early stages when the tank was being set up.) 'But he's rather an unusual man, the PM,' said Lord Rothschild. 'Why do I find him unusual? Because I find that he listens very carefully to what I say and he absorbs it and thinks about it. I also think he's unusual because he's very resolute and, as he himself says, "my enemies say that I'm obstinate, my supporters say that I'm resolute". I find him resolute — the few occasions that I meet him — and I think he's very good at his job.'

Rothschild is 62, and earns £14,000 as head of the CPRS. His background is academic, with forays during the war into espionage and bomb disposal. For 10 years, before joining the tank, he ran the research department at Shell.

He has, say his friends, 'led an extraordinarily autocratic life, couldn't really be a politician in a democracy because of having to be liked and be likeable'.

There is an arrogant — even outrageous — side to him, and he can bully lesser men than himself; but, in Whitehall, if he has met his match it is first and foremost with Sir Burke Trend. 'I happen to work in the same building as him,' said Rothschild on BBC TV. 'I greatly admire him.' *Pause.* 'With his *penetrating* intellect.' Rothschild, whose intellectual standards are high, is said to admire Trend as the only man in Britain who can dictate a White Paper orally within three hours. On paper, however, the two men would seem to be on a collision course and that is irresistibly translated by newspapers into a clash of personalities.

Sir Burke's often indefinable power derives from organising the smooth flow of papers in and out of the Cabinet, making up the Cabinet agenda, deciding who sits on what committee and, most important, he plays the co-ordinating role where more than one ministry is involved. He can control who sees who — which amounts to an ability to actually direct policy.

A quiet word in Sir Burke's ear and problems can melt away. For 10 years he has been the incorruptible master of the Cabinet's business. Rothschild's role, however, is to put up reports to the Cabinet untainted by the normal give-and-take of Whitehall policy-making. The think tank's role is undeniably to produce 'creative tension', to make people think a little harder which, in effect, means throwing grit into the machine. Mostly it submits reports which are discussed early on in the policy-making process, but it can and does send reports straight to the Cabinet, or even the Prime Minister, and this is where the working of Burke Trend's operation may be disrupted.

The CPRS was designed to help ministers penetrate the gloss which departments tend to wrap their policies in. All too often ministers making collective decisions in the Cabinet have neither the time, the power, nor — except in rare cases — the acumen to do it themselves. In Cabinet they were often badly informed by their own department heads about the policies of their colleagues, by which time many valuable opinions had been buried. 'We should get in on the bottom,' say members of the think tank, 'sit on inter-departmental committees and detect the line which isn't put forward. This is very difficult to do with a neatly-worded Cabinet Paper. This is a very skilful and professional document and when it comes round 48 hours in advance of the Cabinet meeting, most Ministers won't know about it. Our job is to try and give them more resources to ask intelligent questions. If, for example, you asked the Department of Health and Social

Security if you can raise pensions, they might say you can't do it for five or six months.

'And that answer is based on information from a computer in Newcastle, and the view is that it was always impossible in the past and it's impossible now. The department will bang on and, when it comes to the Cabinet, the ministers will have to rely on the heads of their departments. If you can apply just a little informed criticism, just to make the department think rather hard, you might make it find a way to a better solution. It's cultivating the skills of the intelligent outsider and pursuing them far enough so that they have validity.'

But Rothschild might come up against Trend when, as often happens, the tank itself only gets to hear of the policy 48 hours in advance — the time lapse between the announcement of the agenda and the actual Cabinet meeting. That is when it needs the patronage of Heath. If it doesn't have time to get an agreement or to insert an untainted report, it sends a minute to Heath. Trend is therefore faced with problems. Throwing a conflicting view into the ring at a late stage makes discussion longer and agreement more difficult. If it is an unorthodox view it makes the task of getting it implemented more difficult.

How much political influence, then, has Lord Rothschild acquired? He himself says: 'Politics, in the normal sense of the word, don't enter into the lives of civil servants.' That is also meant to embrace the think tank.

But the subject causes alarm in Whitehall. Civil servants are bound to become involved in party politics, especially when they are concerned with keeping Government strategy on the rails — the think tank's main function. Whitehall is so nervous about constitutional improprieties being levelled against it that it won't even discuss the think tank. A Treasury Press Officer said it was 'too political' a matter to be discussed — there he slipped up badly. Appealing to 10 Downing Street — which, more and more, becomes the only place you can get information — to see two members of the Treasury who had been connected with the beginnings of the think tank, I was told that the two gentlemen would 'not necessarily be backward in coming forward'. They never broke cover.

Rothschild also subscribes to the mythology that there is a distinction between party politics and government policy. In fact, he dismisses the argument as 'semantics', and when Richard Crossman in a TV interview said of the strategy meetings: 'This is the most political activity a civil servant could indulge in,' Rothschild replied: 'Of course, the government's strategy is political, but the consequences of a political input are not necessarily political in themselves.'

'What the PM wants is analysis,' he told me, 'a logical analysis of the situation, and that's what he gets. If he wants some political advice he certainly wouldn't come to us — he would go through his political advisers. If our analysis is politically unacceptable, then it's politically unacceptable. And we have told the government some pretty unpopular things.'

But set against that are the views of some members of the think tank themselves. 'To be effective,' said one, 'you must be political.' Another said that the tank took over where the civil service became apolitical. And a third said: 'Whether we're political or not can be judged by whether we're controversial. The nearer you get to final decision-making, the nearer you are to Parliament and controversy. The stuff of our everyday work is, "What should we do?" Often the best advice would make us look foolish, and one wouldn't suggest things obviously against the PM's prejudices.'

But the monitoring of government strategy is surely a role where the charges of 'political' activity stick. The think tank's advice on strategy was said to have been very useful in finally persuading ministers that the government was right to go back on the Tory manifesto and introduce a Prices and Incomes policy.

The whole argument comes to the crunch at the six-monthly strategy meetings at Chequers, when members of the think tank meet the Tory ministers. Soon after the Chequers session they meet the middle and junior ministers at No. 10. It turns out therefore that the think tank is talking poltical strategy to no fewer than 80 Tory ministers, a third of the Parliamentary party, and thus a large section of the Tory Party grass roots. Some see this as simply a glorious PR operation for managerial efficiency by Heath — a day out at

Chequers. But there the think tank meets and mingles with the Tories, reports on the Government's performance and thrashes out strategy. If that is not political, Rothschild is right in dismissing the whole thing as semantics.

'I don't think we'd say in these meetings that a minister had short-comings,' said Rothschild. 'We might say a little more effort could be put into something, like those school reports. Quite a good term's work but a little more effort on the Greek is indicated. Seems curiously uninterested in algebra.'

This, however, is no neutered strategy. It is based on the manifesto on which the election was won, and on deliberate alterations to the manifesto. The think tank, by explaining and interpreting Conservative strategy and keeping it in the minds of ministers, is undoubtedly being partisan to that manifesto. More important, strategy concerns the future, and especially how to win the next election — on which all other strategy depends. Does Rothschild, among his charts, have one that shows on a graph the optimum time to call a General Election? Members of the think tank, after all, are asking ministers at Chequers questions like, 'You can't win the next election unless you bring inflation down to 2½ per cent. and halve unemployment. What are you going to do about it?' But there is growing talk inside and outside Whitehall that this function should be put back in the party political headquarters. There is even talk of creating a Department of the Opposition.

It is worth remembering the plans the Tories had for the think tank, and the reform of central government at the outset. They wanted their unit to be a large and powerful agency to 'manage the machinery of government', and saw it working 'in a much more personal way' for the Prime Minister, to quote one of its planners. 'We underestimated the collective role it plays for the Cabinet,' he said. But the argument with Whitehall centred on the problem central to all politics — the allocation of resources, which meant choosing priorities. Alarmingly, no-one was planning expenditure more than five years ahead.

The Tories wanted to take public expenditure responsibility out of the Treasury altogether and lodge it with the new unit. Their major instrument for this was PAR (Programme Analysis and Review), a monitoring unit in each department which would analyse and challenge all public expenditure. When a team of eight businessmen was brought into Whitehall to improve managerial efficiency (all but one have since left), they seized on the task of launching PAR. Rothschild, however, was said to have held them in such contempt that he refused to have anything to do with PAR for a whole year, so it developed in the Treasury — 'not without an ulterior motive', to quote a Treasury source. For this Rothschild is criticised by the machine. PAR, however, has not developed into what the planners hoped would be 'a major instrument of political power'.

In the final analysis the think tank is vulnerable — despite Prime Ministerial patronage — because it depends on Whitehall for information, and therefore on its tolerance. Rothschild says: 'So far they've been very good to us.' But it is the life-blood that could dry up if the think tank began seriously to obstruct the machine. Rothschild has said that he can't know for certain whether he is getting all the information. 'We've got to know what they know to do battle with them and argue on equal terms,' said one think tank member. 'Departments have to decide whether to give it to us or risk that we report with incorrect information. But departments are not monoliths. At every point in policy-making you find some guy who doesn't agree. Therefore there is always erratic support for our activities. and we do have the threat that we can use our access to the Prime Minister, and make rude remarks. That is really why we can operate.'

Still the Whitehall barons and the Treasury knights are complaining that Rothschild doesn't take enough account of how the machine works, that he is not patient enough to get his ideas accepted before sending his reports in writing to Cabinet committees and the Prime Minister himself.

Although the think tank or some central unit may be a permanent part of a Prime Minister's armoury, it is still, in the mind of its members, somewhat insecure. 'The trouble is,' said one think tank member, 'that people don't really know how to live with this organism. I can't say we're established.' Professor Robert Neild, Cambridge economist, was a member of the Fulton Committee and an early advocate of a central advisory unit. He was also thought to be on the list of probables to head it. 'Maybe,' he says, 'we need to try a more open approach, something like French planning, where you have more quasi-autonomous agencies which go in for long-run analysis of policy options.

'It needs to be done as publicly as possible because these are very important political decisions. They dictate the nature of society in the future, and a well-ordered society is one that debates these matters and has information before it, and not gathered away and scrutinised in dark gloomy rooms in Whitehall.

'The whole of British government is excessively cagey, which is a great pity.'

It is more likely, however, that the think tank will eventually be merged into a new Prime Minister's Department, run perhaps by Sir William Armstrong, after the retirement of Sir Burke Trend this year. (Sir William was made a Privy Councillor in the New Year's Honours.) The question remains of whether there will be adequate checks and balances on Prime Ministerial power under this arrangement — or whether the Cabinet system will suffer. Alternatively there are two plans, spelled out by Sir Richard Clarke in his lectures on central government: either there will be a single department of Treasury, Civil Service Department and think tank — a giant monolity of power; or there will be two departments at the centre: a Ministry of National Economy and Finance — which would be the Treasury minus control of public expenditure — and a Central Management Department, which would deal with the public sector and incorporate the CPRS and the Civil Service Department in a kind of US-style Budget Bureau. This might also be under the direct control of the Prime Minister.

Whatever does happen, it is rumoured that the next head of the think tank will come from inside the machine, the official reason being that a replacement for Rothschild's brilliance will be hard to find on the outside. Rothschild, by sheer force of personality, has secured what was generally thought to be an impossible position even to hold. He won't go down as long as Heath's patronage lasts, and as long as the grandmother's footsteps keep on coming.

Bibliography

The following bibliography provides a guide to the most recent books and articles about the Cabinet. Excluded from the bibliography are the large number of biographies, autobiographies, and memoirs of Prime Ministers and other Cabinet members. If the reader is interested in such works he is referred to the comprehensive bibliography in R. M. Punnett, *British Government and Politics* (London: Heinemann, 1968) pp. 475–81. It has not been possible to provide a collection of articles written on the Cabinet by political journalists or written by members of the Cabinet themselves: these are numerous and can be frequently found in the daily and Sunday press, and in periodicals such as the *New Statesman*, the *Spectator*, *Crossbow*, *Socialist Commentary*, the *Listener*, etc.

Alderman, R. K., and J. A. Cross, *The Tactics of Resignation* (London: Routledge & Kegan Paul, 1967).

Amery, L. S., *Thoughts on the Constitution* (London: OUP, 1964).

Barker, A., and M. Rush, *The Member of Parliament and His Information* (London: Allen & Unwin, 1970).

Benemy, F. W. G., *The Elected Monarch: The Development of the Power of the Prime Minister* (London: Harrap, 1965).

Benewick, R., and R. E. Dowse (eds.), *Readings in British Government and Politics* (London: UP, 1968).

Berkeley, H., *The Power of the Prime Minister* (London: Allen & Unwin, 1968).

Birch, A. H., *Representative and Responsible Government* (London: Allen & Unwin, 1964).

———, *The British System of Government* (London: Allen & Unwin, 1967).

Brown, A. H., 'Prime Ministerial Power', Parts 1 and 2, *Public Law* (1968) pp. 28–51, 96–118.

Buck, P. W., 'M.P.s in Ministerial Office, 1918–55 and 1955–59', *Political Studies*, Vol. 9 (1961) pp. 300–6.

———, 'The Early Start Towards Cabinet Office, 1918–55', *Western Political Quarterly*, Vol. 16 (1963) pp. 624–32.

Chester, D. N., 'Who Governs Britain?', *Parliamentary Affairs*, Vol. 15 1962) pp. 519–27.

——— and F. M. G. Willson, *The Organisation of British Central Government* (London: Allen & Unwin, 1968).

Crossman, R. H. S., *Inside View* (London: Jonathan Cape, 1972).

Daalder, H., *Cabinet Reform in Britain, 1914–63* (Stanford UP, 1964).

Ehrmann, J., *Cabinet Government and War, 1890–1940* (Cambridge: CUP, 1958).

Finer, S. E., 'The Individual Responsibility of Ministers', *Public Administration*, Vol. 34 (1956) pp. 377–96.

Fry, G. K., 'Thoughts on the present state of the Convention of Ministerial Responsibility', *Parliamentary Affairs*, Vol. 23, no. 1 (1969—70) pp. 10—20.

Gordon-Walker, Lord, *The Cabinet* (London: Fontana, 1970).

Groth, A. J., 'Britain and America: Some Requisites of Executive Leadership compared', *Political Science Quarterly*, Vol. 85, no. 2 (June 1970) pp. 217—39.

Heasman, D. J., 'The Prime Minister and the Cabinet', *Parliamnetary Affairs*, Vol. 15 (1961—2) pp. 461—84.

————, 'The Ministerial Hierarchy', *Parliamentary Affairs*, Vol. 15 (1961—2) pp. 307—30.

————, 'Ministers' Apprentices', *New Society*, 16 July 1964, pp. 16—17.

Heclo, H., and A. Wildavsky, *The Private Government of Public Money: Community and Policy inside British Politics* (London: Macmillan, 1974).

Hinton, R. W. K., 'The Prime Minister as an Elected Monarch', *Parliamentary Affairs*, Vol. 13 (1960) pp. 297—303.

Jackson, R. J., *Rebels and Whips* (London: Macmillan, 1968).

Jennings, I., *Cabinet Government*, 3rd ed., (Cambridge: CUP, 1959).

Jones, G. W., 'The Prime Minister's Power', *Parliamentary Affairs*, Vol. 18 (1964—5) pp. 167—85.

King, A., 'Britain's Ministerial Turnover', *New Society*, 18 Aug 1966, pp. 257—8.

————, *The British Prime Minister* (London: Macmillan, 1969).

————, and A. Sloman, *Westminster and Beyond* (London: Macmillan, 1974).

Leonard, R., 'Snakes and Ladders', *New Society*, 9 Oct 1969, p. 558.

————, and V. Herman (eds.), *The Backbencher and Parliament* (London: Macmillan, 1972).

Lindsay, T., and M. Harrington, *The Conservative Party, 1918—1970* (London: Macmillan, 1974).

Loewenstein, K., *British Cabinet Government* (London: OUP, 1967).

Mackintosh, J P., 'The Prime Minister and the Cabinet', *Parliamentary Affairs*, Vol. 21 (1967—8) pp. 53—68.

————, *The British Cabinet*, 2nd ed., (London: Stevens, 1968).

————, *The Government and Politics of Great Britain*, 3rd ed., (London: Hutchinson, 1974).

Madgwick, P. J., 'Resignations', *Parliamentary Affairs* (Winter 1966) pp. 59—76.

Marshall, G., 'Ministerial Responsibility', *Political Quarterly*, Vol. 34 (1963) pp. 256—68.

————, and G. C. Moody, *Some Problems of the Constitution* (London: Hutchinson, 1967).

Moodie, G. C., *The Government of Great Britain* (London: Methuen, 1964).

Morrison, Lord, *Government and Parliament*, 3rd ed. (London: OUP, 1964).

Neustadt, R. E., interviewed by H. Brandon, '10 Downing Street: Is it Out of Date?', *Sunday Times*, 8 Nov 1964.

————, 'White House and Whitehall', *The Public Interest*, No. 2 (1966) pp. 55—69.

Playfair, Sir Edward, 'Who are the Policy-makers?', *Public Administration*, Vol. 43 (1965) pp. 251—68.

Punnett, R. M., 'The Labour Shadow Cabinet 1955—65', *Parliamentary Affairs*, Vol. 18 (1964—5) pp. 61—70.

————, *British Government and Politics* (London: Heinemann, 1968).

————, *Front Bench Opposition: the Role of the Leader of the Opposition, the Shadow Cabinet, and Opposition Spokesmen in British Politics* (London: Heinemann, 1973).

Rose, R., *Politics in England* (London: Faber, 1965).

———— (ed.), *Policy-Making in Britain* (London: Macmillan, 1969).

————, 'The Making of Cabinet Ministers', *British Journal of Political Science*, Vol. 1 (1971) pp. 393—414.

Seymour-Ure, C., 'The "Disintegration" of the Cabinet and the Neglected Question of Cabinet Reform', *Parliamentary Affairs*, Vol. 24 (1971) pp. 196—207.

Smith, B., and Hague, D. C. (eds.), *The Dilemma of Accountability in Modern Government* (London: Macmillan, 1971).

Stankiewicz, W. J., *Crisis in British Government* (New York: Collier-Macmillan, 1967).

Turner, D. R., *The Shadow Cabinet in British Politics* (London: Routledge & Kegan Paul, 1969).

Whale, J., *Journalism and Government* (London: Macmillan, 1972).

Williams, F., *A Prime Minister Remembers* (London: Heinemann, 1960).

Williams, M., *Inside Number 10* (London: Weidenfeld & Nicolson, 1971).

Willson, F. M. G., 'Routes of Entry of New Members of the British Cabinet; 1868—1958', *Political Studies*, Vol. 7 (1959) pp. 222—32.

————, 'Entry to the Cabinet, 1959—68', *Political Studies*, Vol. 18 (1970) pp. 236—8.

Wilson, H., interviewed by N. Hunt, *Whitehall and Beyond* (London: BBC, 1964).

————, interviewed by N. Hunt, 'The Prime Minister and the Machinery of Government', I and II, *Listener* 6 and 13 April 1967.

Wiseman, H. V., *Parliament and The Executive* (London: Routledge & Kegan Paul, 1966).

Index

Aberdare, Lord, 13n
Abramovitz, Moses, 243n
Alderman, R. K., 6n, 34n
Allen, Sir C. K., 263n
Allen, Sir Douglas, 279
Alt, James E., 33-54
Amery, Julian, 81
Amery, L. S., 94n
Anderson, Sir John, 251
Apter, David, 30n
Armstrong, Sir William, 279, 292
Aspinall, A., 245n, 252n
Asquith, H. H., 39, 79, 143n, 163, 267
Atlee, Clement, 10, 39, 42, 87, 90, 91, 92, 95, 123, 144, 147, 164, 186, 251, 253, 268
Attorney General, 82
Avon, Lord, see Eden
Avril, Pierre, 55n

Bailey, Stephen, xxiii
Baldwin, Stanley, 39, 42, 51, 79, 83, 95, 143n, 163, 195-6, 253, 267
Balfour, First Earl (A. J.), 81-2
Balogh, Lord, 277
Bank Holiday proclamation, 103-4, 106-8
Barnes, J., 143n
Barnett, M. J., 131
Beaverbrook, First Baron (W. M. Aitken), 82n, 88
Beer, Samuel H., 121n
Belgium, 22
Beloff, Max, 244n, 246n, 247n, 250n
Bevan, Aneurin, 6, 81, 84, 85, 88, 89, 91, 92, 96, 144, 204, 258, 268
Bevin, Ernest, 90, 91, 132, 209, 251, 258, 268
Birch, Nigel, 86, 94
Birkenhead, Lord, 79
Blake, R., 143n
Blondel, Jean, 56n
Bowring, N., 263n, 264n
Boyd-Carpenter, John, 173
Boyle, Sir Edward, 85, 145n, 173, 174
Bridgeman, Viscount (W. C.), 93
Bridges, Lord, 135n
Bright, John, 90

Brittan, Samuel, 130n, 134n
Broad, L., 266n
Bromhead, Peter, 257n
Brooke, Henry, 161, 219
Brown, A. H., 1n
Brown, George, see George-Brown, Lord
Brundrett, F., 260n
Budget, 158, 197-8, 200
Bullock, Alan, 132n
Burns, J., 82, 90
Burton, I. F., 18n
Butler, D. E., 10n, 35n
Butler, R. A. (Lord Butler of Saffron Walden), 84, 161, 173, 176, 180, 193-209, 210, 251, 252, 265

Cabinet, see also Ministers, Prime Minister
   appointments, see Ministers
   committees, xvii, 126-8, 132, 194, 205, 212, 247, 253
   composition, xviii, 6, 8, 245
   decision-making, 132, 193, 207, 221-41
   functions, xiii-xiv
   institutional development, xvii, 242-71
   and Lobby, see Lobby correspondents
   meetings, 221-41, 246
   Office, 126, 132, 163, 247n, 250, 277-9, 282
   powers, xiv-xv, xix, xxv, 202
   reform, proposals for, 269-71
   reshuffles, 9, 49-52, 67, 172-3, 175
   Secretariat, xvii, 247-8
   size, 5, 43, 208-9, 244-5
   structure, xx-xxi
   study of, xi-xxiv
Cabinet government, 34, 109, 193-209
Callaghan, James, 210
Campbell, Peter, 56n, 253n
Campbell-Bannerman, H., 45
Campion, Lord (G.), 246n, 264n
Canada, 59, 67, 72
Carr, Sir Cecil, 263n

Carson, Sir E., 81, 82
Casey, Sir Richard, 254
Castle, Barbara, 123
Cecil, Lady G., 78n
Cecil, Lord Robert, 81, 82, 83, 90, 92, 267
Central Policy Review Staff, xvii, 277-92
Chamberlain, Sir Austen, 46, 143n, 253
Chamberlain, Joseph, 78, 81-2, 88, 89
Chamberlain, Neville, 48, 84, 94, 97, 163, 267
Chancellor of the Duchy of Lancaster, 5, 83, 166, 254, 265
Chancellor of the Exchequer, 7, 50, 59, 62, 63, 67, 77-8, 110-17, 134, 172-3, 197-8, 200, 210-20, 253n; *see also* Government Departments – Treasury
Chataway, Christopher, 174
Cherwell, Lord, 263
Chester, D. N., xviii, 1n, 34n, 46n, 243n, 244n, 246n, 249n, 250n, 258n, 260n, 262n, 263n, 264n
Chilston, E. A. A., 78n, 91n
Churchill, Lord Randolph, 51, 77-8, 87, 88, 89, 91, 93, 94, 95, 96, 162
Churchill, Sir Winston, 8, 9, 38, 39, 45, 79, 84n, 85, 93, 94n, 95, 96, 97, 163, 165, 176, 193-4, 199, 251, 265, 268
Civil servants, *see also* Central Policy Review Staff
 and Cabinet ministers, 121-36, 199, 212, 258-60
 expertise of, 128-31, 213, 260-1
 and government advisers, 130, 261-2, 277
 requirements, 122-31
 turnover, 130
Clarke, Sir Richard, 292
Coady, M., 187n
Cole, M., 143n
Colonial Secretary, 81
Colvin, I., 82n
Colvin, I. G., 84n
Committees, *see* Cabinet
Common Market, *see* European Economic Community
Commons, House of, 10-13, 23-4, 27, 122, 133

Conservative Party, 13, 45, 123, 141, 173-7, 179, 206
Cooke, C., 268n
Cousins, Frank, 13, 80, 81, 86-7, 95, 99
Craig, F. W. S., 141n
Cripps, Sir Stafford, 81, 90, 92, 251, 265, 268
Crises, 20, 46; *see also* Suez
Crookshank, H., 265
Crosland, Anthony, 33n, 34n, 107
Cross, J. A., 6n, 34n
Crossman, R. H. S., 34n, 36n, 96, 169
Curzon, Lord, 81, 92

Daalder, Hans, xiii, xxv, 33n, 34n, 242-76
Dalton, Hugh, 90, 96n, 251, 258
Dalton, M., 268n
Deedes, William, 164, 167, 168, 169, 172, 173
Defence Council, 125
Deputy Prime Minister, 251-2
Derby, Lord, 82
Derry, J. W., 142n
Devaluation of Sterling, 188
Disraeli, Benjamin, 42, 45, 78
Dogan, Mattei, 56n, 253n
Doig, Jameson, 16n, 23n
Donnelly, Desmond, 268n
Douglas-Home, Sir Alec, 6, 182
Drumalbyn, Lord, 5
Drury, G., 18n
Du Cann, Edward, 174
Duff-Cooper, A., 81, 84-5, 93
Dugdale, Blanche E. C., 143n
Dugdale, Sir Thomas, xv
Duncan Committee, 121n

Eccles, Sir David, 173
Ede, Chuter, 197, 265
Eden, Sir Anthony (Lord Avon), 8, 45, 49, 80, 81, 84, 88, 89, 92, 93, 94, 95, 96, 97, 109, 161, 165, 202, 203, 251, 254n, 265, 268
Einzig, Paul, 159n, 160n
Eliasberg, Vera F., 243n
Ensor, Sir Robert, 35n
Equal Franchise Bill, 79
European Economic Community, xiv, xvi-xvii, 160, 204-6, 252
Evans, Harold, 166, 170, 185

Feiling, K., 84n, 142n
Ferranti, Basil de, 174

Finer, S. E., xv, 3n, 34n, 262n, 263n
Finland, 22, 62-4, 68, 73
Fitzmaurice, Lord Edmond, 142n
Foord, A. S., 142n
Foot, Michael, 84n, 94n
Foreign Secretary, 30, 50, 59, 62 63,
    67, 83-4, 103-10, 252, 265, 267
Fox, James, 277-92
France, 22, 55-6, 62-4, 68, 73, 200
Franks, O., 259n
Fraser, T., 81
Freeman, Jennie, 10n, 35n
Freeman, John, 85
Fry, G. K., 1n
Fulton Committee, 1, 28n, 121n,
    127n, 129-30, 131n

Gaitskell, Hugh, 85, 91
Garcia, Thomas V., 130n
George-Brown, Lord (Brown, George),
    xvi, 99n, 103-10, 132, 221n
Gilbert, M., 84n
Gilmour, Iain, 124n
Gladstone, W. E., 35, 42, 51, 78, 162-3
Gollin, A., 81n, 82n, 99n
Gordon-Walker, Lord (Patrick), xiii,
    xvii, 1n, 17n, 28n, 126n, 221-41,
    254n, 268n
Gott, R., 84n
Government, changes of, 36; *see also*
    Stability
Government departments
    Admiralty, 84, 93-4
    Agriculture, 50, 59, 62, 63, 256,
        258
    Aviation, 50, 257
    Commonwealth Relations, 50, 255,
        256, 285
    Defence, 59, 62, 63, 67, 86, 248,
        252, 261, 284
    Dominions, 253
    Economic Affairs, 132
    Education and Science, 25, 50, 59,
        62, 63, 83, 173, 193
    Environment, 5, 25
    Foreign Office, 50, 59, 62, 63, 67,
        85, 103-10, 249, 253, 256
    Health and Social Security, 25, 257,
        258, 288
    Home Office, 18, 25, 59, 62, 63,
        130, 210-20, 256
    Housing, 124, 130, 173, 258
    Labour, 50, 257, 258

Overseas Development, 130
Pensions and National Insurance,
    256, 257, 258
Power, 130, 257
Scottish Office, 25, 173, 255
Supply, 257, 258
Technology, 86-7, 125, 284
Town and Country Planning, 257,
    258
Trade and Industry, 5, 50, 59, 62,
    63, 67, 85, 125, 130, 255, 284
Transport, 123, 130, 256, 257, 258
Treasury, 20, 50, 59, 62, 63, 67,
    93, 110-17, 130, 132, 134, 158,
    163, 199, 210-20, 243, 249, 253,
    254, 256, 261, 279, 290-1
Welsh Office, 255
Works, 258
Government Information Services, 162,
    164n, 165
Government–press relations, 164-70,
    184-90; *see also* Lobby
    correspondents
Gregg, John, 80
Grey of Fallodon, Lord, 254n
Grove, J. W., 245n, 246n
Gunn, L., 125n

Hailsham, Lord, 80, 216
Haldane, R. B., 44, 267n
Halifax, Lord, 93
Hamilton, Lord, 51, 94
Hankey, Lord, 247n, 268n
Harris, John S., 130n, 186
Harrison, Wilfred, 260n
Hart, Judith, 169
Headey, Bruce, 18n, 34n, 121-39, 152n
Healey, Dennis, 105
Heasman, D. J., xxi, 16n, 33n, 252n,
    254n, 255n
Heath, Edward, 5, 10, 11, 13, 19, 147,
    150, 151, 164, 170, 205, 272,
    278, 282, 284
Henry, Laurin, 21n
Herman, Valentine, 55-76
Hewart of Bury, Lord, 263n
Hewison, R. J. P., 246n, 247n
Hicks-Beach, Sir M., 51, 94
Hill, Charles, 159n, 162n, 166-7, 168n,
    169, 173n, 174, 176, 177n,
    178n, 179n, 180n, 185, 248
Hoare, Sir Samuel (Viscount
    Templewood), 83-4, 93, 143n, 267

Home Secretary, 59, 62, 82, 161, 210-20, 265; *see also* Government Departments — Home Office

Hore-Belisha, Lord, 258

House of Commons, *see* Commons, House of

House of Commons Disqualification Bill, 265

House of Lords, *see* Lords, House of

Howe, M. de Wolfe, 267n

Howell, David, 281

Hunt, Norman (Lord Crowther-Hunt), 193-209

Hurwitz, Leon, 56n

Italy, 22, 62-4, 68

Ireland, 62, 72

Industrial Relations Act of 1971, 123, 158

Jackson, Robert, 55n

James, R. R., 78n, 94n

Jeffries, Sir Charles, 255n

Jellicoe, Lord, 281, 284

Jenkins, Roy, 104, 108, 124-5, 210-20

Jennings, Sir Ivor, xiv, 83n, 121n, 246n, 259n, 263n

Johnson, F. A., 246n

Jones, T., 247n, 267n

Joseph, Sir Keith, 173

Kilmuir, *see* Maxwell Fyfe

King, Anthony, xi, 34n, 52n, 56n, 59n

Kingsley, J. D., 259n

Kitson Clark, G., 31n

Labour Party, 6-7, 43-4, 88, 90, 105, 127, 140-1

Laski, H. J., 260n

Laver, Michael, 69n

Law, A. Bonar, 253, 267

Law, Richard, 254

Leader of the House of Commons, 157-8, 253, 254, 265

Leader of the Opposition, 141, 146-7, 158

Leader's Consultative Committee, 141; *see also* Shadow Cabinet

Leaks, 160, 163

L'Etang, H. J. C., 267n

Liberal Party, 44-5

Lindsay, Martin, 268n

Lloyd, Selwyn, 109-10, 172, 174, 176, 179, 180, 200-1

Lloyd George, David, 46, 49, 79, 82, 87, 88, 162, 163, 245, 247, 250, 253, 264, 267

Lloyd-Hughes, Trevor, 169, 186

Lobby correspondents, 157-183; *see also* Government—press relations impact, 172-83 meetings, 157-9 specialisation, 189-90 uses, 157-62

Lord Chancellor, 5, 80, 173

Lord President of the Council, 25, 50, 85-6, 252, 253, 254

Lord President's Committee, 196-7

Lord Privy Seal, 5, 50, 204, 252, 253, 256-7, 265

Lords, House of, 11, 27

Lowe, Richard, 22n

Lyttleton, O., 254

MacDonald, J. Ramsay, 39, 79, 87, 88, 95-6, 108, 163, 267

McKenzie, R. T., 88n

Mackenzie, W. J. M., 245n, 246n

Mackie, M., 121n

Mackintosh, John P., xiii, xiv, 1n, 35n, 78n, 82n, 84n, 93n, 250n

Maclay, John, 173, 174

Macleod, Iain, 6, 81, 154, 180, 265

Macmillan, Harold, 5, 8, 10, 51, 86, 90, 95, 110-11, 124, 161, 164, 166, 170, 172, 173, 174, 176, 178, 179, 180, 181, 182, 185, 201, 251, 252, 258, 268

Macridis, Roy, 56n

Madgwick, P. J., 34n, 77-102

Malmesbury, Earl of, 142n

Mann, Dean, 16n, 23n

Manningham-Butler, Sir Reginald, 173

Mansergh, N., 262n

March, James G., 134n

Marples, Ernest, 17n

Marshall, Geoffrey, xv, 3n

Maudling, Reginald, 173, 180

Maxwell Fyfe, D. P. (First Earl of Kilmuir), 85n, 173, 174, 176, 178, 179n, 182n, 268

Mayhew, Christopher, 81, 86, 89-90, 92, 93, 94, 96, 99

Middlemas, K., 143n

Miller, W. L., 121n
Mills, Lord, 5, 173, 174, 263
Milne, R. S., 259n
Ministerial reorganisation, 47-52, 58,
    64-9
Ministers, *see also* Cabinet, Prime
    Minister
  and backbenchers, 266
  competence of, 7, 12-14, 23-4
  constraints on, 20-1, 26
  continuity in office, 20-3, 28,
    34-42, 58-64, 69-75
  criteria for appointment, 6, 7,
    12-14, 27-9
  experience, xxi, 2, 15-16, 19, 27,
    29, 34, 36-8, 42-6, 148-55; *see*
    also Shadow Cabinet
  hierarchy of, 254
  number of, 5, 10-12, 255
  personal characteristics, xxii, 136
  relationship to Lobby, 159
  responsibility of, xv, 27, 78, 127,
    153, 201- 262-4; *see also*
    Resignations
  roles of, 17-19, 24-5, 93, 122-3,
    154
  and senior civil servants, 121-36
  of State, 254-6
  tasks and requirements, 2, 16-25,
    131-5, 193-4, 215-20, 244,
    268-9
  turnover in appointments, *see*
    continuity *above*
Ministers without Portfolio, 5
Ministries, *see* Government
    departments
Mitchell, Joan, 85n
Monck, Bosworth, 247n
Montagu, Edwin, 81, 82
Moodie, Graham, xiii, xiv, xv, 3n
Morley, Lord, 82, 90, 143n
Morrison, Herbert (Lord Morrison of
    Lambeth), 90, 91, 96, 147n,
    221n, 248, 251, 254n, 258,
    264n, 265n, 266n
Mosley, Sir Oswald, 83, 87

Neustadt, Richard, 127, 136n
New Zealand, 62, 67
Nicholson, Sir H. G., 88n
Nicholson, Max, 121n
Noble, Michael, 173
Nutting, H. A., 85

Oakeshott, M. J., 20n
Ogilvy-Webb, Marjorie, 164n
Olson, Mancur, Jr, 8n
Opposition, 140-56; *see also* Ministers,
    Shadow Cabinet

Parkinson, C. N., 245n, 255n
Parliamentary Committee, 140-1; *see*
    also Shadow Cabinet
Parliamentary Private Secretaries, 5,
    163
Parliamentary questions, 122, 145, 212
Parliamentary Secretaries, 5, 256-7
Parris, Henry, 30n
Pearce, Roy, 55n
Permanent Secretaries, 124-6, 211
Playfair, Sir Edward, 125, 134n
Plumb, J. H., 55n
Policy-making, xvi, xix, xx, xxiii, 34,
    74, 123-4, 160
Pope, John, 58n
Postmaster-General, 169
Powell, Enoch, 6, 81, 86, 92, 116, 173
Press, *see* Lobby correspondents
Prime Minister
  appointments by, 6, 7
  changes of, 47-9
  experience of, 15
  patronage, 9-11
  power of, xi, 33, 98, 103, 109-10,
    194-6, 201, 242n, 249-50, 277
  public relations, 157, 162-72, 185-7
Public expenditure, 77, 86, 89-90,
    112-15, 243
Public Relations Adviser of the Prime
    Minister, 157, 161, 163, 164,
    170-1
Punnett, R. M., 19n, 140-56

Race relations, 215
Reform, *see* Cabinet — institutional
    development, proposals for
    reform
Reid, T. Wemyss, 142n
Research, government-sponsored, 262
Resignations, 51, 77-102, 103-17, 179
  constitutional value of, 97-9
  on policy grounds, 80-7, 89-90
  political context of, 87-94
  as political strategy, 94-7
Richards, P. G., 265n, 266n
Riddell, Baron G. A., 82n
Ridley, F. F., 126n

Ripon, Marquis of, 45, 252
Roberts, M. M., 142n
Robson, W. A., 242n, 263n
Rose, Richard, 1-32, 34n, 121n
Ross, J. F. S., 266n
Rothschild, Lord, 277-92

Salisbury, Fifth Marquess of, 85-6, 95, 251n
Salisbury, Third Marquess of, 11, 39, 41, 42, 77, 78, 91, 97
Samuel, H., 83
Sandys, Duncan, 255, 258
Sankey, Sir J., 80
Select Committee on Offices or Places of Profit under the Crown, 265
Selsdon Park Conference, 149
Seymour-Ure, Colin, xi, xxiv, 157-83
Shadow Cabinet, *see also* Opposition
  and Cabinet appointments, 19, 150-1
  composition, 140-1
  experience of ministers, 148-55
  modern, 145-8
  and opposition effectiveness, 147-8
  origins and evolution, 141-5
  selection, 140-1
  specialisation, 143-4, 145-6
Shonfield, Andrew, 134n
Shore, Michael, 107
Siegfried, André, 56n
Simon, Herbert, 81, 82, 134n
Snow, C. P., 249n, 261n, 263n
Snowden, P., 83, 93, 108
Solicitor General, 5
Stability, 55-6, 65
Stanley, David, 16n, 23n
Stanley, O., 84, 94
Stankiewicz, W. J., 121n
Steering Committee on Economic Policy, 126
Stein, Michael, 55n
Stewart, Michael, 107

Stokes, Richard, 255, 258
Strang, Lord, 1, 254n
Suez crisis, 202-3
Sweden, 64, 68, 73
Swinton, Lord, 165, 198

Taylor, Michael, 56n, 69n
Thomas, J. H., 108
Thorneycroft, Lord (Peter), xvi, 81, 86, 89, 90, 92, 93, 96, 110-17
Trend, Sir Burke, 279-80, 281, 286-8, 292
Trevelyan, Sir Charles, 81, 83, 88, 92
Trevelyan, G. M., 143n
Tunstall, Jeremy, 160n, 162n, 170n, 184-90
Turner, D. R., 142n

United States, executive appointments in, 21

Vernon, R. V., 262n

Walling, R. A. J., 142n
Watkinson, Harold, 173, 174
Weir, L. MacNeill, 88n
Wheeler-Bennett, J. W., 251n
Wigg, George, 169
Williams, Francis, 92n, 123n, 163n, 164, 167n, 186
Williams, Marcia, 169n
Williams, Shirley, 80
Willson, F. M. G., xviii, 12n, 14n, 15n, 16n, 27n, 34n, 45n, 46n, 244n, 249n, 255n, 262n
Wilson, Harold, 7, 9, 10, 11, 13, 44, 45, 51, 85, 90, 96, 97, 103, 107, 108, 109, 123, 130, 132n, 147, 151, 162, 164, 169, 182, 185-8, 221n, 277, 286
Wiseman, H. V., xiv
Woodward, E. L., 35n
Woolton, Lord, 198